Praise for Sister Helen Prejean's

RIVER OF FIRE

"Sister Prejean's radical openness and bracing honesty about her own faith journey is as refreshing and compelling as it is demanding and questioning. If you've ever wondered what 'faith' asks of you, you must read this book. It will turn your world upside down as you witness the conversion of a pious, sheltered nun into a fiery, faithful freedom fighter for the poor and the marginal. It set my own heart on fire, as I followed her quest to set the heart of the world aflame with passion for justice." —Serene Jones, author of *Call It Grace: Finding Meaning in a Fractured World*

"Sister Helen Prejean is one of the great moral leaders of our time. Her superb new memoir, *River of Fire*, is the inviting and inspiring story of her early days as a Catholic sister. A born storyteller, Sister Helen leads you, with her fierce intelligence and lively wit, from her entrance into a novitiate that still practiced the traditional ways of spiritual formation, to the volcanic changes wrought by the Second Vatican Council, to the initial stirrings of understanding what 'social justice' meant in action. *River of Fire* is a book to read and treasure, and Sister Helen's is a life to celebrate and honor." —James Martin, SJ, author of *The Jesuit Guide to (Almost) Everything*

"Helen Prejean's account of her journey to 'get Jesus right' is rich in warm insights, tenderly human, and a full account of life in the American Church during the last sixty years. She is a beacon of authenticity and fidelity to the margins."
—Gregory Boyle, founder of Homeboy Industries

Sister Helen Prejean

RIVER OF FIRE

Sister Helen Prejean, CSJ, a member of the Congregation of St. Joseph, is known worldwide for starting a dialogue on the death penalty. After witnessing the electrocution of a condemned man in a Louisiana prison in 1984, Prejean wrote the bestselling *Dead Man Walking* and set out, through storytelling, to bring citizens close to the hard realities of government killings. Her mission has taken her to every U.S. state and to the Vatican, where her personal entreaties to two popes helped to shape Catholic opposition to the death penalty. When not on the road, this lifelong Louisianan loves to share Cajun jokes, eat Southern cooking, play card games, and write, exploring her fascination with the Divine spark she believes is in everyone: to seek truth, love ardently, and meet, head on, the suffering world.

www.sisterhelen.org

Sister Helen Prejean is available for select speaking engagements. To inquire about a possible speaking appearance, please contact Penguin Random House Speakers Bureau at speakers@penguinrandomhouse.com or visit www.prhspeakers.com.

RIVER
OF FIRE

RIVER
OF FIRE

*On Becoming an
Engaged Citizen*

Sister Helen Prejean, CSJ

VINTAGE BOOKS
A Division of Penguin Random House LLC
New York

Grateful acknowledgment is made to the following for permission to reprint
previously published material:

HOUGHTON MIFFLIN HARCOURT PUBLISHING COMPANY AND THE JOY HARRIS
LITERARY AGENCY, INC.: "Sunday School, Circa 1950" from *Revolutionary Petunias
& Other Poems* by Alice Walker, copyright © 1970 and renewed 1998 by Alice
Walker. Print rights throughout the United Kingdom and electronic and audio
rights throughout the World are administered by The Joy Harris Literary Agency,
Inc. Reprinted by permission of Houghton Mifflin Harcourt Publishing
Company and The Joy Harris Literary Agency, Inc.

LIVERIGHT PUBLISHING CORPORATION: Three lines from "be of love(a little)" from
Complete Poems: 1904–1962 by E. E. Cummings, edited by George J. Firmage,
copyright © 1935, 1963, 1991 by the Trustees for the E. E. Cummings Trust,
copyright © 1978 by George James Firmage; "no time ago" from *Complete Poems:
1904–1962* by E. E. Cummings, edited by George J. Firmage, copyright © 1950,
1978, 1991 by the Trustees for the E. E. Cummings Trust, copyright © 1979 by
George James Firmage. Reprinted by Liveright Publishing Corporation.

The Library of Congress has cataloged the Random House edition as follows:
Name: Prejean, Helen, author.
Title: River of fire : my spiritual journey / Sister Helen Prejean, C.S.J.
Description: First edition. | New York : Random House, 2019.
Identifiers: LCCN 2018051678
Subjects: LCSH: Prejean, Helen. | Sisters of Saint Joseph—Biography. |
Nuns—United States—Biography.
Classification: LCC BX4705.P691673 A3 2019 | DDC 271/.97602 B—dc23
LC record available at https://lccn.loc.gov/2018051678

Vintage Books Trade Paperback ISBN: 978-0-307-38903-9
eBook ISBN: 978-1-9848-5541-1

Title-page and part-title-page images: copyright © iStock.com/IgOrZh
Book design by Victoria Wong

www.vintagebooks.com

Printed in the United States of America
10 9 8 7 6 5 4 3 2 1

For my beloved community,
the Sisters of St. Joseph,
and Sister Margaret Maggio, CSJ,
sister, friend, and co-worker

Ask not for understanding,
ask for the fire.

—St. Bonaventure

Contents

Preface

They killed a man with fire one night.
Strapped him in an oaken chair and pumped electricity
   into his body until he was dead.
His killing was a legal act.
No religious leaders protested the killing that night.
But I was there. I saw it with my own eyes.
And what I saw set my soul on fire—
a fire that burns in me still.

In the 1980s I was living in an African American housing project in New Orleans called St. Thomas. This was a departure from my previous life as a Sister of St. Joseph, largely spent among white suburban Catholics, teaching in Catholic schools or directing religious education in Catholic parishes. I had joined the Congregation of the Sisters of St. Joseph at the age of eighteen, inspired like many other young women of that era by a desire to serve God with my whole mind, soul, and heart. At that time we had a clear idea of what that meant. But times would change.

First came the transformative event in the Catholic Church of a global council called Vatican II (1962–65) that inspired women religious to return to the Gospels and rethink their mission in response to the needs of the world. And then gradually I underwent my own transformation—following a path first charted by Jesus that led to the poor, and to those whom many dismiss as "throwaway" people.

One day I received a request to correspond with a prisoner on death row. I didn't know that in responding to that request I would be taking the first steps on a path that would forever transform my life. That journey culminated in my book *Dead Man Walking* (1993), which was made into an Academy Award–winning film by Tim Robbins (1995). Suddenly, I was thrust into public debate, and soon found myself known as the Death Penalty Abolitionist Nun.

Once when I was inside the Louisiana death house awaiting an execution, Captain John Rabelais, a guard, asked: "What's a nun doing in a place like this?"

Here is an account of my journey to the killing chamber that night and the spiritual currents that pulled me there.

It's a river I'm riding.

I invite you to pitch your boat into its current and come with me.

Introduction

What it's always been about for me is the spiritual energy, the power that flows through us, lights us up, and enlivens whatever we touch. For me, that energy has always been connected to God. Call it Mystery. Call it Grace. Call it the luminous center we touch sometimes and don't know what to call it, but we know that being in its presence fills us with confidence and peace.

I learned as a child that I was created to love God with my whole heart and mind and soul and to love my neighbor as myself, and Jesus, God's Son, would show me how to do it. And the goal of it all: to make it through this life so I could be happy with God forever in heaven. Getting to heaven was really, really big. Catholics call it the "Beatific Vision." Seeing God face-to-face.

Wouldn't it be wonderful to love God so much that I wouldn't be selfish ever again, or obsess about myself and what I need and what I want and what I feel? Wouldn't it be drop-dead wonderful (a requirement, actually—the dropping dead) to be so free of ego? Just imagine being so on fire with love for God that I could be a martyr and sing and make jokes even while they were torturing me. Like St. Lawrence on the gridiron being roasted to death and quipping to his executioners: "I think I'm done on this side. Time to turn me over."

That's what I call spiritual power.

At the age of eighteen I chucked every worldly pleasure I knew to pursue it. I entered the convent to become a nun.

Needless to say, convent life in the late 1950s was a very different kind of world. How different? Maybe this description of our life back then can help ease you in:

A young woman entering a Roman Catholic religious congregation expected that most things would remain the same for the rest of her life. Once she chose a nun's vows of poverty, chastity, and obedience she would have very few decisions to make—ever again—about her lifestyle and work. Upon arising each morning she would put on a long and flowing black, brown, or white dress and the medieval-style head wrap and veil that the members of her order had donned for generations. She would eat meals in silence, with the sisters seated in order of rank. Standardized prayers would be recited at the convent at specific times throughout the day. She would be assigned work as a nurse or a teacher in a Catholic hospital or school, but other activities outside the convent, including family visits, would be rare and highly regulated. Contact with lay persons would be restricted to workplaces and medical visits. Superiors could open and review the letters she received and wrote. The sister would be required to ask her superior, in ritualized fashion, for permission to use objects such as soap, stationery, and thread. Exclusive ("particular") friendships with other sisters would be discouraged for fear that they would undermine community harmony.

The standard manual for sisters, "A Catechism of the Vows," explained that this highly regulated life best "fixed" the sister in a direction that steered her toward "perfect union" with God. The constant discipline and regulation would, ideally, mold the sister into an "interior woman" who concentrated her attention on the bringing about of the "perfection" of her soul through an overcoming of herself and the ways of the world, both of which were related to temptation and sin. As a symbol of the surrendering of an old self, a young sister would be given a new name upon profession as a novice. As the bishop granted the new name he would typically pronounce, "Behold a new (sister's name) which I give you on His part, to enable you to overcome the devil, the world, and yourself." The purpose of the vows of poverty, chastity, and obedience—but most especially obedience—was to help protect her from the "three objects of human concupiscence," namely, riches, sensual pleasures, and the "irregular love" of her own ideas. Through constantly practiced, freely given obedience to superiors in matters large and small, she would learn to "overcome every inclination to self-will," and therefore be a finer instrument of God's will. Through the practice of humble obedience she would "kill the greatest tyrant, the greatest enemy of perfection, her disordered and unruly self."*

That is a good description of the world I encountered when I joined the Sisters of St. Joseph. (*As if* a purely sociological description could ever capture a way of life that for many centuries had produced its fair share of loving, generous beings and mystics.) But that world would change. And so would I.

---

*Darra Mulderry, "What Human Goodness Entails: An Intellectual History of U.S. Catholic Sisters, 1930–1980," PhD dissertation, Brandeis University, 2006, 1–2.

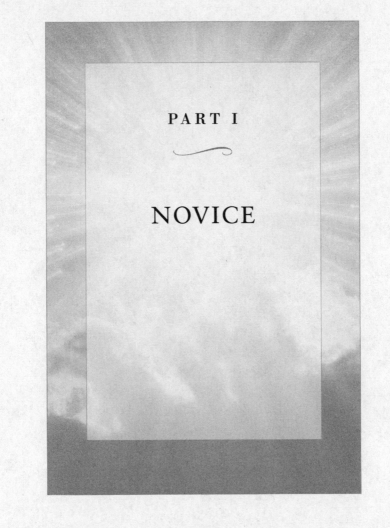

PART I

NOVICE

Bride of Christ

Be perfect just as your heavenly Father is perfect.

—Matthew 5:48

In the name of the Father, and of the Son, and of the Holy
  Ghost. Amen.
I adore Thee, O my God! I thank Thee; I offer myself to
  Thee without reserve. My Lord Jesus! When shall I be
  entirely Thine and perfectly according to Thy heart? My
  God and my all! I love Thee with my whole heart. In Thee
  do I place all my hopes.

—"Prayers on Awakening and Arising,"
Formulary of Prayers for the Use of the Sisters of Saint Joseph

At the close of the evening meal I'm performing what our
Holy Rule calls a "practice of humility." Along with a few
other Sisters I'm kneeling at Mother Anthelma's table to ask
for a penance. Pinned to my veil is a placard that states my
failing: "Most uncharitable," but I have to announce my fault
out loud, too: "Mother, please give me a penance for having
mean and unloving thoughts about another Sister." The idea
behind the practice is that by declaring our faults publicly, we
might be stirred to strive more earnestly to overcome them.

When you're going to do a practice of humility, you go to
a drawer in the dining room and select your failing from a
wide selection of placards: "Unrecollected," "Proud," "Gossip," "Selfish" . . . You pin it on and wear it during the meal. In

among the placards there is also a string with a piece of broken dish tied to it. That is worn around the neck for failing in the vow of poverty by breaking something.

Among us novices, when we know a fellow novice's failing in poverty ahead of time—like the time Sister Eugene broke a toilet seat—we're over the top in anticipation about how she will phrase her failing to Mother. If she says "toilet" anything, the solemnity of the practice will be extinguished by hoots of laughter emanating from the novitiate side of the dining room. It doesn't take much to set us off. With no TV or radio, we're starved blind for entertainment. One time our table of six giggled through the entire meal, losing it every time we glanced toward Sister Anne Meridier, who'd pinned the placard "Unrecollected" upside down on her pious little head. It doesn't help matters that meals are supposed to be eaten in solemn silence.

I have to say that the main reason I'm wearing this "Most uncharitable" placard is because of Sister Roseanne (not her real name). She has one of those bossy, pushy personalities, and in the close, constricted life of the novitiate . . . well, that can drive you nuts. Sister Roseanne had rushed to be the first one to arrive at the novitiate on entrance day, knowing that the "band" (class entering together) would be referred to as "Sister Roseanne's Band." It burned me up that she did that, which proved to be but a small harbinger of her dominating character. And now that everything in the novitiate is recoded into religious ideals, she's doing her level best to be Number One Novice—even in holiness.

Well, to be truthful, competition gets me going, so at first sound of the 5:00 A.M. bell (*the bell is the voice of God*) the two of us throw on all ten pieces of the holy habit—kissing dress, veil, and rosary as we go—and race lickety-split to be first in the chapel for morning prayers. All it took to launch the race was a casual remark of our novice mistress that a *really fervent* novice would not only be on time for prayers but would hasten to the chapel early so she could have a few extra minutes with our blessed Lord. That was it. The race was on.

Another thing that galls me about Roseanne is that during meditation—she sits *right behind me* in chapel—she's always fiddling and rustling. She can't keep her hands still, cleaning one fingernail with another, *click, click, click,* and sighing deeply, one sigh after another. They reverberate seismically through the chapel—where, with everyone quietly meditating, you can hear your own breathing. So imagine *click, click, sigh* behind you constantly when you're trying very, very hard to quiet your soul and enter into the depths of mystical prayer with God.

At our weekly conference, our novice mistress, Mother Noemi, talks to us about putting up with one another's faults and foibles. Now, there's a new nun word, *foible,* part of a whole new lexicon I'm learning, like *edifying* (good example), and *modesty of the eyes* (eyes lowered to avoid distractions), and *religious decorum,* which covers a multitude of actions: speech (demure, never raucous), walking (never swinging arms), singing (like the angels with clear notes and blending voices), politeness (answering "Yes, Mother," "Yes, Sister"; avoiding nicknames), and even blowing your nose in nunly fashion (with men's large white handkerchiefs).

And now *foible,* a quaint little word if ever there was one. I've seen it written but never heard it used by real people in real conversations. Well, ol' Click may well be the Foible Queen of the World. As far as I know, I don't have too many foibles, but you can never be sure. As Mother says, self-knowledge is hard to come by; we all have blind spots because of pride, which we're born with as Daughters of Eve, and pride blinds, while humility opens the eyes of the soul.

Lord knows I need humility just to handle Click. I'm praying for a divine infusion of grace to overcome all the mean-spirited things I hope happen to Roseanne, the most benign of which is that Mother will move her place in chapel and foist her onto other poor souls. And it is such thoughts that now bring me to my knees at the feet of Mother Anthelma.

I'm nineteen years old, the year is 1958, and I've already made it through the first nine months of probation (called "postulancy") and am now a first-year novice at St. Joseph Novitiate in New Orleans. More than anything in the world I want to be a holy nun in love with God. I want to be a saint. And, according to Catholic teaching, by joining the religious life I'm choosing the most direct route to sainthood. By my vows I will become a spouse of Jesus Christ.

Or, rather, as I am learning, I *am chosen* by Jesus because you can't simply declare yourself chosen and become a nun just like that, because that might be self-will, not God's will. Jesus said, "You have not chosen me but I have chosen you," so you have to be invited and you have to pray long and hard, listening to your deep-down soul to hear the call. Then you have to ask admittance to the community, and merely because you're asking doesn't mean they'll accept you, and I prayed and prayed and wrote and rewrote my application to Mother Mary Anthelma, the superior, asking to be admitted to the novitiate. I also had to have my parish priest, Father Marionneaux, write to Mother Anthelma to assure the community that I was a Catholic in good standing. The novitiate, where I am now, is the training ground, the place where you and the community see if there's a "fit."

In senior religion class at St. Joseph's Academy, where I

went to high school, Father William Borders taught us that religious life, or the Life of Perfection, is the "highest" state of life for a Christian, higher than marriage and the single life. That's because the other states of life must be lived in the *world,* which is full of traps, seductions, and temptations—all lures of Satan, who is hell-bent, you better believe it, on separating souls from God.

I still have a pocket-sized New Testament given to me by my sister, Mary Ann, on my entrance day into the community. In it she inscribed:

> To my favorite sister, Helen [I'm her only sister,
> her little joke]
> I hope that you shall be very happy. You are one of
> God's children who has been chosen to be in His special
> family. I'm very proud to tell people that I have a sister
> in the convent praying for me. I will need your prayers,
> Helen, for the way of life I have chosen is a worldly one,
> and I'll have many obstacles in my way. I shall remem-
> ber you always in my prayers. May you love God al-
> ways and stay close to Him, as you are now.
>
> All my love,
> Mary

The *highest* state of life? A life of seeking *perfection?* Bride of Christ? I always did have high ambitions. When I was in eighth grade I announced to Sister Mark and my classmates that I intended to become either the Pope or president of the United States. A joke, of course, thrown out with a thirteen-year-old's flippancy, and everyone laughed, but even then I harbored within my young breast a desire for greatness. After all, as president of our class had I not already exhibited solid, if

not brilliant, leadership? When Maxine, our dearly loved class-
mate, was forced to leave us because her father was transferred
away from Louisiana to the other end of the world—somewhere
way up north like Detroit—had I not given a stirring speech of
farewell, which moved many to tears, including Maxine herself (and almost me myself, had I not hung strenuously onto
my self-control)? I reached this pinnacle of emotion in my
speech simply by pointing out that Maxine's passage from us
was truly a form of death, for we, remaining in Baton Rouge,
would probably never see her alive again this side of the grave.
My speech stunned my classmates. It was my first intimation
of the power of words.

Who knows what fame as an orator I might have achieved
in the "world"?

But I'm chucking it all to embrace the hidden, prayerful life
of a nun. I'm only a teenager, but I know what I want. I want
to withdraw from the "world" and its temptations so I can
contemplate and achieve union with God. Jesus had told Pon-
tius Pilate, "My kingdom is not of this world," and it is this
spiritual kingdom I'm after. So, whatever happens in the
"world" is of no concern to me, except I know to pray cease-
lessly for sinners, especially for the conversion of atheistic,
Communist Russia. I am well aware that, hands down, atheistic Communism is the single greatest threat to Catholics, who
alone possess the one true faith, and to the United States of
America, the unparalleled leader of the Free World.

During these two and a half years of training I will not listen to or read the news except for really big Catholic news like
the election of a new pope. So I know nothing about young
black men such as Emmett Till in Mississippi, beaten to death
around this time for supposedly flirting with a white woman,
nor do I know that in my own state of Louisiana a portable

electric chair is making its way to New Orleans and other cities to kill criminals—overwhelmingly black men or boys summarily convicted of raping or murdering whites.

What do I know (or care) about that? For sixteen centuries the Catholic Church has unerringly taught (all Church teachings are free of human error, of course) that the state has the right—indeed, the duty—to keep society safe by imposing the death penalty on violent criminals. It's clearly a question of self-defense for society, just as countries in war have a right to self-defense. Besides, if a criminal is truly remorseful and accepts death as just and rightful punishment for sin—"The last will be first," Jesus said—that criminal can win a place in heaven along with St. Peter and the Blessed Mother and all the saints. Isn't gaining heaven the purpose of everyone's earthly existence?

As for poverty and injustice, when you think of it, haven't there always been poor people in the world? Isn't that simply the way the world is? That's what we were taught. Kids in India starve and we in the United States have abundance. But if poor people accept their sufferings as God's will, they can achieve an awful lot of eternal merit and win the heavenly crown, just like criminals who repent. Didn't Jesus say to the Good Thief who died beside him on the cross, "This day you shall be with me in Paradise"? Besides, Jesus didn't seem to think poverty was all that terrible. He even seemed to think poverty offered spiritual advantages. "Blessed are you who are poor," he told the crowd. Maybe it was because all peasants in Galilee were poor or like himself, a craftsman, barely a notch above.

In high school, I once met some poor black families in the countryside outside of Baton Rouge when our Catholic Students Mission Crusade took them Thanksgiving baskets. Very nice baskets, packed with a lot of Christian charity: turkey, yams, corn, milk, bread—even cranberry sauce, to top off the festive meal. Three of us in a Jeep had to drive off the road and across a field to reach some shacks—tiny wooden frames with tin roofs and a front porch—and a whole bunch of kids pouring out the front door as we drove up. I asked the mama how many kids she had, so that we could hand out candy.

"Six," she says, counting heads.

Then, out of the door comes another kid.

"Make it seven," she says.

I loved it—told the story for months to my white friends. From my culturally superior perch I thought I had black folks all figured out. *I mean, what do you expect, with all these women having litters of kids by different fathers and lending them out to kin to raise? I guess it is close to impossible to keep track.* At our congregation's health clinic in New Roads, a rural town about thirty miles out of Baton Rouge, a story circulated about Mandy, a black patient, who every year came to the clinic to have her baby. As she was leaving with number four, one of our Sisters said, "Bye, Mandy, see you next year."

"No, you ain't neither," said Mandy. "We done found out what's causin' all dis."

That's black folks for you, we thought. Not a care in the world. Like the kids, squealing with delight, helping us carry the Thanksgiving goodies onto the porch. It was November and some of the kids were barefoot, and a few had runny noses, but there they all were, smiling and giggling and happy as larks that these white ladies were delivering candy and good eats for everybody.

I used to think that poor people are happier than most of us. Their minds aren't screwed up with conflicted philosophical notions about the meaning of life. They just live. No worries about house payments or even the expense of having babies. They just collect monthly welfare checks from the government. It's been that way forever in Louisiana, which had a huge slave population to work in the cotton and sugarcane fields, and black people still compose a hefty percentage of the state's population. I'm not prejudiced, I'd tell myself, I'm Christian. I love all people, whatever their skin color. And I get along with "Negroes" as well as I do with anybody. I was always the one in our family who hung out in the kitchen the most, chewing the fat with the servants.

Here at the motherhouse all the servants are black—Bernice with Sister Bernard in the laundry, Lily Mae with Sister Joseph Claire in the kitchen, and Monroe with Sister Mercedes in the yard. We novices work right alongside them, cutting up vegetables and peeling potatoes or folding sheets and towels in the laundry. When I'm a professed Sister I'm looking forward to being on the "home missions" team in summer, teaching black kids their catechism in Morganza, another rural Louisiana town. After all, they're God's children, too. And when God looks at souls, He doesn't see black or white. He only sees who's in *sanctifying grace* and who isn't.

One day, as the river of consciousness deepens, I will radically change my way of thinking about all of this. But not until I burst out of my cocoon of privilege. Don't hold your breath. It's going to take a while.

Later I'll also realize just how much my faith is riddled with fear. So much fear that I'm even afraid of Jesus. Yes, I know he is my Savior, but he also has this no-nonsense, tough judge side. In the Gospels he makes no bones about the Last Judgment, that the saved—the sheep—will come with him into heaven, while the goats are separated out and sent to hell. It's clearly there in the Gospel of St. Matthew, and I can just picture myself jockeying around in the final push, trying to get away from the goats and in tight with the sheep but knowing there's no hiding, no blending in with the crowd when it comes to this final, very particular, judgment from which no human is exempt. As I'm at last approaching Jesus, getting close, I can hear him and see him point to this one and that one: *You! Over here with the sheep, welcome into heaven.* But terrifyingly, also: *You, goat! Not you! Away from me into eternal hellfire,* and I can picture the poor goat bleating pitifully, *Bahhh, bahhh, I wanna be with the sheep,* but off he goes, prodded and shoved with the other goats into eternal perdition. Which would I be? Sheep? Goat? All eternity, hanging in the balance, and I'm praying like mad, "Please, Jesus, please, let me be with the sheep."

A vivid imagination can be a curse.

The morality I know I learned straight from the Baltimore Catechism, and there I learned that all it takes to end up in hell with the goats is one mortal sin. One single, solitary mortal sin. That's it, and you burn forever. Which drives me to pray to Mary, the Mother of Jesus, who is finally and surely the only fail-safe access to God's mercy because she has true compassion, as only a mother has. For me, finally, Mary, Our Lady of Mercy, is the only one I can really count on.

But enough for now about distorted ideas of a cruel God. Life in the novitiate is bumping along with its ups and downs when a huge, dark influenza cloud hits us, felling almost all but a few of the novices. It flattens me for nine days. Mother Noemi tells us stories of saints who used the occasion of illness to offer up their sufferings for the conversion of sinners. Mother is a stickler for religious decorum even when you're sick as a dog.

The Holy Rule prescribes that you are supposed to lie in

bed in nunly fashion: legs straight, not bent; arms by sides; hands holding a rosary or crucifix—the reverent posture you'd assume if Jesus suddenly appeared to you. The mind game I always play with that scenario is that if here and now Jesus deigned to appear to me, I'd be so shocked out of my mind that whatever posture I was in, irreverent or not, would get frozen. Thus, the logic went, I could lie in bed any way I wanted to. I figure if Jesus were to go out of his way to appear to me, would he care one divine whit what posture he found me in? Honestly.

But here is the bad thing about being sick in the novitiate, the thing that speedily dissipates whatever virtue I possess: You are always under surveillance. Always. And without fail every time Mother visits the dormitory, she singles me out and corrects me for my posture in bed. She finds it slovenly, irreverent; she says I am "lying in bed like a cowboy." (A cowboy?) She always seems to pick on me, and normally (when I can *breathe*) I can take my share, but I am sick and *very, very* tired of trying to pray and be holy all the time.

My saintly sentiments have long ago flown the coop, and all I can think about is Mama and how loving and attentive she was when we were sick, how she'd be fixing us special things to drink and eat, custards and ice cream or ice chips to ease our sore throats. But here, supposedly the dwelling place of God's chosen ones—here it is hell warmed over. Nine days and nights . . . hence, the state of my weakened and brittle soul when Mama and Daddy come on visiting Sunday, and Mother decides that despite a low-grade fever, I am well enough to visit.

I handle the visit okay. I don't cry in front of my parents. (Good nuns don't cry.) But after Mama and Daddy leave and after I have silently wept my way through the psalms of evening prayer (which are studded with tear-jerk phrases such as "Forget your father and your father's house"), I wait for Mother in the darkened room that she always passes on her way back to the novitiate from the chapel. And when I call out to her and she steps into the room, the nine days and nights of raw throat and boredom and fever and reprimands for un-nunly posture all erupt. It isn't so much anger—I haven't gar-nered enough selfhood yet to muster real anger toward a superior (the voice of God for me); it is more sheer vulnerabil-ity and confusion: *Why are you always fussing at me? I'm sick. I feel terrible. Aren't you supposed to be tender toward the sick? We're stuck in this sick room all day and don't even have a deck of cards or Scrabble or any kind of game to play. All we're supposed to do is pray, pray, pray!* I cry full force and don't notice or care how loud I am. I think I ended with: *And you call yourself a Mother?!*

I don't remember Mother's exact response but I got its import—her utter sincerity in her role to train us (as she had been trained) to be "strong women of faith." And the very next day Mother arrives at our sick room with chess and checkers, decks of cards, and, of all things—ice cream. Her conversion toward tenderness is so immediate that I feel embarrassed, humbled even, that I had let her have it with both barrels. But once we are all well again, forget the tenderness, it is back to business as usual: Boot Camp for Brides of Jesus.

The Day I Left Home

I tell you solemnly, there is no one who has left . . . brothers, sisters, father . . . or land, for my sake and for the sake of the gospel, who will not be repaid a hundred times over.

—Mark 10:29–30

It's a very ancient rite of passage I'm now performing, leaving home and everything familiar to be initiated into a new way of life, much like the young boys in ancient times who were taken from their mothers and put through frightening, painful ordeals that forced them to face their fiercest fears and learn to tap inner spiritual resources they didn't know they had. That's what I'm doing now.

And I'm handling it all okay until the subject of the parakeet comes up. Everything is packed in the station wagon, ready for the trip to New Orleans, all my new black-and-white nun clothes in my trunk, Louie and Mary Ann already in the car, Daddy and Mama ready to turn their daughter over to God, me in my white, tiny-blue-flowered dress with the puffy sleeves, dressed up pretty and poised for leaving the nest, holding it all together until Mama has to go and ask if I fed Billy Boy, and that's what undoes me and I lean over the deep freeze in the kitchen and start bawling.

I'm leaving home today, leaving all my young Helen years, leaving my precious family, my house, my bed, the spacious yard with the big oak trees where we could go barefoot in summer and play softball with the Barbay boys. I'm leaving all that, leaving my home with the tall grasses in the back lot where you could make a hideaway and stay for hours if you wanted to and no one could find you.

I'm leaving home. Forever.

When you become a nun, you can never again step into your family home—not for a meal or a family reunion or a marriage or anything except for the death of one of your parents, and even then, if they live in a city away from the convent, you may have to decide whether you'll visit before they die so you can say farewell or wait and attend the funeral. As a nun you are strictly forbidden to sleep away from the convent.

I'm leaving Mama and Daddy's bedroom, where we gathered each evening for the family rosary, the bedroom where one late afternoon I waited for Daddy to get home from work so I could show him my exciting new skill—"Hey, Daddy, look at this," and I slowly, deliberately tied the brown laces of my oxford shoes into a perfect little bow. I'm leaving the special Daddy-Helen times—I was always his little *petitsie*—and I'm leaving Mama and her lavishly affectionate love. I am leaving the sweet, sweet sleep in my double bed there in the bedroom with Mary Ann always by my side.

I'm leaving everything: the fireplace in the breakfast room, where late one night when all the others had gone upstairs to bed, I stayed at the round oak table and wrote in a feverish frenzy my first short story—under the constraint of having to weave ten spelling words for Mrs. Herthum's class into the narrative. It was a very, very dramatic story, about a man who went to war where "bullets fell like rain," but the man by a miracle of God survived and returned home. True, he had lost one leg, but he was *alive*, not dead, only one leg but alive!

Alive! I couldn't wait to read it in spelling class. When unsuspecting Mrs. Herthum asked who would like to read the sentences composed from spelling words, up I shot and read my piece with as much fervor as I had written it, and all went well until Janice Calabrese let out a loud, disrespectful cackle at the part about bullets falling "like rain."

And now I'm leaving the oak table and the breakfast room and everything I've known of home—now on this eighth day of September, the birthday of Mary, the Mother of Jesus: a perfect day to give your life to God.

I'm crying my eyes out as I get into the car, but deep inside myself I'm calm and resolute and, in a way, I've already left, already given myself over, already sealed the decision in some deep soul place beyond thinking or even willpower, a place inside with a call so deep that all I can do is say yes, and I am all aflow in the yes, not whining and afraid like a coward (a state I struggled against all through childhood). I'm ready, I'm doing it, I'm leaving—only to be brought to tears by a little yellow-green parakeet named Billy Boy.

We were bonded, Billy Boy and me. I taught him to talk—first, his name, which he rumbled in his throat perfectly, like a little old mustachioed man. But soon it was clear the bird was capable of saying anything I whispered into his little parakeet ears: *Billy Boy Prejean is a dir-r-r-ty bird . . . Hi ho, Silver . . . Hail Mary, full of grace, the Lord is with thee . . . drop-dead stupid* (though the bird sometimes mixed it up: *dirty Billy Boy . . . Hi ho, Mary . . .* and *the Lord is with Prejean*). The thought of leaving this feathered, articulate wonder—knowing that without me his vocabulary will freeze and there will be no more new words for him—is all too much to deal with. But it's time to get into the car; it's time to go.

I sit between Mama and Daddy in the back seat and we all

say the rosary and cry all the way to New Orleans. Mary Ann drives, her eyes straight ahead, with Louie, now in eighth grade, sitting up front with her, unusually quiet, subdued by the import of it all.

By the time we reach the novitiate building, on Mirabeau Avenue in New Orleans, I have cried away the tears, and as we cross the overpass on Wisner Boulevard, I see the novitiate building in an empty field, and I say, almost to myself: "My new home." The car pulls up, and I get out and bound through a side door near the chapel and announce, "I'm here! I'm here to become a bride of Christ!"

"Lord, help us—who is this character?" wonders one of the novices who happens to be standing near the chapel entrance. Her name is Sister Christopher (family name: Ann Barker), and she is standing there because she is the sacristan, preparing the chapel for benediction, the culminating event of the day. Six years later, when she becomes my closest friend, she will recall my arrival and laugh and tell me about it in vivid detail.

Thus, on a September day, the stream of my Helen-life joined the wider river of women by showing up for novice training with the Sisters of St. Joseph.

Origins

As far back as I can remember, I've had a vivid sense of being alive. I'd close my eyes and there it was, the feeling: *I am. I'm me. I'm alive, having all these thoughts in my head, which only I know.* It still amazes me that I'm alive and thinking—I am always thinking—and I can't get over it when I open a book and I'm allowed to descend into the inner sanctuary of another's thoughts. It still amazes me.

I also have a strong sense of family. I am Helen Theresa Prejean, the daughter of Louis Prejean, Sr., and Gusta Mae Bourg, and my older sister is Mary Ann and she was born ahead of me on May 13, 1938, but I was born the very next April 21st, so I turn a year older before she does, and for twenty-two days every year we're the same age. For a *little* sister this is a Very Big Deal. Louis, Jr.—we call him Louie—was born five years after me, but when he was a little baby he caught pneumonia and almost died, and one night, when all the doctors said his life hung in the balance, Mama prayed all night long and marked little crosses all over his stomach and chest with water from the miraculous spring at Lourdes and promised Mary, Mother of Jesus, that if Louie lived, he would be dedicated to her and wear blue and white until he was six years old. Which is exactly what happened.

Our family always had a fierce devotion to the Blessed Virgin Mary. We said the rosary every night, and on long family trips we said three rosaries a day—that's over 150 Hail Marys and eighteen Our Fathers and Glory Bes—which, along with the purely spiritual benefits, proved to be a surefire Catholic Prozac for three squabbling kids in the backseat. This backseat Peaceable Kingdom was put in jeopardy by the goal Mary Ann and I set to make Louie cry in every state we traveled through, and there were a lot of them—about thirty over the course of ten summers. You can see why we had to say a lot of rosaries.

When Mary Ann and I go to play in the front yard, Mama warns us that we must *never* cross the ditch onto the highway. I especially need dire warnings because I'm a dreamy kid, always sort of looking around without seeing things. I'd like to say it's because I'm deep in thought. Maybe that's part of it, because it's still true about me that what I'm thinking about is almost always stronger than what I'm taking in from the outside world. So you can understand that as a kid I needed a lot of parental protection.

We call our house "Goodwood"—that's also the name of the neighborhood because of the big trees. It's a big two-story house on five acres of land with oak and gum and sycamore trees towering close by our bedroom windows on the second floor, and at night we can hear crickets and tree frogs—when they're loud, Mama says they're singing for rain—and sometimes an owl, which is *verrry* scary (they can see you but you can't see them). Mary Ann and I don't want the owl to see into our bedroom, so we two little girls in pink nightgowns bury our heads under the pillows with our two little behinds pointing upward.

Summer sounds: whir of the attic fan, cool breeze coming through tall windows, clink of ice in the water pitcher as Mama in her nightgown brings it up the back stairs to us in our beds, and once in bed with lights out, a healthy dousing with holy water from Mama "to keep the devil away." Always night prayers. Always morning prayers. Faithfully, without fail, kneeling by the side of my bed.

I have olive skin like Mama's. It's kind of tan even on my stomach, which never gets sun; it's just natural, and at summer's end I'm always the darkest kid around. When school starts again in September, some kids will call me "Blackie," which makes me cringe because of all the prejudice against black people, and I surely don't want to be lumped with *them*.

One time an older Bahlinger girl, sister of my close friend Charlotte, said, "Come here, Helen, you little black nigger." She laughed and tried to act like she was teasing, but I was offended. "Don't you call me a nigger! I have an *olive* complexion like my mama. I'm a tanned white person!" And so it went. But sometimes I didn't fight back. I kept silent and burned with humiliation and just wanted the hurtful words to pop and disappear like a bubble—or I'd quickly change the subject. Later, much later, I'd learn about racial prejudice, but then I had no idea about how culture blinds us, immerses us, makes us feel comfortable and convinced that the way we do things is the way things are—and rightly so.

Mama and Daddy grew up on sugarcane plantations on the west side of the Mississippi River near Baton Rouge, both of French Cajun stock. Mama's family name is Bourg (a city in France) and Daddy is a Prejean (*pres,* French for "prairie or field," and *jean* for "John" somebody or other: John of the prairie). The story of Prejean ancestry goes that two rather prolific Prejean brothers, exiled from Nova Scotia by the British in the eighteenth century, made their way to Louisiana and sired a bunch of Prejeans, who did more than their fair share of populating southeast Louisiana. But for a long time, whenever someone would ask me if I was Cajun, I'd always say, "No, I'm French—our family came directly from France. My daddy speaks French, not Cajun patois, and during World War I he was a translator in the army in Washington, D.C."

Daddy's mama, Stella Gassie—we called her "Mamom"—spoke mostly French, but I don't remember her ever saying a word, because by the time I knew her she had already had a stroke, and all I remember is being brought into her bedroom, where she lay paralyzed, cared for like a little baby by Attee and Lee Lee, two maiden aunts, and her room always smelled like baby powder, and the aunts always petted her and talked to her in cooing tones like you do to an infant. Daddy had taught Mary Ann and me to say *"Je vous aime beaucoup,"* and that's what we'd whisper in her ear, but she didn't smile or say anything back, so the visits were mostly to please Daddy. When Mamom died, it felt inevitable, and neither Mary Ann nor I cried, but Daddy did. When we saw her with her eyes closed in the coffin, it wasn't much different from the way we always saw her in bed.

Mama's side of the family, the Bourgs, are French, too, mostly. Grandpa Bourg, Mama's daddy, ran the store for the owners of the Allendale plantation, in West Baton Rouge, and before that, other plantations, too. He'd talk about how the "niggers" were always trying to cheat him, but he showed them—he'd secretly hold his thumb on the scale when he was weighing lunch meat or cheese and inch up the price a bit. It was only right to offset the lazy, good-for-nothing "niggers" trying to get one over on him. Though he did admit that occasionally you'd meet a "good one," and those few he always treated with respect.

Mama's family was so poor that to get extra warmth in winter they used to layer newspaper between the bedsheet and the blanket. Like Daddy, she and her siblings walked to school, and in the winter, as they walked along the levee, with the cold wind cutting through them—"like a knife," as she said—they'd put their coats on backward to have a solid wall of warmth in the front. They knew their mama, Annette, felt bad about their having to walk on cold, rainy days, but what could she do? No car. Not even bicycles. They always brought sweet-potato sandwiches to school. It was the only staple they always had plenty of.

Only Grandpa's authority as store boss, the meager salary he got, and his white skin raised him a notch above the black folks. It was just a small notch above, and maybe that's why he was so prejudiced. Black people on plantations were never paid in cash. In return for their labor, workers ran a "tab" at the plantation store, and that was a big part of Grandpa's job—keeping track of who owed what and what they might buy on whatever remained from their monthly pay.

This same plantation-store system was still in place in New Iberia, Louisiana, in the mid-1970s and early '80s when two of our Sisters taught literacy to black sugarcane workers there. The Sisters' efforts among the workers were not looked upon kindly by the plantation owner or the Catholic pastor of the church. The priest did not at all like his biggest donor, the plantation owner, being upset by the "liberal nuns" sowing discontent among his workers—whose needs, he assured anyone who would listen, were "well provided for." Without cars, the workers were not free to leave the plantation and shop elsewhere. Educating black plantation workers was labeled a "political" activity.

It seemed perfectly natural that our family would have two black servants working for us: Ellen, in her blue-and-white uniform, cooking and helping Mama in the house and "minding" us—polishing our shoes and taking us for walks—and Jesse, under Daddy's supervision, doing yard work. Mama and

Daddy were always kind, and Daddy used his influence to get a job for Jesse at the Esso refinery and arranged for them to purchase their own house in the Negro section of Baton Rouge. But that took a while. Meanwhile, Ellen and Jesse lived in the servants' quarters behind our big house. They always ate in the kitchen and never used the family bathroom—only the servants' toilet in a tiny room near the carport. They called Mary Ann and me "Miss."

I would not have the opportunity to meet African Americans as peers until I was forty-two years old, when I moved in as neighbor in the St. Thomas housing development in New Orleans. But we need to go quite a ways down this river of time before we come to that.

Daddy had eleven brothers and sisters, then ten, when one of the twins died. When Daddy first attended school, he spoke only French but learned English fast, facilitated greatly by a pop on the hand with a ruler every time a French word came out of his mouth. But there must have been in his soul some deep love of language because he always seemed to relish words, purchasing his own copy of a dictionary as soon as he could get one and setting himself the goal of memorizing a page every day.

Family pride in Daddy started early. "Watch that Louis Prejean," relatives would say. "He's got brains. He's going to amount to something." After finishing Brusly High School, Daddy worked as an elevator boy and at other jobs to pay his way through Baton Rouge Business College, and he got his first big career break when he landed the job of secretary to U.S. senator Edward J. Gay of Louisiana. This took him to Washington, D.C., and the dream of his life—law school. He had access to the senator's law library—part of the deal he made when he was hired. He knew what he could do. *I'll be*

*the best secretary you've ever had, and in return you give me
access to your law books.* That was the deal, so here's Daddy
pursuing the Great American Dream, working for the senator
during the day and taking classes at night at the Columbus
School of Law—a small institution founded for Catholics by
the Knights of Columbus that later became part of Catholic
University.

Mama had zest, humor, and mischief. Gusta Mae, her
Mama named her, and it suited her, especially the *Gusta* part,
which is close to "gusto," which she had in abundance. She
could hold a room with her stories. When Daddy met her, he
didn't stand a chance. Although he was a well-known forty-
year-old bachelor in Baton Rouge with a reputation for never
sealing the marriage deal with women he dated, when Gusta
Mae's gravitational force lured him in, he was a goner. When
they met, she had recently finished nursing school at Our Lady
of the Lake in Baton Rouge, run by the Franciscan Sisters, who
were hoping she'd be a nun. Such a prize—this joyous, pious,
Catholic young woman, who often joined them for early morning Mass, even when she had worked late the night before.

"No, sirree!" Gusta Mae told them. "I'm going to marry a
good Catholic man and have a family." And like all good Catholics of the day, she and Daddy hoped for a big family. They
even ordered a large dining room table with twelve chairs.
When, after two years of dating, Daddy proposed, saying they
could set the wedding date when a certain piece of real estate
was sold, Gusta Mae checked the newspaper every day, and
when she saw the property had been sold, sent the announce-
ment of the wedding to the newspaper herself.

It was fun being her kid. She made everything a game,
warmed our clothes by the fireplace on cold February days,
surprised us on hot summer days, as we worked in the yard

with Daddy, all of us dripping with sweat. Here comes Mama with the brown pottery pitcher, full of ice-tinkling, freshly made lemonade with bright yellow disks of lemon floating on the top.

Always in the evening there were prayers. Before getting into bed at night, there were Daddy and Mama kneeling by their bed, saying their night prayers. Mama was upright but Daddy knelt at a slant like a slide with his arms and head resting on the bed, and Mary Ann and I liked to ride down his back, and he'd let us do it.

At night when Daddy would be reading his newspaper, we'd sneak up and suddenly bat the paper out of his hands. Mary Ann was shy. She'd do it once, maybe, and Mama would hear me egging her on to do it again. "Come on, Mary, he's not gonna do us nothing." I had complete confidence in Daddy, and it was from him that I got intellectual curiosity and a love for books and reading and tips about public speaking. It was Daddy who urged us to keep a travel diary when we took long family trips, and I was the only one who did it. Like Mama, Daddy was a great storyteller and joke teller, and I can still remember a few of his classics. He *loved* Groucho Marx. ("These are my principles and I'm sticking to them. If you don't like these, I have others.") It was wit he loved, which led to a lot of wordplay at the dinner table, which still happens when Mary Ann, Louie, and I get together. Most of it pretty corny stuff. Daddy also introduced us to *Roget's Thesaurus,* and I felt proud just to be able to pronounce the name.

Daddy had definite opinions about politics, and a quick temper. The one and only time he ever talked directly to Governor Huey Long, he called him a goddamn son-of-a-bitch dictator and hung up the phone. The only time he cussed was when he talked politics. We girls were not allowed to cuss, of course. It was part of Southern women's gentility, and I held off doing it for a long, long time.

Whenever Daddy came home in the evening from the office, Mary Ann and I would be waiting in the kitchen to hug and kiss him. Mama was always telling us about Daddy being our "breadwinner" and working hard for us so we could have our clothes and toys and house. Until I was in high school, I didn't realize he was eighteen years older than Mama. All I knew was that Mama was Mama and Daddy was Daddy, and they loved each other and were a team, so what did age have to do with it?

Every morning and evening Mary Ann and I would kneel at Mama's knee to say our prayers to the Blessed Mother and Jesus to help us be good children. We'd repeat the words of the prayers after Mama, and one day a significant request was added: "And please, dear Jesus, send us a little brother." Five years later along comes Louie.

I was old enough to be secure in myself and ready to be Mama's helper with my new little brother. When Mary Ann went to school in first grade and I was left alone with Mama, I was by her side as she sewed and cooked, watching her and chattering away like a chipmunk, giving my constant commentary on life, liberty, and the pursuit of happiness. Unsolicited, I proffered new information I was learning. "Mama, I know the difference between a cow and a bull. . . . The cow has a lot of little bitty tits and the bull has just one great big tit." Sometimes at night I'd overhear Mama and Daddy in their bedroom, talking and laughing. *Guess what Helen told me today.*

Talking—easy, friendly talk in southern Louisiana—is the most natural thing in the world to do. Mama talked to *every-*

body, her friends on the phone, cashiers, even to the telephone operator when she got a wrong number.

Mama gets most of my questions.

"Where do we live?"

"Baton Rouge—it's French for 'Red Stick.' "

And she explains that Baton Rouge is our city and Louisiana is our state, and guess what? Daddy's name, Louis, is in our state name.

I write it down, proud of it, and show it to Frances Paula, a childhood friend.

Frances Paula is one of six children in the Holiday family. Our mamas had been in nursing school together and our families are close. We argue fiercely about whose daddy has the best job, makes the most money, whose house is the best. On the house bit I win hands down because our house is a big two-story house, plus I'm quick to throw in that our yard is bigger than theirs—that we have five whole acres of land.

Frances says, "Oh, yeah? Well, our house is closer to Our Lady of Mercy Church."

This gives me pause. Jesus in the tabernacle—the Real Presence right down the street? Tough to beat and she knows it, and she caps it off with: "And our house is close to a drugstore, and we can walk there any time we want and buy things."

I'm ready. "That's nothin'. Mary Ann and I walk to Duke's drugstore, which has a gumball machine and you can get a lot of stuff with four pennies and in the summer Mama lets us walk there barefooted."

"We go barefooted, too."

"My daddy is a lawyer and people pay him cash on the barrel just to get his *advice* [the barrel thing I'd picked up from a cowboy movie]. He's paid ten or fifteen cents for every word he says. That's why we're going to be rich. My daddy's a millionaire."

"No way. Do you know how much a million dollars is? No way."

And so it goes, jousting our way toward selfhood.

I guess I started out as a pretty violent kid. Mary Ann and I were always arguing and fighting. I mean slugging it out—punching. We never scratched or pulled hair, and a cardinal rule was that you could never slap in the face. I see now that a lot of the violence originated with some tough childhood friends. Once, for self-protection, I ordered boxing lessons by mail. In a magazine I had seen the ad that showed a weak, skinny guy at the beach—you could even see his ribs—and a big, muscular guy comes along and taunts the skinny guy and kicks sand in his face, and when I saw the scene, I knew just how the skinny guy felt, so I clipped out the coupon for the free "You, too, can be a he-man" booklet, but by the time it arrived, I had drifted on to other pursuits.

Besides the tomboy stuff, I liked girl play, too, but only with certain friends. With Charlotte Bahlinger I played paper dolls and with Harriet Jacob I played with real dolls, which we bathed and fed and dressed like we were their mamas. Harriet and I also practiced gymnastics and hatched glorious plans to give a major neighborhood performance and charge admission, which would include a glass of free lemonade, but she was the only one who could do a full back bend. No matter how hard I tried, my back wouldn't bend. But I could do almost perfect cartwheels.

I wanted badly to be famous for something, and for the first fifteen or so years I thought sports would be my gateway to fame. I was short but a fast runner, and in races or jump-the-sticks I always ran the fastest and jumped farthest. During recess when it was softball season, I was always chosen captain and always pitcher.

During high school at St. Joseph Academy, *the* team to belong to was the Red Sticker Basketball Team. Mary Ann was a star forward, and whenever there were tournaments, she often received a medal. I had every bit as much enthusiasm for basketball as Mary Ann did, but I was a bit challenged. I was too short, and I was a terrible shot. I could move around the court very fast, I could dribble and pass, but I was lucky if I netted four points in the entire game. I lacked the skill—the poise Mary Ann had when she'd feint one way, wheel around and stand, arm raised, ball poised on her fingertips, and *swish*. I was far too jerky in my movements to ever be accurate. But what I lacked in skill, I made up for with whirling-dervish energy and enthusiasm, and I excelled at out-jumping players far taller than me at jump balls. Maybe that's why our coach, Sister Alice Marie Macmurdo, kept me on the team: for my relentless, fierce hustle. And no doubt my inability to score made me hustle all the more. Like the preacher's note to himself to put punch into his sermon: "Ending weak, yell like hell."

I compensated on the court for my lack of skill in another way as well: I prayed. You never saw a more devout player than Prejean, number three, as I stood on the line for a free throw. After all, we were a Catholic team, and public school teams came to expect sprinklings of prayer from us throughout the game. Before the game there was always the huddle and some Hail Marys and an Our Father, and always this rousing cheer: "For when the one Great Scorer comes to write against your name, He writes not that you won or lost *but how you played the game, so PLAY IT WELLLLLLLLL!*"

Lord knows, with people like me on the team we needed a

lot of help. Nobody prayed on court more than me. I even chose the number three for my jersey in honor of the three persons of the Trinity. It didn't help that I never practiced and that all I cared about, really, was the pure social engagement of it all—being part of a team and dressing in uniform and riding the bus to out-of-town games. True, I didn't shine much on the court, but shine I did on the bus with classmates and friends. I knew a million jokes and loved to tease, and when we harmonized, I sang soprano like an angel.

In retrospect I realize that I never did really *like* basketball. What I wanted was a way to excel, to rise above the crowd, to be somebody special. Which is fine, but playing basketball also evoked in me a far less praiseworthy trait—with a strong greenish hue.

The truth was I was playing basketball mostly as a way to gain fame. One clue that I was in it for the wrong reason was the constant feeling of jealousy I had for my teammates who scored a lot of points. Not the older girls—they were out of my orbit. It was the athletic prowess of my peers that got my goat. Why wasn't I at least happy that they could be counted on to score some decent points for our team? What about that made me so sad? I could tell they really loved the sport. They'd be there in the gym on their own time before school. And after school, there they were, practicing free throws and layups and set shots. I never did that, even though we had a basketball net in our backyard. Later, when I find out about purity of intention in the spiritual life, I'll learn that jealousy is a symptom more than a cause, and it raises the question, *What does she have that I urgently wish I had?* Surface answer: I want to be high scorer like her. Deeper answer: I want to have her passion for the sport itself.

But I didn't want to put in the effort. I just wanted to get medals. I never worked toward the delicious feel of a ball arching perfectly through the air, all in a flow from my fingertips, and knowing it was going right into the basket. I didn't know about "acting by not acting" that the Tao teaches. Later, I'll learn this bedrock principle of the spiritual life: *Do what you do for its own sake, not for the benefits you get from it.*

EVERY SUNDAY WE go to Mass at Our Lady of Mercy Church.

I learn that going to Mass is the single most important thing a human being can do on this earth to save souls. This is because the Mass is the reenactment of Jesus's sacrifice of his life on the cross, which gained infinite merit, also called grace, which is heavenly currency having the power to save souls from the fires of hell. I learn Catholic doctrine from the Baltimore Catechism in Sister Lawrence's first-grade religion class: about grace and indulgences and sacraments and holy water and how the Catholic way of salvation works.

I learn that Catholics are really, really lucky because we have the one true faith and Protestants don't. For one thing, we have the Real Presence of Jesus in the tabernacle in church, but Protestants think the bread is only a symbol. They don't accept the authority of the Pope and a whole lot of other things. True, Protestants can go to heaven by God's mercy, but it's going to be tough for them to make it without all the Catholic help, and that's why we are never to set foot in a Protestant church or attend a Protestant service. I'm very glad I'm a Catholic, and feel sorry for my friend Caroline because she was unlucky enough to be born a Protestant, and her parents don't even take her to church.

Sometimes when Caroline and I play dolls I try to give a good example—you know, very, very indirectly—by suggesting that maybe we could take my doll, Marie Noel, and her doll (I forget her name) to church. I pray for Caroline and her family because if they don't get it right before they die, they'll either go to hell, which is sad, or else they'll spend eons in purgatory, which burns you in fire, too, but you can get out one day after maybe four million years, when you're purified enough to enter heaven with Catholics, and you get to see God face-to-face and you're blissfully happy and nothing can make you sad, and if you want it, you can have an ice cream cone every fifteen minutes or your pet dog or anything at all that makes you happy. That's what Sister Mary Lawrence taught us, and it's God's truth.

I'm scared to death of hell, and it's going to take me a long time to break free of the fear. (Later on, when I'm studying to be a nun in the novitiate, one afternoon when I am kneeling before a statue of Mary and asking her to intercede with Jesus for me—for the umpteenth time—I finally figure out that the reason I'm always praying to Mary is that I'm scared to death of God.)

In my formative years, fear of hell is so interwoven into Catholic teaching that almost subliminally, no matter how much God's loving mercy is talked about, the Big Fear always wins, hands down. The doctrinal language specifying what you can do to go straight to hell is called "mortal sin." It means a sin so terrible that it can cut you off from God for all eternity. And what is eternity? I remember Sister Lawrence in her long black dress and veil with a giant rosary hanging by her side, and I can see her standing by her desk in the front of the classroom helping us get our six-year-old heads around the concept of eternity. Picture an enormous steel ball as big as earth and every million years a bird flies by and scrapes its beak against the ball—only a tiny scrape—well, children, the millions and billions of years it would take for the steel ball to wear down to the size of a marble would mark *only the beginning* of eternity.

All I know is that it's the most terrible thing to be cut off from God forever, and you can't climb out of hell no matter how much you beg and cry. And I'm terribly aware that I don't suffer well; I'm the biggest crybaby ever. I cry when Mary Ann gives me a "frog" in my arm, which means hitting the muscle with your knuckles in the most tender part of your arm, which sends a shock through your whole arm. I cry when Mary Ann and her friend Kathleen or Lydia Ann do magic tricks and won't tell me how they do them.

There was only one time in our entire childhood when Mary Ann cried and I didn't, and that was when we got our tonsils out. My throat was hurting, too, but I didn't cry, and it was the only time. She was always braver and stronger than me. So I can't begin to imagine how much crying I'll do if I go to hell—with no Mama to hold me and tell me it's going to be okay. That would be the saddest of all because Mama would be up in heaven and I could never reach her, and at the thought of it my mind just shuts down—it's too terrible to think about. Once, playing "imagination" with my friend Harriet Jacob, she dared me to make myself cry. We were upstairs in a bedroom, and I stepped inside the bathroom and got behind the door and pictured Mama dying and that was that.

The sin that was always mortal and could land you in hell in a heartbeat was any kind of sexual sin, which always started with impure thoughts. As girls we were taught to dress modestly (shorts not too short, dresses that amply covered bosoms) so as not to be "occasions of sin" for boys, who seemed always to have a ready inclination toward sex. It was just the way they were made, and we girls—the responsible ones—had to help them. I knew you weren't supposed to ever touch certain parts of your body yourself, even though it was your own body. Much less allow boys to touch you.

I didn't know about sexual intercourse for the longest time. Sex eluded me. I thought the power of the spirit was so strong a force that when a man and woman kissed, if they wanted a baby strong enough, the woman would get pregnant simply from the couple's mutual will. I was just so convinced that the power that could move heaven and earth and make anything happen was spiritual power. Hadn't Jesus said that if you have faith enough, you can say to a mountain: "Cast yourself into the sea," and it will up and jump into the sea? Is that spiritual power or what? I lived in the realm of the miraculous, so why not a direct intervention of God in the birth of babies, too? Hadn't the Holy Spirit overshadowed Mary to conceive Jesus in her virginal womb?

Mama tried to explain how it worked, and she insisted— she said it more than once—how beautiful "the sexual act" was, that God had created us man and woman, and the reason that only married people could have sex was because only people who were committed to each other for life could provide a loving home for children.

But there was an undercurrent of fear around the "beautiful" act. In the catalogue of sins, killing someone might be justified and not a sin at all, but sexual sins were always mortal sins. Even *thinking* about sex in a way that caused arousal was a sin. Killing umpteen people in war—even dropping an atomic bomb on the enemy (if it served a good purpose, to end a war)—wasn't a sin. But masturbation was always a sin, and a mortal sin at that. That's what the Baltimore Catechism taught. All of which made sex a Very Scary Area. One slip on its slippery slope and you found yourself burning in hell.

At Mama's urging, Mary Ann and I always wore a Mary

medal (called a miraculous medal) around our necks, and when Mary Ann got married at Our Lady of Mercy Church, after pronouncing her vows (to a wonderful man named Charlie), she went and knelt before the statue of Mary to put her marriage under her patronage. Nun rules did not allow me to attend her wedding, but Eliza Commeaux, a close family friend, came to see me at the convent immediately afterward and told me all about it, describing in some detail how impressed everyone was to see young Mary Ann kneeling in prayer before Mary before leaving the church for the reception.

Before I joined the Sisterhood I had never had a close boyfriend, so my purity was untested. I had never experienced even one close, lingering kiss. From seeing movies and hearing popular songs, I often wondered what intimacy with a man might be like. How special for a woman to be singled out, chosen, sung to, admired, given roses and candy and told over and over in poems and endless protestations how beautiful she is, how desirable she is! That must be the most secure, most exhilarating feeling in this world.

At least for a weekend or two.

It's the settling in for life, promising to find happiness with just one person, that gave me pause.

I wanted more.

New Habits

Since the Sisters of the Congregation are not strictly cloistered and must go out into the world to devote themselves to the practice of charity and works of mercy, it is necessary to receive as subjects only those who possess the qualities and virtues required to edify the neighbor and safeguard the subjects themselves from all danger.

The following qualifications are required:

Applicants must be of legitimate birth. Their parents must have led an exemplary life and must not have incurred any defamatory judicial sentences. They must have good health. . . . They must be free from debt. They must, above all, be straightforward, and must possess a sound and practical judgment. Those who are notably lacking in judgment must be excluded.

—"Formation of Subjects,"
Rules and Directory of the Sisters of St. Joseph

When I joined the Congregation of St. Joseph (CSJ), in 1957, Catholic girls right out of high school were entering religious life in droves. Between 1950 and 1965 the number of religious women in the United States rose from 147,000 to 179,974. We had eighteen members in our band—a tiny number compared to our cousin CSJs in the Northeast (same founder, different branches), who routinely had a hundred or so young women a year entering the community. After the Second Ecumenical Council of the Vatican (1962–65) the number of aspirants to religious life would plummet, and nuns would leave the convent in large numbers. Some would say the number of nuns dwindled because we modernized too much and so lost our distinctive, otherworldly form of life that set us apart from ordinary Catholics.

For now, I'll just say that the huge mind shift of Vatican II about Christian vocation and holiness—that every baptized Christian is called to holiness, not just nuns and priests—in confluence with women coming into our own intellectually, socially, and politically, had more than anything else to do with the diminished number of nuns. Until Vatican II, Catholic women flocked to religious life in large part because it was held up as such an esteemed option for Catholic women who chose not to marry. In contrast, the lifestyle of single women was considered a shadowy half-life existence at best: unable to get a husband and not generous or holy enough to become a nun. But, no doubt, with fear of eternal damnation as a driving undercurrent in so many Catholic lives, the single biggest advantage to becoming a nun was that you were practically assured eternal salvation. (Whoever heard of nuns going to hell, except in jokes? Or even getting a traffic ticket?)

An aside: The traffic-ticket nun waiver extends into current time. A few years ago I'm driving on Interstate 10 from Baton Rouge to New Orleans and occupying myself in an intellectually satisfying way by reading a book I have propped up against the steering wheel. I glance down at it for a few sentences, then look up at traffic, and so on—up and down—and everything is going smoothly until I become conscious of a blue flickering light on top of a car riding alongside me on the left, and, lo and behold, I'm looking into the faces of two rosy-cheeked, no-doubt-rookie policemen, now speaking over the loudspeaker and ordering me to pull over. They pull over behind me and I reach into the glove compartment for insurance papers, which

I do speedily in situations like this, because the insurance forth-rightly names Sisters of St. Joseph as the car owners, and I hope the "nun card" might effect a merciful outcome.

Meanwhile, the rookie cops have zapped my license plate and a digital voice informs them that they have a nun on their hands. I now take my sweet time with the insurance papers because I can hear them in deep theological discussion about their situation, and one is saying, "Rick, for God's sake, she's a nun. We can't give her a ticket; we'll go straight to hell!" No use rushing such a discussion, so, papers in hand, I slowly walk to the back of the car, and the younger of the two (he looks like he's twelve years old) tells me in a worried, very concerned tone that they had been cruising alongside me for ten minutes and that I'd go fifty miles an hour, then seventy, sometimes eighty, then drop to forty, and that I must never, ever read while driving, that it is a very, very, very dangerous thing to do, not just for me but for others. They are so totally sincere and concerned that I promise on the spot never, ever to read while driving ever again. I mean it. And I haven't done it since. True story. No ticket.

The CSJ congregation I joined got its start in France in 1650, one of the first innovative religious communities to allow women to leave the enclosure of the cloister to serve the people. Until then, joining a "nunnery" meant sealing yourself off from the world to devote yourself to a life of prayer and penance. In seventeenth-century France, where women were severely constrained and options were limited, for some women, at least, joining this new form of Sisterhood with its freedom to work with people in need must have seemed like a heady adventure. Married women had a hard lot. Many died during childbirth, and usually the very best a woman could hope for in a husband was *amitié,* friendship, and even that was asking a lot. Confessional manuals of the time reveal that fathers had "absolute" rights over children and wives, and disobedience to the paterfamilias was treated as a mortal sin.

A woman's average age when she married was twenty-four, and most women gave birth to a child about every two years. Childbirth was precarious, and because so many women died giving birth (one in five, or even worse in bad times), a live birth and an alive mother were an occasion for celebration. But getting born was but the first step in a hard, brutal life in which starvation and malnutrition, plagues, blights, epidemics, and wars cut lives short. As always, peasants—90 percent of the French population—fared the worst. Misery and desperation among peasants led to a rash of rebellions close to the time of my congregation's founding in 1650.

Enter this scene six women in Le Puy-en-Velay, whose names I give you because so often in literature, including the Bible, women remain nameless. Our founding women were Françoise Eyraud, the leader; Marguerite Burdier, whose spirit so breathed life into the group that she was known as its "soul"; Claudia Chastel, who alone could sign her name; and three Annas—Anna Vey, Anna Brun, and Anna Chraleyer. A Jesuit priest, Jean Pierre Medaille, who met the women in the course of his preaching in their towns and villages, organized them into a spiritual association devoted to piety and service "of the dear neighbor" and gave them a simple "rule" (a set of instructions) by which they governed themselves.

This was a vote of supreme confidence at a time when women were thought to be governed by "cold and wet humors," and thus incapable of fully exercising logical thought. Nor did the theology of the day about women as "Daughters of Eve" help to bolster confidence in women's gifts. Churchmen preached untiringly about women as temptresses, considered to be more "physical and bestial" than human. No surprise then that many churchmen believed that women were more prone to heresy than men, and so should be separated physically from men in church and not trusted to express opinions on spiritual or theological subjects.

In the spiritual manuals of the day, topping the list of womanly virtues were purity, obedience, and utter submission and resignation. Every spiritual writer of the day stressed that to attain union with God demanded nothing less than "annihilation of self." Such language, and the attitudes that accompanied it, seeded itself throughout my congregation's constitution, formulary of prayers, and "maxims of perfection," and were still in evidence when I joined the community. But there were some timeless spiritual gems in there, too, and I can still say some of them by heart:

"*Never leap ahead of grace by imprudent eagerness, but quietly await its movements, and when it comes to you, go along with it with gentleness . . . and courage.*" I ought to have this maxim tattooed on my forehead, so badly do I need its counsel. I'm a "leaper," all right. (I claim to be "spontaneous.") But it's true, at the least provocation I'm prone to jump into action headlong, and only in retrospect check back to see if, perhaps, the motivating spark was divinely inspired, or, once again, simply that trigger-happy ego of mine ready to spring. Thank God for my wise community.

"*Always speak favorably of others and value highly the good in them, excusing in the best way you can, the deficiencies they have.*" (A tough one, especially dealing with the Clicks of the world.)

"*Never think of tomorrow unless it has some necessary*

link with today, but entrust it entirely to providence." (Ahhh . . . the wellspring of Buddhist wisdom: staying attentive to the present moment.)

If a single motto were written above the portals of the novitiate, it would be "Enter here to die to self to be reborn in Christ." Of course, it might have helped to have something of a developed "self" to die to. Most of us were just kids right out of high school—idealistic, inexperienced, malleable, and trusting. So, no surprise that our descent into the novitiate experience, with its practices of humility, bolstered by the novice mistress's public reprimands, and extremely limited social contacts and relationships with everybody else in the world, might be—to put it mildly—detrimental to healthy personal development.

Choosing to perform a practice of humility is one thing. But Mother taking you apart limb from limb in front of everyone is shattering. Not just for me, but for others, some of whom I can tell have zero confidence to begin with.

When Mother singles you out for correction, you follow the novice protocol: Drop to your knees, lower your veil, and receive her correction in silence. You never, ever, no matter the circumstances, defend yourself. Corrections can be about anything: being even a few seconds late for class or community prayers, not keeping modesty of the eyes, speaking out of turn, calling attention to yourself (a big one; you're never supposed to stand out)—anything. I'm moving into my second year of novice training and studying attentively the Holy Rule (which includes a chapter on the novice mistress), so I really should have been able to keep a tighter lid on these wayward lips of mine.

Here's what our Holy Rule says about the role of the novice mistress:

The novices will often remind themselves that the novitiate is a time of trial. . . . Neither will they be astonished at the trials to which the superiors submit them in order to train them in self-conquest and strengthen their virtue. With this in mind the superiors may impose upon them some salutary humiliations . . . and teach them to give up their own way of seeing and doing things so that the novices may recast themselves in the mold of the rules, the customs, and the methods of the Institute.

Having already weathered postulancy and the first year of novitiate, I'm figuring I'm ready to take whatever Mother dishes out. If Jesus suffered humiliation, why shouldn't I? He was spit upon and whipped and taunted as he hung from the cross. I mean, what's a little humiliation when you know Mother's just following the Holy Rule? She's not being mean; she's simply performing her disciplinary role.

But I never should have cracked that stupid joke.

It happens while we are helping out with a super load of laundry, and we are plastering a ton of guimpes—the white breastplate-like cloths—onto metal sheets. Novices are called in to help with laundry when there's too much work for Sister Bernard to handle. (I like Sister Bernard. She's French, has button-brown eyes and large, overhanging cheeks, and a big, warm heart. When we play around instead of working, she says, *"Grand parleur, petit faiseur."* ["Much talk, little work"], but the twinkle is there and we tease her back, "Whatcha mean, Sister? Whatcha mean, *parleur*-ing and *faiseur*-ing?")

But there's no teasing Mother.

Today, because of the huge load of linens, not only guimpes, but bandeaus (forehead coverings) as well, we work all morning and into the afternoon. Mother gave us *benedicamus* for part of the day, so we could talk as we worked, and that's probably what does me in—me, the roaring extrovert who loves to chatter and tease (learned with some proficiency at the Prejean dinner table). So, here we are with zillions of linens to do, not hard work, really, kind of fun, rolling up sleeves and sticking hands into the sticky, blue-white, gelatinous starchy goo, slathering it onto white linen cloths, then plastering the cloths onto a metal sheet. The way you starch linens (who knows? you might need this in another life) is that after you rub the glob of starch all over the linen, you start in the middle and press the heels of your hands firmly over the cloth, careful to work the air bubbles out at the sides. And what joy in the work of art after the linen has dried in the sun and you peel it off and it's smooth as glass. It takes a while to get the hang of it, though. Imagine the look on the faces of the professed Sisters—veteran nuns, who have professed vows—upon seeing the craters and pockmarks in their guimpes, which the poor things have to wear for a week. They know all too well who got shanghaied into laundry duty.

Back to laundry duty and my loose lips . . . By early afternoon, when Mother dips in to see the progress of the work, Linen Mountain still sits mighty high in the laundry basket.

"How's it going, Sisters?" Mother asks.

And in I go: "Oh, fine, Mother. Ten thousand down, only thirty thousand to go."

All it takes is one look from Mother, and lickety-split I am on my knees for ten minutes.

Until then—except for the bed posture thing—her corrections hadn't perforated my self-confidence. But Mother keeps at me, and I begin to feel demeaned.

"A generous young Sister would have spoken about progress made, not complain. You're always seeking to call attention to yourself. A humble, generous little Sister would make light of the task. A prayerful little Sister would never . . ."

At first, inside myself, I'm holding it together, thinking, *Mother is just doing her job to keep me humble just like the Holy Rule says.* But she is going after my motives, my character. It's bad, and I feel myself crumbling inside. *Maybe Mother can see that I don't have what it takes to be a good nun.* In conferences, Mother has made it *very clear* that she has the power with the higher-ups to block our profession of vows if she doesn't think we are mature enough. The ultimate threat: *You have been tested and found wanting.* I picture Mama and Daddy's shock and disappointment. Their daughter too immature to profess vows with her group—like a kid in school, held back a grade—all because of *one teeny wisecrack,* obviously a joke.

Afterward I run upstairs to the dorm room and cry my eyes out. Sister Kathleen Bahlinger, a childhood friend, one year ahead of me, sees me crying and says, in her German matter-of-fact way, "You'll learn."

Until now, I have had a pretty secure self to hold on to. In junior high I was always elected president of my class, and in high school I was student-body president, accustomed to initiating projects, writing essays that won contests, holding forth at a podium in front of the student body and faculty. And I received top honors at graduation. But here all the rules are different. The whole idea is to die to self. But it's harder than I thought.

My family bolstered a vigorous sense of self in all of us. I was loved, delighted in, rocked as a baby in Mama's arms far longer than the law allowed. Mama told me that when she'd rock me and sing to me, I'd settle in under her arm, and when she felt my body go slack, she'd slowly rise to put me in my bed, when from under her arm would come the peremptory command: "Rock!"

Now in my life—this. Which seems to stand in some contrast to the ideas of Father Jean Pierre Medaille, who, despite his use of the annihilation-of-self argot of seventeenth-century spirituality, presupposed the first members of the new congregation to be substantive women. With a minimum of supervision he drew up a basic rule of life that set the women's energies free to go into the streets, discern a course of action, and serve the people. He trusted that a deep spiritual life in community would give them the inner compass they needed. In the seventeenth century the first Sisters, dressed as widows (which freed them to travel the streets unaccompanied by a male companion), ministered to the hungry and homeless, the imprisoned and orphaned, the diseased and illiterate. Soon small communities of "Daughters of Joseph" began to appear across the southeastern countryside of France. The communities of two or three began the day with prayer and gathered in the evening around the hearth for a meal, prayer, and conversation about how the work of the day had gone.

The effort of each Sister to remain attuned to the promptings of the Holy Spirit, combined with collective discernment in addressing the needs of society, has been a hallmark of our community, as it is of other *apostolic* (in contrast to contemplative) religious orders. When, in the 1960s, Vatican II invited religious orders of women to recover once again the spirit of our founders so we might better adapt our service to the needs of the people, American nuns responded with amazing—and, to some, alarming—alacrity.

The truth is that by the 1940s religious orders of nuns had pretty much lost the spirit of our founders—the "*charism* of the community," as we called it. The uniform Code of Canon

Law (spiritual regulations that govern the Catholic Church), imposed on the Holy Rules of nuns, had pretty well blotted out distinguishing characteristics of particular congregations. As a result, all rules looked alike, and you couldn't tell a Franciscan from a St. Joseph or a Benedictine from a Notre Dame or an Ursuline. Naturally, in the authoritarian mode of the day, every revised rule gave top value to the virtues of obedience and submission. Members were to be obedient to superiors, and superiors, in turn, were to be unquestioningly obedient to bishops and other members of the hierarchy.

Those were the days when we were called the "good nuns" and "obedient daughters of Mother Church." Or, in playfulness, because of our black-and-white dress: "penguins." We dressed in black all the way down: veil, wide-sleeved blouse, petticoat, long serge skirt, stockings, and old-lady-lace-up shoes. The only white was the band around our faces, covering forehead, ears, and neck, and a wide, starched guimpe, which covered our breasts. The guimpe proved something of a challenge for our buxom women because it refused to lie flat and tended to stick out like a shelf. Not exactly helpful on the modesty end of things. (There were no guimpe-stick-out worries for me. Mine hung down flat as a Kansas prairie.)

Another aside: When we nuns head out onto the streets of New Orleans, the black garb can scare the willies out of little kids, especially little black kids, who have never come within a hundred yards of a nun. And in New Orleans, with its colorful citizenry, laid-back lifestyle, and penchant for storytelling, there in the mix of Mardi Gras and Bourbon Street nun anecdotes abound.

Woman One: "What's that coming?"

Woman Two: "Catholic nuns."

Woman One: "Why they dressed all in black like that?"

Woman Two: "They married to Jesus; he died on the cross."

Woman One: "Well, they sure in deep mournin' about it."

It would take Vatican II for us nuns to dress once again as ordinary people. As luck would have it for the poor, shocked Catholic faithful, unaccustomed to seeing even a lock of our hair, much less legs, arms, and—Lord have mercy—bosoms, the time of our "coming out" happened to coincide with the time when miniskirts were in vogue. So, not only were the "good nuns" going wild, we were going hog wild by wearing skirts that stopped at the knees, or, with some of the young ones, above the knees—or even pantsuits. Shock waves reverberated through clergy and laity alike, but the wisdom among us was that if we nuns were going to join our contemporaries, we sure as heck weren't going to look frumpy. (That remains a matter of opinion; some folks claim they can easily pick out a nun in a crowd.) Even now, years later, I still encounter folks who grump about the day of doom for the Catholic Church when we nuns "defrocked" ourselves.

Back in eighteenth-century France, the new form of "unenclosed" religious life quickly attracted new members from upper-class "elites" and peasants alike, both eager to be part of this fresh opportunity for interiority, spiritual friendship, education, and work in the public square. Within the first five years, in the Le Puy area alone, twenty CSJ communities sprang up, and before the French Revolution in 1793 chopped the sapling congregation down to the ground, a hundred or more additional sister communities had been established around France.

At first, the Revolution targeted only cloistered nuns, not active communities who tended the poor and sick and were seen as fulfilling a social purpose. But as the Revolution unraveled into paranoia during the Reign of Terror, it became increasingly difficult for the Daughters of Joseph to avoid taking the "patriotic oath," which aimed to cut off Catholics from Rome. Under threat of death, Catholics were forbidden to associate with priests who refused to take the oath, or, worse, anyone who attempted to hide such priests. During the Terror many Sisters in the fledgling community were imprisoned, and five were guillotined.

Having myself accompanied six human beings to execution, I feel irresistibly drawn to the women's suffering and fear—especially thirty-one-year-old Sister Toussaint Dumoulin, who at the time of her arrest protested vehemently that she had been away from the convent in Dauphine when a priest had come there to hide. The young woman's pleas fell on impervious ears. In June 1794, she and the priest and two other Sisters—Sainte-Croix Vincent and Madeleine Senovert—were tried and sentenced to death.

Their agonized wait was extended by a month—first, because the small town had no guillotine and one had to be transported across the country, and then because officials had to recruit someone from another town who knew how to operate it. And all the while as she waited in her dungeon cell, Sister Toussaint's loud cries of innocence reverberated throughout the prison. On July 8, 1794, she and the others were led to the guillotine erected in the town square where, at the sight of the first severed head, she fainted. As her limp body was carried across the square, some of the townspeople cried for mercy, but to no avail. The executioners carried out the bloody task and reached for the next victim. In another town, two other Sisters were executed during the Terror: Sister St. Julien Garnier and Sister Alexis Aubert. Many others awaiting execution were spared at the last minute by the death, on July 28, 1794, of Maximilien Robespierre, zealous leader of the Terror.

Sister St. John Fontbonne, a fiery, determined woman who was among those who escaped the guillotine by a hair's breadth, set about reassembling the scattered Daughters of Joseph in Lyon. We CSJs credit her with refounding the congregation, and you'll find her serene, strong face in every motherhouse.

Back at work among the people, it did not take the women long to find their way to girls and women desperately in need of education and work skills. Starvation and malnutrition were rampant, and having enough to eat became such a fixation that there arose a mentally frenzied state known as "hunger disease." The quest for food began right after birth in small babies. What chance of survival did children have, especially girl children and young, single women? In Le Puy, many women found work making lace, though those with strong bodies did manual work as well, some of them working side by side with men, digging ditches.

The education of women soon became a top priority for the newly founded congregation. A large boarding school for young women arose in Lyon close to the convent, a model multiplied throughout the world and across the United States and Canada when, in the 1830s, CSJs made their way to North America, and to Baton Rouge, Louisiana, and, eventually, blessedly, to me.

Becoming Fire

FIRE
God of Abraham, God of Isaac, God of Jacob
not of the philosophers and of the learned.
Certainty, certainty, heartfelt, joy, peace.
God of Jesus Christ . . .
The world has not known Thee but I have known Thee.

—Blaise Pascal

Blaise Pascal, the seventeenth-century French philosopher, turned to the image of fire to convey his encounter with the divine. He so wanted to remember the encounter that he recorded it on a small piece of paper and sewed it into his coat and carried it everywhere.

I want to pray with fire like that. Learning how to pray is one of the main goals of novitiate. You can't be a saint if you don't know how to pray. The fire, the mystic union, is God's pure gift—so all the prayer manuals say. And it's far from automatic. It's grace; you can't achieve it by your own efforts. When I show up to pray, even if I wait humbly for long hours or even when I make sacrifices to add "weight" to my request for divine favor—none of this amounts to a hill of beans when it comes to mystical graces.

We have this one novice who must have the gift of mystical prayer. She kneels stone-still in chapel during the entire time of meditation, and you can just tell that she is deeply into it. She also seems to stay in a state of prayer (we call it "recollection") during the day, too, because she maintains really good modesty of the eyes. You never catch her looking around at everything.

As for me, I found out that too much modesty of the eyes could be dangerous. One time when I was experimenting I had lowered my eyelids too far and had a traffic accident in the hallway. While rounding a corner I ran squarely into Sister Barbara Hughes just as she was bending over a bucket wringing out a mop. She went down, I didn't, and I can still see her uncomprehending look as she stared up at me from the floor. From this I learned that lids lowered way down—maybe to seven-eighths—is too much.

And in the chapel I just can't be stone-still. I always have to move around a little, though not as bad as Click, and it usually takes a while to still my mind, which jumps around with distractions like popcorn. Actually, my mind jumps around almost all the time.

One of the main reasons I'm seeking a nun's life is that I know it will give me chunks of time for prayer and spiritual studies. I need the silence it offers, freed from the empty chatter and trivial conversations at which I excel. I need the time it opens up for retreats and spiritual reading and study, and—maybe most important of all—to be in the company of other spiritual seekers.

I have my prayer models, like Thomas Merton, a cloistered Trappist monk at the Abbey of Gethsemani in Kentucky. *The Seven Storey Mountain,* the story of his conversion from worldly life to monk, seized my imagination while I was still in high school. Merton had led an alcohol-sodden, pleasure-seeking life, but an intellectual life, too, which included years of study at Columbia University in New York. One day (like all big soul events, it must have been building inside him), the mysterious power of "vocation" drew him off the busy streets of New York into the dark quiet of a Catholic church. It was all so casual; he hadn't intended to go into the church—he wasn't even a Catholic—but as he ducked into a pew and knelt down he felt his soul go quiet, and a feeling of peace came over him. He didn't know what the quiet meant, but he knew his soul had been waiting for it, and he sought to follow the quiet and the peace it gave him.

Soon after that experience Merton asked to become a Catholic, and things moved quickly. In a few short years he found himself at the gates of Gethsemani asking to be admitted to the abbey. He had thought his vocation was to be a novelist. He loved literature, especially James Joyce; he read all the time, hung out with aspiring writers, and tried his own hand at writing novels (the manuscripts rejected by publishers sat in a drawer), while stalagmites of books were stacked high in his apartment.

But no. Here he was jettisoning a writer's life (or so he thought) in exchange for a life of silence and prayer in strict separation from the world. Then, lo and behold, there in the monastery he found himself in one of his first acts of obedience to the abbot writing a book. His spiritual memoir, *The Seven Storey Mountain*, published in 1948, quickly became a bestseller, amazing and surprising everyone in the publishing world. Merton was all the rage when I was in high school. You had to put your name on the waiting list weeks in advance to check *Mountain* out of the school library.

I loved reading about his young, wild, and lonely life in which he searched and searched and then heard God's call to the purest, loftiest call of all calls: to be a Trappist monk. Carved on the entrance gate of the Abbey of Gethsemani are the words "God alone," and they mean those words. Once inside the walls you surrender your life to silence, fasting, and chanting the Divine Office seven times a day, rising to pray at 3:00 A.M., then interspersing prayer with hard physical work in the fields throughout the day, until Compline as the sun sets and evening comes. You never, ever eat meat and seldom eat fish—only on feast days. You never have wine or beer. You talk only through sign language. You never leave the monastery except for emergencies, and then only with permission from the abbot. And you sleep on a hard board and are supposed to meditate on death as you fall asleep.

In a way, by the life you're leading, you're already dead to this earthly life. But the upshot—the glorious, wondrous benefit of it all—is that in giving all to Christ you will greet death joyfully, recognizing it as the gateway into heaven and eternal communion with God, whom you've already known in prayer. What's more, amid all the other spiritual benefits that accrue to faithful monks, you have the satisfaction of knowing that your penance and prayer, when united with Christ's sacrifice on the cross, has special power to save souls from hell. What earthly life could be worthier than this?

Maybe if I had more spiritual pluck, I would have chosen the cloistered life, and I did consider it for one weekend in high school while I was on retreat, when the silence and solitude were delicious and God felt as close as my mama talking to me in the kitchen. But the weekend ended and I came home to Mama's wonderful garlic-studded roast, rich brown gravy on rice, and garden-grown snap beans, and . . . well, that quickly booted out a cheese-and-vegetables-only penitential cloistered life. I'm part Cajun, and love of food runs deep. Not to mention that life of *total* silence. Never talking? Talking for me is like *breathing*. And, besides, no talking would mean no teaching, and so even though I admired the heck out of Thomas Merton, that put the coda on the cloistered life.

Still, even though I'm joining an apostolic community, not a cloistered one, I know that prayer is at the heart of our life. As the Holy Rule says:

> In order to be good teachers, the Sisters will strive to re-
> main calm, often recalling the presence of God, and they
> will be most faithful to their prayer life so that they may
> not lose the interior spirit in the midst of their occupa-
> tions. [A prayerful Sister] knows how to permeate all her
> teaching with the profound convictions she draws from
> the careful meditation on the Gospel.

Now, here in the novitiate, I know this is what I want most of all: to know Jesus intimately. I'm taking copious notes from my reading and from Mother's conferences about how the saints prayed—the steps they took, one by one, to find the quiet, fertile place where I, too, can meet the living Christ and refashion my life. I have already been introduced to methods of prayer by my high school teacher Sister Jane Louise Arbour. Every spring she would take long walks with me in the spacious green yard of St. Joseph Academy and talk to me about prayer, and one of the most repeated lessons was that you have to devote time to prayer whether you feel like praying or not. You have to commit yourself to times of prayer and present yourself before God faithfully, even if—Sister Jane's words— "you feel you're wasting your time and you feel dry as a stick."

Sister Jane had a special devotion to St. Thérèse of Lisieux, who entered a cloistered Carmelite convent in Normandy at the age of fifteen and died of tuberculosis nine years later, in 1897. In Thérèse's last days, her spiritual agony proved to be even more horrible than the physical torment she endured. In her spiritual autobiography, Thérèse shares the spiritual desolation she felt: "[God] permitted my soul to be invaded by the thickest darkness, and that the thought of heaven, up until then so sweet to me, be no longer anything but the cause of struggle and torment."

It was the mocking voices that got to her the most—voices whispering that her experiences of sweet intimacy with God were nothing but illusion, pure fantasy. But when the end came, Thérèse's face relaxed and cleared and she looked intently at the crucifix and said, "Oh, I love him. . . . My God, I love you."

I'm learning that this is one thing all saints seem to have in common: They all die well. They all pull it off at the end, even if in agony. St. Joan of Arc, burned at the stake on charges of heresy and the unpardonable sin of cross-dressing (she wore men's clothes in battle), cried out in agony as flames engulfed her body, but witnesses attest that she kept her gaze riveted to Jesus on the cross held before her and cried over and over: "Jesus! Jesus! Jesus!"

I shudder at the thought of dying like that.

I just know I'd never be a good martyr. I burned my hand once making brownies and I nursed my wound and talked about my wound and held up my poor burned hand for all to see and sympathize with. Burn at the stake? For something as trivial as holding beliefs considered to be a little unorthodox? Be burned alive for *that*?

I know I wouldn't make it through even a preliminary interrogation. I'd say anything they wanted me to say, confess any sin, even make up new sins if it helped. I'd babble like a brook, squeal on anyone, betray my own family. I'm such a coward.

Martyrs are big-time saints. I'm looking for a way into sainthood for run-of-the-mill, regular folks like me. There must be a way to be holy for cowardly people, too.

So I was very ready when Sister Jane Louise introduced me to the spirituality of the "little way" of St. Thérèse. No big heroics. What makes the "little way" little is that you do very, very ordinary things, such as washing dishes or weeding the garden or doing the laundry—with love for God. The "Little Flower," as Thérèse is affectionately known, taught that these insignificant acts, if done with great love, are as pleasing to God as history-changing, heroic deeds.

Thus was laid down in my soul a foundational principle of the spiritual life that guided my actions for a long time: the type of activity I engage in—what I do—doesn't matter as long as I do it out of love for God.

I know better now.

I know that acts are far from being equal in value, and that in the face of critical suffering and injustice, refusal to act is immoral. Or as Annie Dillard puts it:

> [We] diddle around, making itsy-bitsy friends
> and meals and journeys for itsy-bitsy years on end . . .
> raising tomatoes when we should be . . . raising Cain, or
>   Lazarus.

If, at this part of my journey, I had encountered Dorothee Soelle's book *The Silent Cry: Mysticism and Resistance,* in which she speaks of "mystics who have turned their backs on the world, who politically are totally resigned and swallowed up by their own narcissism," I wouldn't have had a clue about what she meant. I'm happy to be apolitical. The way I see it, *really* spiritual people are *above* politics. After all, when you're in communion with God, the Lord of History, in command of the rise and fall of nations, why be concerned with picayune, ephemeral politics?

When I go to the chapel for meditation, it's the intimacy I'm after, the feeling of God's presence, close and sure—*I am with you,* as God spoke to Moses and Abraham, and to the prophets and to Jesus. Speaking and listening is the life-breath of prayer, especially the listening part. It takes steady spiritual practice to learn to get past anxiety-laden, surface chatter into Deep Soul.

St. Teresa of Ávila called prayer "a conversation with Christ, who loves us," or, simpler still, "a conversation between friends." Ah, yes, *friends.* I've got to learn to relate to Jesus, because in this tidal pool of the novitiate it's the only deep relationship I'm allowed. So, I welcome—*I need*—the safe, private space of the hour of silent meditation each day that our Holy Rule mandates. I need to hear God telling me: *You please me. I delight in you.* With my daddy when I was little it was like that. He'd be reading the newspaper, and I'd sneak up from behind and kiss him on the neck, and I knew he was pleased and he'd call me his *petitsie.* So confident was I of his love that when I had scary dreams he was always the one I'd wake up in the middle of the night. Mama was grumpy when you woke her up—so it was always him, and he'd come and lie beside me in my bed until I fell asleep.

I need intimacy with *somebody.* As days move into weeks, then months, then years of novitiate life, loneliness settles in. Close friendships—or "particular" friendships, as the Holy Rule calls them—are forbidden, and zealously monitored by Mother's watchful eye. At recreation I'm careful not to seek out Sisters I really like two or three nights in a row. Learning new things in classes and through reading helps fill the emptiness somewhat. But all the learning and new facts and interesting ideas in the cosmos can't substitute for a relationship. I'm beginning to realize the starkness of the life I have chosen.

Some of the loneliness I expected. I knew it would be hard to leave my family and close friends. I've always had close friends. *So, okay,* I say to myself, *this is your life now. God is sufficient.* "My grace is sufficient for you," as God told St. Paul.

I'm trying to believe that part about God's grace being sufficient for me. Trying. Maybe it was easier for St. Paul. He was, after all, *Saint* Paul, and I'm, well, just me, a work very much in progress and not so sure sometimes about "grace," which can feel pretty airy sometimes. There is one thing, however, one thing writ large that I'm very, very sure of: I am so ready to be done with this novitiate and its close, tight scrutiny and confined activities. I am so ready to kick off my training wheels and become a full-fledged member of this community.

After two and a half years, novitiate ends and I profess my vows.

Praise God!

PART II

TEACHING AND LEARNING

In the Classroom at Cabrini School

They will study the character of their students and will try to understand them and win their confidence so that they may be better able to help them. . . . Each teacher will be allowed full initiative to choose the means most apt to encourage joyful effort among the pupils in her classroom. . . . A Religious who has a truly supernatural outlook knows how to permeate all her teaching with the profound convictions she draws from the careful meditation on the Gospel; her lessons and her personal example are for her students, even though they may be unaware of it, a continuous religious instruction.

—"Sisters Engaged in Teaching,"
Rules and Directory of the Sisters of St. Joseph

At last I stand before them, my very first class—eighth-grade girls and boys at St. Frances Cabrini School in New Orleans. The girls in white blouses and blue pleated skirts (like I used to wear), and I in my respectable black widow's garb of the seventeenth century (a tried-and-true authority prop for any greenhorn teacher in a Catholic school).

My arrival caused something of a stir, not because anyone knew who I was but simply because I was a newcomer nun on the Cabrini faculty scene. Fresh out of Mass on a Sunday in late August, parents and kids strain to read the posted list of classes and teachers for the 1962–63 school year. *Who's the new nun? Sister Louis Augustine? Hope she ain't Sister Louis*

Disgustin'. (Squeals of laughter). *Hope she doesn't give tons of homework. . . .*

I'm assigned to teach religion and English to seventh and eighth graders.

I had hoped to teach high school. More than hoped—it was my life dream. "Missioning Day" laid me low. There we all were, after Mass, waiting silently in the chapel as Mother Anthelma and her assistants glided softly to hand each of us our assignments for the year, the vow of obedience kicking in big-time now, the dizzying suspense of it, praying, beseeching Thy will be done, O Lord. . . . Grace, give me grace to accept thy holy will. . . . Then the dull, aching thud as I read the small white slip of paper.

> Sister Louis Augustine,
> It is the will of God for you
> to teach at St. Frances Cabrini School.

Junior high? What am I lacking? What didn't the superiors see in me that I wasn't selected to teach high school? Hadn't I been chosen as one of the first to attend Dominican College to get my bachelor's degree before going into the classroom—one of the first ever? Most Sisters started teaching right out of the novitiate and had to inch their way toward a college degree by attending ten to fifteen years of summer school. Clearly the superiors had believed in my abilities enough to send me to college. They must have thought I had a decent enough intellect. Our congregation doesn't have colleges, so high school teachers are considered our top-notch educators.

They don't think I'm mature enough.

What a blow! My first experience of the costliness of giving over agency of my life to others—exactly the opposite of a self-directed life. Obedience, as I am finding out, does more to suppress the ego in one fell swoop than a thousand practices of humility. What is required of me is to obey blindly and to trust God's providence—God, who can "write straight with crooked lines."

Yeah, right. I'm terribly off stride. I'm used to achieving what I set out to do.

After the missioning ceremony, everyone is in the lobby talking excitedly about who is going where, and I can't be more upbeat: "I'm going to Cabrini, a great school. Sister George is principal; I hear she's the best!"

I want to teach high school so badly I can taste it.

What makes it harder to take is that two of my peers who attended college with me were chosen to teach high school. Obviously they were deemed more mature than I am. I was so used to being a leader in high school, so used to being the best.

Under the tutelage of the nuns in my high school years, I almost exploded with all I was learning and the gifts of my personality that were coming alive. What big business deal or scientific discovery or clever invention could possibly compare to the satisfaction, the joy, of opening the minds and hearts of young women? Chaucer knew the power. In the *Canterbury Tales* he says of the Teacher: "Gladly wolde he lerne and gladly teche."

Chaucer knew that knowledge is power, and that teaching others means that you'll always be digging for more knowledge. If you're teaching, you're learning. (Although I must confess that I was only just beginning to taste the joy of learning for its own sake; I was too caught up in trying to make top-notch grades to please others, too bent on proving myself. I treated "secular" studies—everything except theology—as second-best, inferior, worldly.) I'm sure I thought that teaching high school was the most exalted profession because of what I had experienced at St. Joseph Academy.

The nuns in my high school had what I wanted: spiritual power. They had the power to change our consciousness, to open realms of truth and possibilities that we never knew existed. They welcomed questioning and debate. They taught us to think critically (except when it came to the teachings of Holy Mother Church). They urged us to be kind to everyone, even those we didn't like. They were a force. Their presence filled the room.

But it was their humanness that drew us most of all, and we loved any glimpse of it we could get. If we saw a wisp of hair emerge through the face linens, we'd whisper and point, or when gusty winds blew long black veils aside, we craned our necks to catch sight of close-cropped hair. *Hey, she's a blonde!* Or, *It's jet black!*

"Do nuns shave their heads?" "Do nuns have menstrual periods?" "Do nuns drink beer?" "Do nuns like rock and roll?" (Elvis was making his mark.) "Do nuns play poker?" Our curiosity was endless. And because it was an all-girls school, we were like family—playful, teasing, blurting out one-liners, performing practical jokes. Like hanging Sister Alice Marie's chalk holder from the ceiling light or hiding in the storage room behind the chemistry lab, all smashed together, giggling, anticipating the moment of the great discovery of the student-less classroom. And like the time Sister Mary Veronica, our seventy-five-year-old Latin teacher, stood en garde by the window as the Catholic High guys cruised by and honked: "You keep writing, girls," she said. "I'll wave."

"You just know the nun's wave for the guys had to be the thrill of a lifetime," said Renee McGuiness, our class wit.

Our nuns were fun. Their affection for us was tangible. They challenged our minds, taught us how to read critically, savor good literature, argue logically, work algebraic equations, write cohesively, give a persuasive speech. They told us stories of funny things that happened in the convent, cracked jokes, and wrote spiritual or witty sayings on the chalkboard. I still remember one: "Some of the biggest imprints in the sands of time have been made by heels." Not exactly a showstopper, but strong enough to imprint itself on my brain cells to this day.

Our nuns coached our sports and rode with us in Beetlebum, our school bus, to basketball games, and we'd sing fun songs such as "Bill Grogan's Goat" and "Sippin' Cider Through a Straw," and if it was a night game and coming home the nuns needed quiet time for their evening meditation, we'd all be quiet or sing Palestrina's *O Sacrum Convivium* and *Ave Maria* and other hymns to put them in the mood to commune with God. And there in the quiet dark, I'd try to pray, too, the most basic of prayers: *God, puleeeze let us win this game,* and maybe, when you boil it down, that is the rock-bottom foundational prayer, which in times of crisis never really leaves us: *Please, God, just this once, stretch the rules of the universe for me—do this one miracle for me.*

And at basketball games in our gymnasium, when we all stood up to sing our alma mater, a hush would descend on the crowd, even on unbelievers there just for the game—even they could sense our rapt attention and devotion as we sang:

Lift up your voices to our alma mater,
pledge her your loyalty as long as you shall live.
always remember the spirit and the way
of sanctity, joy, and action, dearest SJA.

We weren't just a school—we were a family.

Our Sisters gave us such freedom to be ourselves that I tried my first curse words out loud during an exam in Sister Alice Marie's geometry class. I got a "D" in conduct because of it and voluntarily resigned from the student council for the rest of the semester (better to resign and look virtuous than to be kicked out). I knew I was way out of line, that I got what I deserved, but I could also feel the love that informed the discipline. (This was in the fifties, when genteel Southern ladies refrained from even uttering a "darn" or the scrubbed "Got-dog-it" in place of a bona fide curse. I suspect the "Got-dog-it" may be confined to the Deep South. I've never heard it outside Louisiana.)

In my high school years I prospered. I ran for student body president and won, and I started making my mark in oratorical contests when I was only a freshman. With coaching from my lawyer daddy, I led our student council in teaching the rules of parliamentary procedure to the entire student body (about 250 students and 20 faculty members), then had a practice session in the gym. When I stood at the podium before my peers, I knew to wait for their respectful silence before I spoke. I never doubted that I would command obedience and respect in a classroom. It's one of the reasons I knew I'd be a good high school teacher.

Then came the mission assignment.

Twelve- and thirteen-year-olds? Anybody could teach little kids.

Alone in prayer I come to grips with my crushing assignment. I tuck in my soul and do my utmost to shoulder the rejection. Only then can I open a space in my soul to love the kids entrusted to me. "It doesn't matter where you start out," the voice whispers. "Just be a good teacher."

Now, here I am at St. Frances Cabrini facing twenty-five middle schoolers. Despite the initial disappointment with my assignment, it doesn't take long to get hooked. What's not to love? All these fresh, young faces looking up at me. "Don't smile until Christmas," veteran teachers counsel new teachers. "Let them know right off who's in charge; don't get friendly too soon."

I introduce myself.

"Good morning, class, I'm Sister Louis Augustine," and I write my name on the chalkboard, right under the bulletin board, where I had posted in large red block letters: "Come, Holy Spirit." Invoking the help of the Holy Spirit is the staple prayer of Catholic schools, the prayer par excellence for school openings and before taking tests. At my elementary school of Sacred Heart, in Baton Rouge, we began every school day, unless it rained, lined up by class on the blacktop singing, "Come Holy Spirit, Creator blest . . ."

And I love my students, love them the way Sister Mary Mark loved us when I was in eighth grade. And I love preparing my English and religion lessons in the dormitory at my student desk (the kind you have to slide in from the side to sit down in) next to my bed, the white curtain pulled around to form my six by eight feet of privacy. I have everything I need: religion text and *Voyages in English* (the staple English grammar book in Catholic schools), a stack of papers to correct, and my lesson-planning book. I lay books and papers out across the white bedspread and open the planning book and outline the lessons carefully, detailing exactly what I'll cover in the class and what the assignments will be. I use a ruler and red pen to draw columns to separate one section from another— all very organized, very neat in my lesson-planning book, which I show to my principal, Sister George, every Sunday night.

I plan exact steps to help my students learn nouns and verbs, gerunds and participles, tenses of verbs, how to diagram sentences, give a speech, write a good essay. I explain to them how a "soul journal" differs from a diary. I open up new ways for them to be creative in their journals, freely expressing their private thoughts and feelings in poems or doodles—whatever, which I promise not to read unless they want me to. Day by day I take them through English grammar thoroughly and solidly, and, in the process, learn it myself, which has served me well in my own life—even to this very sentence.

I gradually recognize that the quiet place I inhabit in the dormitory as I plan my lessons is akin to the quiet place in chapel. It is filled with the sense that I have all the time I need to perform the task before me now, which frees me to give myself to it completely, as if nothing else in the world exists. And I taste how very good it is to have this work to do.

And what a clean, good, satisfying feeling on Monday morning to put all the prepared lessons into my book sack and set off for school with a bounce in my step like *Pippa Passes* ("God's in His heaven, all's right with the world"). Come Monday, I know I'm stepping on the first of the moving plates of a teaching week, which won't stop until Friday afternoon at three o'clock. Often enough my work doesn't end right on the dot at 3:00 P.M., because there's volleyball practice or a meeting of the student council (which Sister Mary John and I inaugurated in the school to promote leadership) or the Borromeo Club (to promote religious vocations) or the Sodality (for girls, dedicated to the Blessed Mother to foster piety, purity, and charitable works) or practice for the eighth-grade play—a real hoot and hardly worthy of the name "drama," so padded is the production with dances of maids and butlers, singing gardeners, and angel choirs, all to maximize inclusion of every single kid (savvy as we are that school productions are as much about pleasing parents as they are about developing talent in kids).

I like teaching boys and girls, love the mix, revel in the differences. I talk to my girls after class, coach their sports, listen to their problems, soothe their hearts when they are anguished by a boy's rejection or the treacherous gossip of girlfriends. In class boys exhibit more spontaneous humor in the give-and-take of discussion, and their skits are invariably less polished than the girls' and more outrageously funny—although, in one respect, utterly predictable.

Whatever the subject matter, whatever the theme, I absolutely know we'll be treated at least once to a skit in which one of the guys, dressed like a little old lady, will, in the course of events, proceed to beat the tar out of somebody with a purse. You can count on it. And, although we do make a point of teaching nonviolence in Christianity, an exception always has to be made for the purse-pummeling scene.

I don't run a terribly tight ship, and there's always a lot of teasing, a lot of allowance for repartee. I enjoy the buzz, the live energy, though when the chips are down, they know who's boss. I remember my own sixth grade with a very strict teacher, Sister Emmanuel, and deciding right then and there, in that cut-and-dried, no-nonsense environment, that one bright and shining day when I would become a teacher, learning would be fun and full of surprises and nothing would be predictable and boring and sad.

The rascals size you up quickly. It doesn't take them long to know that I have a soft spot for humor, but they quickly catch my serious side, too. When I invoke my stern voice, one of them intones: *She's ser-i-ous. Tha—a-at's all, folks.* Whenever I have to fuss at them, I never yell—I'm always aware of *willing* the correction, that it comes from a center of calm inside where I'm not really angry, but I have to make my voice sound angry or disappointed and serious. I have learned from veteran teachers that good teachers never raise their voices, and it doesn't take long to predict that the teacher down the hall who is screaming her head off at the kids or pounding the desk or sending kids to the principal's office is not going to make it for long in Middle Hall at St. Frances Cabrini.

As I go about teaching vocabulary, I know the kids have an almost infinite capacity to learn and assimilate words, so, along with the regular vocabulary words, I throw in *supercilious* and *lugubrious, perspicacity* and *lethargic*—and why not? The kids love the challenge and gobble up the words, and then I get the treat of the words turning up in essays or class discussions—sometimes with hilarious results, and all in the tone of: *Hey, Sister, watch me try out my new hundred-dollar words!*

"Isn't this all rather lagubrious [*sic*]?"

(They love using *sic*—probably misspelling words just to get *sic* in there.)

"Fair greetings from your locquatious [*sic*], brilliant student, Frank Silvestri."

Putting new vocabulary into practice leads to interesting exchanges.

Me: "How did you arrive at that interesting insight, Mike Russo?"

Russo: "Perspicacity, Sister—sheer perspicacity."

It is a formidable challenge to teach English grammar to twelve- and thirteen-year-old boys (it seems to come more naturally to girls). I find myself talking to other teachers to marshal up every game I can find to whiz up syntax, punctuation, and sentence structure. So we have baseball grammar, Whiz Kids grammar bowls, vocabulary and spelling bees, and bonus and sweepstakes questions on daily quizzes. At first, I don't realize that I'm teaching gambling skills with the sweepstakes questions, the only way to recover lost points in a grading period. I give daily quizzes to keep them on their toes, and this causes some tension in their young lives.

The way the grading system works, each student begins the six-week period with a hundred points, and the idea is to keep as many of those points as possible. Naturally, attrition happens in tests and quizzes, so questions that offer extra points provide a way to replenish lost points. Bonus questions are best, since they offer extra points without the risk of losing points for a wrong answer. But sweepstakes questions involve bona fide risk: two points won for correct answers but two points lost for wrong answers.

Oh, the angst, the agony of the decision-making process. The kids know that the sweepstakes questions are optional, which is where the gambling comes in. I watch them knit their brows, groan and pray, throw their heads back, cover their eyes, struggle out loud, saying, "Yeah, yeah—what the heck," then erasing furiously, then writing again. I let them struggle. It's good to struggle over the little stuff—it helps strengthen prudential judgment (a virtue of the practical intellect, says Thomas Aquinas). Maybe it'll come in handy one day when they choose a mate or weigh the pros and cons of a business deal—or consider making a flying leap from a predictable, banal, boring life to a life bristling with risk and immense happiness.

Or not.

You never know.

My Writing Life

For the first time I begin to keep a journal and write simply because I want to—a private journal for my own pleasure and for my own eyes. The habit sticks for a lifetime. I look across the room now and see the journal I wrote in this very morning. I'm mustering up humility here as I share my first entry, and as soon as you read it, you'll know why.

What sparked the inspiration to write was a visit to the John F. Kennedy Library Exhibit in New Orleans in 1964, just a year after Kennedy's assassination. One of the photographs in the exhibit captures Kennedy at the podium delivering his inaugural address in 1961 and there, next to the photo, is an excerpt of his original draft of the speech scribbled on a yellow legal-size pad. I can't make out all the words: "*When your country is going* [words not clear] *ask what you can do for your country.*"

I am intrigued by how tenuous it looks, words easily dashed off, easily erased, and surprised by the sheer plainness of content, simply asking citizens to think about what they could do for their country. Of course, I well know—almost everybody knows by heart—Kennedy's memorable challenge: "Ask not what your country can do for you—ask what you can do for your country." It's the counterpoise with the *ask not* coming first that gives the punch, but he had to come to that by first writing the bland, ho-hum, trite stuff. I am fascinated, watching the intimate alchemy of the writing process, watching beige words sparkle into living color. It thrills me, stirs me, makes me want to write something good, something bold.

This is real power.

I sense that maybe somewhere in me I could do this.

But there is another powerful part of the exhibit for me—photographs of Kennedy the orator.

One captures a back view of him, silhouetted at a podium, his arm extended to the audience, shrouded in darkness, and six shafts of light from all sides, lighting him up. The sheer impact of it—one human being speaking words that spark new consciousness and give a new tilt to the world. The force of words—delivery, yes; charm of accent, yes; personal charisma of the speaker, yes—but first and foremost and always, it's the words, the words themselves, and how the words are put together that unleash the energy.

I want to write words like that.

I come out of the exhibit and know, absolutely know, that I am going to begin writing my words in a journal, and as soon as I get back to the convent, I go to the school supply closet and select a plastic "Blue Horse" three-holed loose-leaf binder, fill it thick with pages, and begin to write. In the front of the binder I put the exhibit brochure so I can see it and keep the fire of inspiration hot.

I make the first page a title page, writing slowly, solemnly, deliberately:

JOURNAL
Sister Louis Augustine, CSJ
Private
September 21, 1964

The words come in a torrent, brimming with so much confidence it borders on grandiosity.

> I visited the Kennedy Library Exhibit today and suddenly something sparked in me. I had come into contact with greatness . . . and my own impulse to greatness stirred within me. . . .
>
> These are my thoughts—the most unique thing I can give to the world. These thoughts have never been expressed before, because they are my own and I have never existed before. I shall never exist again. Someday I shall die, as everyone else does. But I am alive now . . . deeply alive. I tingle with warm thoughts, strong impulses, vibrant feelings. My body feels strong, my mind is stimulated with thoughts like sparks running to and fro in the reeds, my heart is warm with the glow of love for Christ, for everyone in the world, and for my new friend, Sister Christopher, who has helped me come alive more deeply, more humanly.
>
> I am! . . .
> I am a person of vision.
> I have a message for the world.
> And I have the feeling that the world will listen to me, because the world today is hungry.
> It is hungry for truth—
> simple truth spoken and lived . . .
> Tonight I needed to voice my thoughts.
> This is only the beginning.

The world waiting for the message of this young prophet? Gag. Yuck. This is so em-barr-ass-ing.

But it's me, all right—I-will-save-the-world me. The buoy-

ancy comes a lot from Mama. Even at Daddy's funeral Mass
she led us out of the church, singing at full volume, "Glory,
glory, hallelujah" from the "Battle Hymn of the Republic." She
wasn't faking it. Her faith carried her through her whole life,
and when she died, she gave herself over and slipped through
the dark wormhole of eternity in peace, after telling us, "You're
okay, you're going to be okay," and shortly before that, to
Mary Ann and me, "Don't gang up on Louie"—a perennial
theme throughout our lives. But there was still the twinkle as
she said it, and we smiled as we cried and promised and thanked
her and couldn't stop thanking her.

What makes me think that people hunger and thirst for my
words? Me, the young, naïve, so-called prophet I claim to be?

It all had to do with the unassailable confidence I possessed
as a Catholic, a solid believer in the one true faith, bolstered by
Christ's saving message of truth and life. And, well, as a consecrated virgin and bride of Christ—I did have, shall we say,
special access and special pull?

Short confession.

When I began writing this book I promised myself I
wouldn't do this—critique my young, full-of-beans self. I told
myself I'd just put myself out there in my outrageousness.

So much for that promise.

I'm finding out that writing a memoir puts your different
selves in tension with each other, and it's hard to just stand
back and let the brassy young upstart have her say. Far more
humbling than confessing "foibles"—that's for sure.

From this first journal I'm struck by two ways I express
things that have stayed with me and still pop up when I write
and speak: the first is "like sparks darting to and fro in the
reeds."

The image comes from the Book of Wisdom (3:7), where it

speaks of holy ones who in the afterlife will shine and dart about as sparks through stubble. The image I get is of these tiny, orange gleams of fire, zinging around in wet, matted reeds and fading almost as quickly as they appear—now here, now over there, not concentrated in one place, all of it intense while it lasts, but pretty intangible and evanescent. Just the way my mind works.

And many times now as I'm standing before an audience to take them into my experiences of the criminal justice system and how death is meted out by our government, I think of those fiery little darts hitting in and out of matted reeds, all with the hope that my words might spark my audience into new insight and compassion they've never experienced before.

At other times at prayer, when I'm in a funk, I feel like I'm the matted reeds—damp, sluggish, resistant to the slightest spark of feeling or insight.

The second way the journal reminds me of how I express my inner life is that I'm always talking about feeling warm and humming inside. And here in my later book *The Death of Innocents* are those very same words, but this time inspired by waiting inside the Louisiana death house with Dobie Williams—waiting for the "strap down" team to come: "Normally I am warm and humming inside, but in that surreal house of death I was cold and paralyzed."

Same words. Same me.

Friendship

All real living is meeting.

—Martin Buber

As nuns we have no personal money to purchase books, but, happily, we who teach at Cabrini live in the convent with Sisters who teach at our high school, St. Joseph Academy, and so have access to all sorts of good books, and we are passing books from one to the other and talking in small huddles about all the amazing new ideas we are discovering. As we are no longer novices, the rule of silence is not so strict for us anymore, and we are loving the new freedom to talk—about everything. I'm reading like mad, have a book under my arm everywhere I go, even to the bathroom. I think reading has to be the most amazing thing ever: to open pages and enter another's interiority, accessing another's thoughts, feelings, tragic mistakes, and stunning adventures. I feel like, for the first time, I'm reading what I want to read. New avenues of freedom and selfhood are opening up. I'm more curious, more focused. Pretty basic freedoms, really, but in some ways new to me. And best of all: freedom to develop friendship.

After years of trying to love only God and everyone else more or less equally "in Christ," I know I can't make it without a close friend. I need to entrust myself, invest myself with another. I need to get past my protected public self and open up the vulnerable parts of myself. Maybe like crabs in the Gulf, when they go deep into the marsh to molt, doing their best to camouflage themselves in the sandy bottom as they shed their hard shells and have to wait and hide in their soft, tender skins until their new shells harden. I'm longing to be able to be vulnerable like that with somebody. Isn't that what true intimacy means?

Like those in any other lifestyle, nuns, too, can develop superficial ways of communicating, always saying the predictable, expected, "spiritual" thing. Yuck! I'm done with that. I want to get past the polite surface and delve deeply into what really matters.

I want to care deeply for someone and, hopefully, have someone care deeply for me. It's not that God isn't enough. It's the opposite, really. If God truly is love, then the deeper I love, the more I know God. That's one really good thing about the Christ-life: It's grounded in love of flesh-and-blood people (as if a rarefied, cerebral, purely mental love life could ever make us happy). Robert Frost wrote a poem about earth being the best place for love, adding that he didn't know "where it's likely to go better."

The name of my first close friend was Sister Christopher. That was her nun name. Her family name was Ann Barker, and I'm forced to write about her in the past tense because she died in 1997; we had thirty-four years of precious friendship. I don't know what dying means. Like Yegorushka, the small boy in one of Chekhov's stories who passes by the cemetery where his grandmother "slept day and night," and all he knows is, "Before dying she had been alive, and she had brought him soft poppy-seed bun rings from the market, but now she just slept and slept."

In faith I hope that Chris wasn't zapped into nothingness, but I have to be honest; I can't reason my way into knowing where she is or how she is. All I can do is trust that the God who called her into existence has received her in death and she's okay. One thing I do know: I keep talking to her and listening for her, and sometimes I ask her help—in the same way, I guess, that I pray to God and the saints. I can't stop talking to her.

It's like breathing.

Chris was the novice who in 1957 witnessed my rather flamboyant arrival on entrance day. It's 1963, we've both made vows, it's summer and we're both at our motherhouse, I to help with the Sisters' retreats, and Chris to prepare for final vows. In the novitiate, Chris was two years ahead of me, so we were together for only the nine months of my postulancy before she was professed and moved to the professed sisters' wing across the yard. Only a football field distance away, but it might as well have been China, so great was the divide between novices and professed.

After I made vows and was going to college and Chris to nursing school, we'd occasionally be together at the motherhouse on weekends and get to talk during evening recreation. I majored in English and she always wanted to know about literature, and I—very much not a nurse—wanted to hear about what it was like to run a post-op hall, what surgery was like, what it was like to witness a baby being born, and what it felt like to be with somebody dying.

Back when we were together in the novitiate a member of my entry group, Pam Crasto, was always talking about Sister Christopher—the prayerful way she came back from communion, the regal way she walked, the way she was entrusted with the special responsibility of cleaning the novice mistress's clothes and room. (It was a very big deal to be trusted to enter the inner sanctum of Mother's bedroom.) I had been given nothing but piddly jobs: cleaning bathrooms, mopping halls, kitchen chores. In the novitiate at recreation, Chris and I never got to talk together longer than a few minutes, and not too often. Mother Noemi saw to that in her zeal to nip "particular friendships" in the bud.

When Chris's entry group enacted a scriptural skit, Chris often portrayed Jesus (I got to be a beggar or sing in a chorus behind a screen). She was tall and had a gentle, spiritual-sounding voice, and in the Jesus role she'd be behind a screen so you could see only her silhouette, which made it all feel shadowy and mysterious and holy.

The skits our entry group performed didn't succeed nearly as well. In fact, we were the ones who got martyrdom scenes banned from the novitiate. All because Sister Anastasia couldn't control herself. As the child martyr Tarcisius, she did all right crumpling to the floor with a heavy groan as Roman soldiers beat her, but not so well when the soldiers moved in for the kill. It wasn't her fault, really. She didn't have nearly enough dramatic training to handle the extreme emotion of dying in the bloodiest manner. (We had the wisdom not to try to show the blood.) Her only training had taken place in a short dry run carried out hurriedly just before the performance.

She maintained her composure pretty well during the first sword thrust, but after that she lost it. As the soldiers moved in with swords slashing, her groans quickly morphed into loud, unstoppable giggles, which, as you can imagine, sent all sense of mystery and pious mood to hell in a handbasket. What was worse, one of the stabbing soldiers was killing herself with laughter, too. It ended very badly, even though we amped up the recording of Schubert's *Ave Maria* as loud as it would go. Even after the bell signaled night prayers and sacred silence was supposed to descend, there was no stopping periodic eruptions of giggles—even *through* night prayers and yet again as we mounted the steps to the dormitory. Anastasia got nicknamed "the Giggling Martyr," and that was the end of martyrdom enactments in the novitiate.

Now, on this July night in 1963 (the sixteenth, to be exact), here comes Sister Christopher descending the stairs into the front lobby just as I swing through the chapel door. I see her coming and wait and ask how preparation for her final vows is going (final, or "perpetual," vows take place after five years of temporary vows), and we start talking and drift out to the long, screened back porch and sit in two rocking chairs there in the dark. It's quiet, no one is up, it's late.

Early on, Chris and I hit on words from scripture that become the mantra of our friendship: "And the soul of David was knit to the soul of Jonathan." I still have these words, printed by Chris on tiny strips of paper pasted inside an oyster shell.

We couldn't be more different. She's tall, I'm short. She's blond and fair. My hair is brown and I have olive skin. She's introverted, while I'm extroverted out the wazoo. I'm a chattering brook. She's a deep well. I'm openly affectionate. She's reserved. I like to relate to a lot of people, she likes to relate to only a few.

One example of how different we are: One time when we are together, I gush out four, five, six things I like about her, and when my outpouring is met with silence, I tease her to say what she likes about me. And all she can say is that she thinks

I am "nice." I go, "'Nice'? Is that it?" And she answers that I'm the one who's the English major.

She's better with words when she writes to me. It's the introversion thing. Her words come slowly from within a private place, and I learn to respect that quietness in her and wait for her to tell me about herself when she's ready. But it takes a while, and I always have to work at it. It's probably my biggest fault that I talk too fast and too often and don't listen enough.

Whenever we're together she always wants to know what I'm reading. As a nurse at our only hospital in the small town of Houma, Louisiana, with no CSJ teaching communities around, she has no access to theology books or literature, the way we teachers do. As teachers we're lucky. We get summers off and are always taking courses and learning new things. Our nurses have to work all year with only a few weeks off for retreat and vacation. The imbalance puts her off and makes her insecure.

Chris's vow-preparation classes are her first taste of the renewal sparked by Vatican II, and she's alive with what she's learning. Sister Alice Marie Macmurdo (my favorite teacher from high school) is teaching Josef Goldbrunner's *Holiness Is Wholeness,* and it's like fresh water on parched earth. Goldbrunner's big point is that if we remain undeveloped selves—if we're unable to give and receive love in a healthy way—we'll always be too needy, too unsure of ourselves to risk the give-and-take that a close relationship demands. How can we be Christ-like by dying to self for others if we don't have a developed self in the first place? Christ doesn't need wimpy doormats.

All of us young nuns are eating this stuff up. We've known the gnawing emptiness of trying to live a style of religious life that cloaks over human emotions and tries to spiritualize everything. Got a problem? Sinking into a hole of depression? Take it to prayer. Want to indulge in something you like? Sacrifice it for sinners. Talking it over with Jesus was supposed to be the answer to everything. Still got a problem? Pray harder.

At last, we get to reclaim our humanness—all of it—including our physical selves, our bodies, our desires, even our sexuality. Until now, anything remotely connected to sexuality was squelched. We're nuns, after all—consecrated virgins with vows of celibacy. Sexuality is out of this picture. The only way we ever heard the words *sex* or *sexuality* was if the word *sublimation* was in there somewhere. That's what we're supposed to do, always and everywhere: sublimate. Turn it over to God, Who will transform our steamy longings into . . . well . . . heavenly things.

Vatican II, with its intoxicating invitation to claim our humanness, is opening all these previously closed doors. And, on the philosophical front, existentialism is making its mark, with an open-ended approach to being human that says *Experience life for yourself, try it out, live it, see by its effects if it's good for you, you decide, it's your life, there's no blueprint.* And all this is unfolding in the psychedelic, authority-challenging, war-protesting, rock-and-rolling, pot-smoking, LSD-tripping, sexually liberated sixties. Movies depict people meeting and hopping into bed just to get acquainted. The message comes from practically everywhere: If you're not sexually intimate, you're not alive—you're not really human.

Know what a nun is? *Got none, never had none, ain't ever gonna get none.* (Bad joke maybe, but its truthfulness makes me smile.)

In such a milieu, we nuns with our vow of celibacy couldn't be more countercultural. Even sociology books classify us as deviants. There's truth in there. A vow that entails forgoing sexual intimacy is not most people's way of being human. And I'm crystal clear that if I don't develop relationships deep enough to stretch me past my boundaries of who-I-think-I-am-and-will-always-be, I'm going to be nothing but a shriveled-up grape, dying on the vine—spiritually exalted bride of Christ or not. I am absolutely determined I am not going to die on the vine. And it is this desire to live a full life, this more than anything, that brings me to this porch late on this summer night, to talk to Sister Christopher.

A bunch of us are reading Saint-Exupéry's *The Little Prince,* and I tell Chris about it, especially the part where the fox teaches the little prince about how to "tame" him—that he can't just walk up to the fox and say, "Be my friend," just like that, but he must "observe the proper rites." That means that each day at the same time the little prince must approach the fox's den so the fox can expect him and be happy at his coming, and each day he is to come a little closer with great care and respect and never in a hurry. Taming someone can never be rushed, and only then, perhaps, will the fox let him tame him.

As it turns out, letter writing will mainly be the "proper rite" for Chris and me to build our friendship. She's in one town, I'm in another, and we don't have the freedom to make long-distance telephone calls, or access to a car so we can visit.

But write we can, and that's one thing I really like to do. It's spontaneous for me, and whatever thoughts and feelings come, they flow right onto the paper—pretty much in a steady flow, and usually in a sharp upward slant on the page, which is my optimistic bent in life. The rule that superiors are to censor Sisters' correspondence is easing up, though because Chris's superior still reads the Sisters' letters sometimes, she puts her letters to me in a public mailbox at the front of the hospital.

I'm not as brazen. Obediently, I still put my unsealed letters on Mother Jean's desk, trusting that she'll respect my privacy and not read them. She's respectful of young Sisters, which in these days of emerging personhood goes a long, long way.

Chris and I talk until midnight, and being there in the dark on the porch, just the two of us, feels private and sacred, and a deep bond forms between us.

The fox ends his instruction to the little prince by saying, "You become responsible, forever, for what you tame," and that will become one of the main themes of our friendship.

I'm ready for the taming.

And—miracle of grace—Chris is ready, too.

In the first years of our friendship, Chris and I face a formidable challenge. She lives in Houma and I'm in New Orleans, so I mostly get to see her at community assemblies, and that's always in a big crowd. Visits are rare, although sometimes Chris volunteers to drive her superior, Mother Evelyn, to New Orleans and sneaks over to Cabrini School to see me. And suddenly there she is—a tall, white-habited nun (our nurses wear white) gliding across the blacktop toward my classroom, and my students go, "Look! A white nun!" and me, delighted, calmly assign them a few pages to read while I step outside for a few minutes. Her surprise visits are always a thrill. I know she chooses to drive Mother on the chance that she might be able to see me, even for a few minutes. Mother Evelyn is a severe soul, and you don't dare be even a minute late, and as soon as you get in the car, prayers begin—first the rosary, then vocal one o'clock prayers, then four o'clock prayers, and then a half hour of silence for meditation. More than fine with Chris, she says, because when you're praying you don't have to keep the conversation going.

My visits to Chris in Houma are never a surprise. They always entail planning of a full-fledged community outing with the superior's permission. As I've said, exclusive friendships are considered the bane of community life, and it's unheard of for a Sister to simply get in a car to go visit a friend in another town. And so, within the confines and restraints, Chris and I keep the life flow of our friendship going by a steady stream of letters.

I tell her about classroom encounters, the latest being a showdown with a red-haired hellion of a girl, whom I like—the kid has spunk—but I couldn't have her blatantly disobeying me and causing mutiny in the ranks, and so I had to take her on. Chris tells of the bone-weary workload when one of her nurses calls in sick and she has to take on the 11:00 P.M. to 7:00 A.M. shift after having already worked the 3:00 to 11:00 P.M. shift. She says that 2:00 A.M. is always bottom-of-the-hole time, when her energies hit zero and all she can think is that if she could only crawl into a spot in the linen room, just curl up and sleep for even fifteen minutes, she could make it.

Our newly budding relationship is still fragile, the way beginnings always are, and in every letter I affirm the meeting of souls that happened so spontaneously in the rocking chairs, and we both know that the bond between us, though real, is mostly still only potential, only promise. No letter of mine ever goes out without my telling her how glad I am that God sent her as a friend to me, and it's a wild, delirious, fanciful dream, but I put out the hope that maybe we might be able to pull off a vacation together at Grand Isle, Louisiana, even though we aren't living in the same local communities. It's the longest of shots any way you look at it, and Chris says she hopes—she prays—Grand Isle can happen, but her superior is not kindly disposed toward adjusting work schedules, or any kind of schedule, for that matter, simply because some young Sister has it in her head to go on vacation.

Chris's biggest hope is that if . . . if . . . if she can line up her nurses to cover all the shifts for a week and not have a nurse go sick, then maybe she can come with me and a group of other Sister teachers to Grand Isle. Her responsibility for the surgery hall means that she can never make firm plans, but in a letter I'm going, yes, Chris, yes, yes, yes, come hell or high water *we are going to Grand Isle,* and I draw a little island with a palm tree and a beach with a starfish on it, and a bright sun with rays shining over everything.

At the convent personal mail is put on top of our desks in the community room, and my heart lifts whenever I walk in from school and see the familiar handwriting and the Houma postmark. I'm starting to learn the medical shorthand Chris uses—the way she puts "c" with a dash over it for "with," for example—and I feel proud of all she knows about medicine and the way she's a real professional. Mama was an RN, and I could tell from her stories how much she felt for her patients, and I can sense that same spirit in Chris.

In one letter Chris tells me about one of her patients—some poor guy with cancer who was going crazy from the pain— and one morning she walks into his room and sees him humped over in the bed trying to drive his head into the mattress. The worst situation, she says, is when a patient is in severe pain and she can't get the doctor on call to authorize an increase of the pain medication. Maybe he's on the golf course or something and won't answer his pager. I tell Chris I couldn't stand that. I'd tear out of there and hunt that guy down. I can't bear to see anyone in pain. I'm sure it's because I'm such a coward myself about pain.

I admire Chris's know-how, the way she takes charge of a situation and is willing to push everything to the max to help her patients. Later, I'll experience it for myself when I have ankle surgery and get a terrible staph infection and Chris drives to New Orleans and steps into my hospital room, and I relax and know everything's going to be all right.

When a group of us teachers finally pulls off a visit to the nursing community in Houma and we all sit down together for lunch, we're amazed at the graphic, detailed hospital incidents the nurses talk about while we're eating. I mean graphic. Like the poor lady brought into the emergency room at 1:00 A.M. with half her gluteus maximus sliced off by her machete-slashing husband—blood everywhere—and their assisting the surgeon for four hours as he stitched the lady's behind back on. I think, *Now, that's real work,* and it makes teaching kids subject-verb agreement and verb conjugations seem pretty airy. There's no end to the nursing stories, but it gets a bit hard to stomach when you're eating delicious baked chicken and the story turns to the abdominal surgery on a very obese man and how the surgeon had to cut through layer upon layer of fat—just like yellow chicken fat, the nurses inform us (*thanks a lot*)—and how the surgeon got his gloves plastered with yellow yuck, and I find that the once succulent chicken in my mouth sort of just sticks there. The nurses aren't trying to gross us teachers out, they're just talking shop as they always do, and they're finished eating in about fifteen minutes flat. All the nurses I know eat fast, and when Chris and I have lunch together I'm always trying to slow her down.

There's a lot I don't know about nursing, but I know enough to know that I'm not cut out for it. I'd be as sincere and compassionate as I could be, but I'd be messing up medications and killing patients left and right. I'm too scatter-brained. I'm also not helpful when someone is throwing up, because I'd be throwing up right alongside the poor soul. By a stretch I could call the impulse compassion, but I know it's only my nervous-jervis gag reflex.

I remember one time in the fourth grade on the playground Sister Rosemona hurt my feelings terribly by ordering me to leave the scene when a kid was throwing up and I was there beside him, gagging and heaving. Sister Rosemona, who was always sweet and never raised her voice to a flea, yelled at me: "Helen, leave now!" It's not like I was *trying* to throw up.

I'm appreciating how grounded Chris is. No fluff about her, in stark contrast with ole Fluff Queen, me, who's always spinning big dreams of winning the young people of America and the whole entire world over to Christ. Sister George, my first principal, would say, "There she goes, that Sister Louis Augustine, her feet firmly planted in midair."

Chris's levelheadedness is good for me, and I hope my vibrancy and optimism are good for her. When the reforms of Vatican II make it possible to visit our families once again, it's a wonderful thing not only to visit our own families but our friends' families as well. And as soon as Mama meets her, the two of them are like gravy on rice, and their obvious delight in each other brings on a riff of mine that is totally efficacious in its result every time the three of us are together. The way it goes is I tell Mama, "I know it—you can't hide it. I can see you like Chris more than me, and I'm supposed to be your own flesh-and-blood daughter," and I cradle my head in my hands and let out a pitiful *boo hoo hoo* to emphasize my deep hurt. It never fails to trigger Mama's "No, honey, no, you know no one can ever replace you." And so, whenever we're together—

clearly to keep the peace—Mama gives us nicknames, calling me her "Chick" and Chris her "Pet," and that's the way it goes.

Chris's mama—I call her "Lady Pennington"—is tall and regal and plays the piano and belongs to a book club and is a teacher and was born on the exact same day and year, September 27, 1911, as my mama. Over time they get to be friends, too, and that makes a four-way web that binds me to Chris even more.

Lady P had a much harder life than Mama. Mama and Daddy loved each other, and all I ever knew was this solid universe of love that held us all together. But out of the blue, Lady P's husband, Chris's daddy, left her and the four children for another woman. Chris was six, and she remembers her mama and daddy arguing late one night in the kitchen and the next day he was gone. The betrayal was deep, and Chris's mama never talked about it, and so Chris and her brother and sisters didn't know what the terrible thing was that happened. They couldn't talk to their mama about it because it made her cry.

The wound of it, the brokenness, stays deep in Chris her whole life. It feels natural for me to trust her but hard for her to trust me, and we always have to work at shoring up trust between us. It takes a long, long time before Chris trusts enough to have a no-holds-barred, voices-raised argument with me, and it's not hard to know why. The last encounter between her parents that she remembers was a loud, angry argument, and the argument broke apart everything and her father left forever. Growing up, I had my sister, Mary Ann, to argue with, scream at, and fight with—I mean, wrestling each other down to the floor and slugging it out. Then it was over and life went on. In my family a good argument simply meant a good way to get blood circulating in your brain, and the rapid-fire exchange taught us how to think on our feet and put out to-the-point, cogent arguments or shut up. Although among us kids there was also a steady stream of ad hominems hurled back and forth at each other:

You're stupid.

You're stupider.

You're stupid to the "nth" power (after learning a little algebra).

You're stupid to the "nth" power plus one.

But for Chris, arguing had always meant the end of the world.

Chris always wonders why her daddy didn't love her enough to stay, and later on, after years of friendship, Chris trusts me enough to confide that one of the main reasons she became a nun was that she knew she could never trust a man enough to marry. Only God, her true Father, could be trusted to be faithful.

Through the steady stream of our letters, Chris and I descend into each other's worlds. She's so submerged in the daily practicalities of medicine, her imagination and spirit are starved. She misses being able to read—something she always had loved to do. Growing up in Houma, she'd spend whole afternoons on the screened front porch with Mark Twain and the Brontë sisters, and any historical novel she could get her hands on. She so delighted in *Jane Eyre* that when she knew she was coming to the final chapters, she forced herself to slow down so the book would never end.

In my letters I introduce her to J. D. Salinger, who in the sixties is all the rage. As an English major in college, I studied *The Catcher in the Rye,* and of all the books I'd read, hands down, the freshest voice in writing I ever encountered was that of Holden Caulfield. There it was, from page 1, this honest kid's voice: "If you really want to hear about it, the first thing you'll probably want to know is where I was born, and what my lousy childhood was like . . . and all that David Copperfield kind of crap, but I don't feel like going into it, if you want to know the truth."

Later, when I write books myself, it's this spontaneous, just-you-and-me-talking voice I'll strive for. But all this writing-voice business doesn't get into my letters to Chris, mainly because I don't even know there is such a thing as having a "voice" in writing. What I am saying to Chris, though, is what a fantastic writer this Salinger guy is, how spiritual he is—the way he blends Zen and Christian mysticism—and for her to always look out for the Fat Lady and little children in his stories, and don't worry about all the *goddam*s—they are just Salinger's way of spicing things up. By hook or crook, I'm telling her, you just have to get *Catcher* and *Franny and Zooey* and read them.

Sometimes I feel like a medieval monk scribe, the way I transcribe long excerpts from books in my letters to Chris. But I know how thirsty she is for imaginative ideas, and I try to give her cool drinks by passing on the new things I'm reading. It's the most concrete way I have to show my care for her. That's what Erich Fromm says in *The Art of Loving*—one of the books I'm reading: that you must practice loving the way you practice music or any art—you must perform deeds to show you care.

In what I'm afraid is exceedingly enthusiastic fashion, I share snippets of my journal with Chris, which probably bowls her over and paralyzes her more than inspires her: "Chris! The thrill of it, to record alive thoughts right as they flow out of my soul like hot lava rising—wouldn't you love to start a journal, too? And you can record exactly how you're feeling and what you're thinking, and . . ."

Poor baby. She's too tired to read, much less write, and she's never been good at spelling (much to the chagrin of her mama the teacher), and it didn't help her confidence much during novitiate at our junior college to suffer Sister Veronica's grading bias against those who had suffered the misfortune of not attending a CSJ school. Chris attended a high school in Houma run by the Marianites of Holy Cross, and this was enough to merit an automatic "C" on every composition she wrote for Sister Veronica. It may have been one or two misspelled words that did her in. Sister Veronica saw misspelled words as proof positive of despicable laziness. "What—with a dictionary at your elbow?"

After novitiate Chris got her RN from the Mercy Sisters, and that was all practical knowledge about anatomy, biology, and pharmacology, and zip on literature or composition, much less creative writing. And so it takes a while for her to feel comfortable writing to me and just letting the words flow, misspelled or not. When she really loosens up, she starts illustrating her letters with little stick-man cartoons, so outrageously primitive they make me laugh out loud.

A year after our friendship began a very big thing happens— we finally get to go on that vacation together for a week in Grand Isle, Louisiana. Chris and I had both spent summers at Grand Isle. Our family had a camp where we'd go for weeks at a time, and Chris's family would go to her uncle's camp. As young girls, we might have passed each other on the beach.

Our vacation crew is fourteen strong, thirteen of us teachers and Chris the nurse. Until now it was always the rule that local communities not only lived together, prayed together, and worked together but also vacationed together. Everybody together all the time. You get the picture . . . and maybe you can imagine the sheer human challenge of it, especially since, grace or no grace, nuns or no nuns, human beings have a way of showing up as themselves, and old Sour Grapes at work and meals and community recreation at home is going to be her vintage Sour Grapes self on vacation, too.

I'm excited out of my mind to be going back to Grand Isle. Once I entered the convent, I never in my wildest dreams thought I'd ever swim and fish in the Gulf again and walk the beach and feel the strong Gulf breeze whistling through my hair. We are all still in full habits, and once we arrive at the camp and settle in, it takes us a good half hour to hash out a sizable ethical dilemma about how we're going to cross the very public highway to get to the beach.

Should we cross the highway dressed in our habits and discreetly disrobe on the beach? Or, should we put on our swimsuits and nonchalantly cross the road in twos and threes and maybe not be noticed? (In summer the island swarms with Catholics, who know how to spot nuns a mile away.)

Poor Sister Jean, our superior, recently appointed, who is nervous about displeasing the higher-ups, has the responsibility of shepherding us through this ethical quandary. She thinks maybe the best way for us to get to the beach is to wear our habits to cross the highway, which is about as public as you get, she says: The Holy Rule makes it clear that the habit is always to be worn in public, especially when traveling.

Traveling? But, Mother, we're only crossing the road.

True, it's not far, but what else is it but traveling in public?

And so it goes, batting out definitions and discerning between letter versus spirit of the Holy Rule. What finally clinches the decision is that one of us lays out a vivid imaginative sketch of fourteen fully habited nuns crossing the highway to a public beach and then . . . well, disrobing en masse before God and everybody there on the beach. Just think of the mountain of black habits there on the beach: Can you picture it? And here come people strolling down the beach and catching sight of . . . *What the hey is that black heap?* The scene might summon an action reporter from a local television station and make top billing on the nightly news.

A week. Chris and I have a whole week of freedom and recreation on an island we both have loved from childhood. It's very much a community affair with fourteen of us in the camp with a long table and benches on each side downstairs and wall-to-wall beds in a dorm upstairs for sleeping. Chris and I pick out the two beds at the end of the row and slide them close so we can lie across them and be close enough to talk at night without disturbing the others. Throughout the week we get up early to fish, and we swim in the surf, going out to the second sandbar in the afternoon when the tide is out. There's a strong breeze coming from the Gulf—you can smell salt in the air and the waves are running high, and we have a giant tractor-tire inner tube that can hold six of us at a time like rub-a-dub-dub, six nuns in a tub, and a lot of squealing and yelling and laughing as we skinny ones attempt to pull up the chubby ones onto the tube, and a lot of mishaps up and down all the way around. The hot sun warms our faces and arms and the water is cool and salty, which makes you feel sticky when you get out, and you can't wait to take a shower. Fourteen people sharing one bathroom? We hook up a hose and put out two large galvanized tubs in the yard and take turns holding the hose for each other as we suds up and rinse off sandy suits and sticky skin and hair. And then, to be all dry and clean, faces reddened by the sun, sitting around the table mounted high with scarlet boiled crabs and cold beer—tell me: Is this heaven, or what? After supper we play cards or read and listen to music, and then gather around for evening prayer before we go to bed. Psalm 42 gives a mantra for the day:

> Deep is calling to deep
> as your cataracts roar;
> all your waves, your breakers
> have rolled over me.

Each afternoon we set aside an hour for silent meditation, and once again I'm walking the beach of my childhood and trying to quiet my soul so I can take in the beauty and the joy. As a young girl I learned to swim in these warm Gulf waters, and I remember one night when our family was on the beach for a wiener roast and I walked away by myself for a while and the gray-white moon was shining across the dark, heaving water and all I could hear was the breathing of the waves, and I thought my heart would break from the joy or sadness or both at the same time. I did not understand what I felt, with my heart longing for, aching for . . . what? I did not know. Nor do I know even now, as I tell you about it. Something as simple as the moon shining on water has a numinous, unnameable quality about it that is unspeakable. What else to call it but Mystery?

Except for Chris, we all teach religion, and with the magma of new, exciting theological ideas flowing out of Vatican II, the books and articles we're reading have made their way onto this island, along with musical albums and novels, and they course through our conversations during meals and on the beach and everywhere else. Chris finds the discussions fascinating, and at night, side by side in our beds upstairs, we talk in whispers about the amazing new insights.

She has brought the copy of Salinger's *Franny and Zooey* I sent her, and we talk about Franny's frenzied efforts to achieve union with God by praying the Jesus Prayer over and over— "Lord Jesus Christ, have mercy on me"—which she got from a book about a Russian peasant who took to heart St. Paul's words about praying without ceasing. Franny is obsessed with the prayer but also in great distress and close to a nervous breakdown.

The clincher comes in the final chapter, when Zooey, her brother, draws her up short and helps her understand that praying the prayer like the Russian peasant is fine and he doesn't ridicule it. But, he says, she's not actually loving the people around her—for starters, her own mother, who keeps bringing her homemade chicken soup, which Franny keeps rejecting. If it's a spiritual life she wants, Zooey says, she can keep saying the Jesus Prayer all she wants, but she'd better start recognizing the "religious action" in her mother's soup and accept it as the act of love it is. And when she performs onstage, she needs to stop complaining about the "stupidity of audiences." She needs to give it all she's got, and do it for the Fat Lady who is listening to the program at home on her radio.

And who is the Fat Lady?

Zooey explains, "Ah, buddy, it's Christ Himself."

Off and on all week, Chris and I talk about the story and where we meet the Fat Lady, and it's not hard for Chris. She meets the Fat Lady every day in the hospital. It's harder for me. I talk mostly in generalities or stretch the meaning to apply to a kid I teach who has alcoholic parents, legitimate enough when it comes to human suffering, but nowhere near what awaits me down the river. (The Fat Lady is waiting for me, and with the consciousness I have, I'm doing my best to make my way to her, waiting for grace to wake me up.)

And now, these days of this miracle vacation, here I am again, the joy of it too full to take in, with this greatest gift of all, Chris, and I thank God over and over. But there's so much frenzied excitement and energy in me, it's hard to stop and be quiet inside so I can taste the wonder of it all. It reminds me of the way specially treated charcoal catches fire when you put a match to it. There's a flare and the flame quickly spreads across the surface of the charcoal in a thin line of red, but only on the surface, and it takes a while for the burning to catch deep inside.

The only time Chris and I can talk privately, just the two of us, is at night in our beds in the dorm, and we have to whisper so we don't disturb the others. Two tall stand-up fans are on at either end of the row of beds, and they help muffle our voices. We're still only beginning to know each other, and she tells me about the tense situation she and the other young Sisters at the hospital are facing with the grueling schedule and unsympathetic superiors, and I can tell things are not very life-giving there and she and the others are suffering, but I don't know what to do about it. We marvel at these days here on the island and how wonderful it feels to fish again and swim, and she especially loves the feel of wind in her hair. We're both terribly excited about the changes coming about in religious life, and we talk endlessly about the new life and possibilities heading our way. It's a good time to be alive, a good time to be nuns in the Church—the way we're moving away from having to renounce everything good and positive, and embracing it instead.

Chris and I are at the beach every chance we get, and I'm delighted that she loves to fish, as I do, and knows how to bait the hook, cast out, and take fish off the hook—even tricky catfish with their poisonous dorsal fin.

A few of us rise at daybreak to fish in the sparkling surf, just as the sun is coming up, and, O, God, the beauty of it, with the relentless surf swirling round our knees, the undertow trying to pull us out—it takes a lot to keep our footing in the shifting sand. Cast out the singing line and reel it in, cast and reel, ebb and flow . . . all your waves, your breakers, have rolled over me. . . . I look across the surf and see this new friend in my life, fishing beside me, and I sense the patience in her, the long patience that comes from knowing how to wait when you fish and that you're never guaranteed anything when you cast your line into the enormous sea.

One evening after supper we sit around to listen to the story and music of Leonard Bernstein's *West Side Story*—a modern version of *Romeo and Juliet*. Sister Kathleen Pittman had seen the musical the previous month, when she chaperoned the St. Joseph Academy seniors to New York City, and she feeds us the narrative bit by bit, interspersed with the songs, which she stops and plays, and it's as if we're there. We can see it, we can feel it, all the way through to the tragic ending, when Tony, Maria's new love, is stabbed in a gang fight. As his life ebbs away, Maria kneels beside him and sings, "There's a place for us, somewhere a place for us."

We're all crying. The music gets to you. The sheer tragedy of it—two young people just meeting and loving and having their whole life before them—*there's a time for us . . . time together with time to spare . . . wait for us somewhere . . .* only to have it all shattered in a stupid gang fight. How fragile life is . . . love is. We can't ever hold on to anything. I'm seized with terrible longing. How do people do it, surrender themselves, invest their lives and happiness completely with another? Why am I not drawn to give myself to one person in marriage like that? Maybe, once you strip off the spiritual coating of my "religious vocation," I'm only a sterile, little, shriveled-up, deluded . . . what? . . . bride of Christ? Nah—just an old maid, afraid to risk it all for the sake of love.

Or not.

When the pain of my solitary, me-alone-life hits like this, I've got to learn to face it head-on, begging for grace to cushion my fragile heart. *Abide in me. This too will pass.* I'm also learning that vacation time can be vulnerable time, unmoored as it is from the daily schedule that moves me in increments through tasks of the day.

After exactly one week, vacation is over, and we pack up everything to leave the island. I'm going back to the convent in New Orleans to teach at Cabrini School and Chris is going back to the hospital in Houma.

Where did the week go? School? Ugh. I'll hit the treadmill on Monday morning and won't get off until Friday afternoon. It makes me tired to think of it. Endless Mondays, endless lesson preparations, endless teacher-and-parent meetings. And to what purpose? Do I really think my teaching kids for nine months out of the year is going to have any kind of real, lasting effect on their lives? Why does everything feel so empty? Isn't vacation supposed to energize, renew, and refresh?

We drive up to New Orleans, and Chris takes the Greyhound bus back to Houma. Once home, we unpack all our things, go to chapel for evening meditation, then in silence close the curtains around our beds in the dormitory to prepare for sleep. My heart feels as heavy as lead. Why be close to anyone, if it means always having to say goodbye? I think of Chris arriving back in Houma. When we hugged goodbye she could hardly talk. Back to the salt mines. She'll be up early tomorrow for the 7:00 A.M. to 3:00 P.M. shift. Back to writing letters. All we have, really, is letters. What kind of close friendship can we sustain with letters? She's a nurse, I'm a teacher; we'll never be missioned together, never live in the same house.

I climb into bed. Grand Isle fades. Monday morning with my eighth-grade English class beckons. *Give me your love and your grace. . . . I can't . . . make it . . . without . . . your grace.* The best thing I can do this night is put this heavy heart to sleep.

Changes

The glory of God is a human being fully alive.

—St. Irenaeus

By the time Pope John XXIII summoned the Second Vatican Council in 1962, questions and new consciousness about Christ and God and the needs of the world were already astir among Catholics, especially theologians and teachers and nuns. We nuns played an enthusiastic role as first responders to the new outlook Vatican II offered, because we had already been tilling the soil in our own intellectual and spiritual lives. Since the early fifties, a small, steady stream from our community had attended summer classes in theology at Notre Dame University and were coming home with copious notes and exciting new books, which they shared with the rest of us. The theology I learned at Dominican College was still old vintage scholasticism, with its abstract reasoning about God the "Unmoved Mover," who is all-knowing, immutable, and all-powerful—which in the end leaves your soul dry as a stick.

The new insights are refreshing and stimulating and help me get my selfhood back after my futile attempts to relinquish it. Imagine my delight to discover (as St. Irenaeus had already figured out in the second century) that God is glorified by persons truly alive, who make active use of intellect, imagination, and decisional power to do something exciting in the world.

The idea that I can be my natural self and use my gifts of intellect and heart is terribly exciting, because my mind has always been alive with questions and ideas, and I'm longing for real relationships with real people, not relationships laminated over with some kind of artificial spirituality (like the very tricky "I love you in Christ"). I'm finding out that the vow of celibacy is a pretty tricky proposition. While we nuns might be setting out to "love all men" (as we unthinkingly phrased it then and cringe to see it written now), we could very well end up loving no one in particular. I am bound and determined not to become what we call a "nunny nun," obsessed with cleanliness and strictness about rules and ending up being pinched and narrow-minded or maybe even downright mean. Not to mention miserable.

As we begin to reclaim our own humanness, we're also delving into the humanness of Jesus and the situations he faced as a first-century Galilean Jew. I have a long way to go to understand Jesus as truly human, because the God part of him has been so ingrained in my mind that I haven't taken the human part very seriously. What I have known is that every time I go to Mass, I join with Jesus in redeeming the world. So whenever a huge problem such as war or famine arises, what I mainly do is pray for God to comfort the people and solve the problems.

The great thing about the theology opening up for us is that scriptural studies are opening up as well—a new thing for Catholics. Until Vatican II, it was always Protestants who knew the Bible backward and forward, and who could quote chapter and verse—never Catholics. We mainly quoted from the questions and answers in the Baltimore Catechism. Martin Luther had laid down the track of salvation by "faith alone," based on God's word in scripture, and Protestants knew they had to dig into the Bible (read it, for starters) and figure out how to live it in their lives. Maybe the biggest reform of all that Vatican II gave us was the mandate to use the vernacular in worship. For the first time at Mass we began to hear the scriptures read in English, not Latin. Before, you had to look up the scripture passage and read it in English before Mass so that when you heard it in Latin you could maybe make a few connections with the text.

Sister Alice Marie tells us that when she talked to one of her professors at Notre Dame about "blind obedience" to superiors as the "voice of God," he had laughed out loud and told her that kind of thinking was good for children, but not for responsible adults. As I listen to Alice Marie, I realize that deep down in my being I had questioned whether life could really be all that cut-and-dried simple as blind obedience was made out to be.

One of the biggest "God" books we were all reading was John Robinson's *Honest to God,* which I literally copied in huge tracts into my journal. By the time I finished Robinson's book, the God of modern "theism" was gone from my life. Gone was the Old Man Judge, the pumped-up-with-human-attributes super being who knows all and sees all and has infinite power (so, why does He allow little children to suffer?) and who dwells "out there" or "up there" and whose anger is assuaged only by penance and suffering and pain. No, Robinson is saying—this anthropomorphic super being is a God of our own projection, and he shares this insight of Paul Tillich, words about God, which are writ large in my journal:

> The name of this infinite and inexhaustible depth and ground of all being is *God.* That depth is what the word

God means. And if that word has not much meaning for
you, translate it, and speak of the depths of your life . . .
of what you take seriously without any reservation.

We are passing books from one to the other and talking in
small huddles about the amazing new ideas we're reading
about. We are, after all, a bunch of young women, terribly curious and interested in just about everything, and the rule of
silence is no longer so strict in professed communities, and we
are loving the new, exhilarating freedom to talk—about everything.

There's Bernard Häring, a brave German theologian, who
suffers intimidation and threats from officials in the Vatican
because of his teaching that Christian ethics should be based
on love, not simply following the letter of the law or fearing
punishment. But of all the books, maybe my favorite is Erich
Fromm's *The Art of Loving*, which I borrow and keep on the
shelf under my pew in chapel. I get up early so I can copy excerpts into my journal. I diligently continue this practice for
weeks and months until finally Sister Mary Smith, watching
from the pew behind me, leans over and whispers: "Why don't
you just ask Mother to buy the book?"

From Fromm I get insights about how to love that stay
with me to this very day. One is that we mistakenly think that
to love well we must search out and find the one right person
to love, believing that this one relationship will teach us all we
need to know about loving. Another key insight, the heart of
Fromm's book, is that to learn the art of loving we must develop the habit of loving all sorts of people: children and old
people and those who seem strange and different and odd. We
must practice loving all these different sorts of people if we

want to become proficient in the art. Only then, he says, will we be able to commit ourselves lovingly and faithfully to one person, knowing that our hearts and needs are far wider than any one person can fulfill. Fromm's insight is similar to Simone de Beauvoir's advice to young women: "Do you want the young men to love you? Love the old people."

My junior high students have me now at a good time. Everything I'm learning is finding its way into my religion classes with them. Years later, as I have encountered my former students along the way, they tell me that what they remember most about religion class is that I was always talking about love. Funny—I remember teaching them about the Old and New Testaments, the sacraments, the Beatitudes of Jesus: Blessed are the peacemakers, blessed are the poor. . . .

One thing I know I did not teach them about was social justice.

I didn't teach it because I didn't know it myself. This situation was deeply related to how I thought about Jesus. I thought Jesus's commandment to love meant simply that I should always be charitable. I had yet to discover the edges Jesus pushed, the boundaries he crossed, and the people in power he upset by standing with the dispossessed. I knew to practice charity only to people around me in my little tidal pool at Cabrini and in my community—not at all a bad life, not a wrong life, all in all a very good life, spent doing good deeds for good people.

Meanwhile, all around us the civil rights movement is exploding. With the leadership of a new young pastor in Montgomery, black people are refusing to go to the back of the bus, staging sit-ins at lunch counters, and pulling off yearlong boycotts and marching on the roads to get voting rights and being battered with fire hoses and beaten with billy clubs and attacked by dogs and having their churches firebombed and their children killed and going to jail rather than resorting to violence, and some white people are joining them on the road as they march, including young college kids, who spend a summer in Mississippi registering people to vote, and some of them are getting beaten and killed, too.

The school year of 1962–63, my first year of teaching—the year that James Meredith attempts to attend the University of Mississippi, only to be repulsed by Governor Ross Barnett—is also the year Archbishop Joseph Francis Rummel orders the desegregation of all Catholic schools in New Orleans. Although Archbishop Rummel had firmly declared compulsory racial segregation morally wrong back in 1956, he believed in the gradualist approach, so no action had been taken until now. Regrettably, my church lagged behind the state and federal governments in ending racial segregation in schools.

New Orleans public schools desegregated in 1960, despite strenuous, continuous attempts of the Louisiana legislature and the governor to block the federal court order. On November 14, 1960 ("D-Day," the White Citizens' Council called it), four little first-grade African American girls walked into the buildings of two previously all-white public schools. A large crowd of white protesters, mostly women and teenagers, tried to block the school doors and stood on the sidewalks where the little kids had to walk and screamed insults and tried to spit on the kids, who were flanked all around by federal marshals. (The civil rights documentary *Eyes on the Prize* has footage of this scene.) Ruby Bridges was one of the kids. The scene of her walking alone amid the marshals was commemorated in Norman Rockwell's painting *The Problem We All Live With*.

Later, in the 1980s, I'll meet Ruby. She will tell me that she didn't realize the crowd of people at the school was about her. She thought it was a Mardi Gras crowd, throwing things, shouting. Nor did she think it unusual that she was the only one in her classroom with her very own teacher, a nice lady, Mrs. Barbara Henry. She thought that was just the way it was for every kid who went to a white people's school. She never knew that her attendance at school had caused all the other teachers to refuse to teach. She enjoyed the lunch they served her every day, not knowing that because of an irate woman's threat to poison her, the school authorities thought it best to prepare her food themselves.

My school, St. Frances Cabrini, in obedience to the archbishop, accepted a few black kids into the primary grades in 1962, but I never met them, because primary hall was over in another wing, and their playground was separate, too. There must not have been a serious problem with parental backlash because the issue never came up at faculty meetings.

But the desegregation of our high school, St. Joseph Academy, was a whole other story. Black teenagers integrating white high schools presented a far greater threat to nervous parents than little kids, although the four little first-grade girls attending the public schools had caused such a ruckus that the story was covered in international news. White parents well knew that little kids grow up to be big kids, and the ultimate fear—the really big, worst fear of all—was stated baldly at a White Citizens' Council rally by Leander Perez, the district attorney of Plaquemines Parish: "Don't wait for your daughters to be raped by these Congolese. Don't wait until the burr heads are forced into your schools. Do something about it now." At another White Citizens' Council rally, chairman Emmett L. Irwin brought on stage several young white children, some in blackface, who, on Irwin's signal began kissing each other. "That's just a little demonstration of what integration means," Irwin told the crowd. In radio broadcasts the White Citizens' Council decried school integration as Communist-inspired.

Enter this arena St. Joseph Academy for girls, founded by our Sisters in New Orleans in 1858. The principal, Sister Jane Aucoin, a spiritual and intellectual leader among us, is at the helm in 1962 during the first year of integration. When the archbishop first announces the decision to desegregate, our Sisters meet and begin to prepare for the momentous social change. Our SJA faculty decide to admit any black young women who apply for the 1962–63 term. They don't set a limit of admitting only a few token black students to appease nervous parents. Instead, they actively recruit students from black elementary and high schools and welcome whoever comes.

Our academy succeeds so well in attracting African American students that it isn't long before white parents start taking their daughters out of the "nigger" school and transferring them to other Catholic high schools, which have admitted only a token few black students. Anguished, disturbing debate goes on at the Catholic high school principals' meetings as Sister Alice Marie, who has replaced Sister Jane as principal, pleads with the other principals to widen their admission policies to admit more black students. "Don't you see what's happening? By having only a token number of black students, you're contributing to white flight." At meeting after meeting, Alice Marie tries to get them to see that if every high school had an open-door admittance policy, parents wouldn't have a "white school" haven of escape. "Isn't this what the Gospel calls us to do?"

She tries.

The other principals are afraid. They don't want to be attacked by the White Citizens' Council over the radio. They don't want to be called Communists. They don't want the Klan burning crosses on their lawns. But mostly they don't want upset parents pulling their kids out of their schools. They'd lose all those tuitions, and with too much attrition, they couldn't make it financially. They are too afraid to hear Alice Marie's point that by admitting more than a token number of black students their white students would have to mix, enter into conversations and debate, and get a real education in a multicultural society.

Each year more and more black students applied to St. Joseph Academy, and each year more and more white parents pulled their girls out, or did not register them as freshmen.

All the things that the other Catholic-school principals feared would happen if they received a significant number of black students, happened to our academy: threatening phone calls, radio call-in shows where SJA was called the "Nigger School," our nuns called Communists. On the night of the junior-senior prom in the school gym, the Ku Klux Klan burns a cross on our lawn to protest the presence of two black couples at the dance.

Unable to make it financially, our academy closed in 1979.

I still feel pride in our Sisters for our principled stand.

When Reverend King's "Letter from a Birmingham Jail" was published, we passed it around and read it. I saw the moral soundness, the integrity of King's actions. I recognized that he was truly living the Gospel of Jesus, refusing to meet violence with violence. I supported him, prayed for him, admired him. But I joined no marches. I wrote no letters to the editor. Cool admiration, but no fire.

But I did learn to play my guitar and sing some of the civil rights songs. There I was in the laundry learning C, A, F, and

G7, the backbone chords of half of the songs, and singing over and over: "The answer, my friend, is blowing in the wind."

A mighty wind was blowing, all right, all over the place, rattling the windowpanes and pushing at the doors in the beleaguered lives of black people all around me.

Until I got Jesus right, I couldn't hear it.

PART III

LONDON,
ONTARIO

Opening Windows

Religions die when their lights fail.

—Wolfhart Pannenberg

Big step.

I'm in a plane heading to London, Ontario. The year is 1966, and after only four years of teaching, I'm leaving the classroom to attend Divine Word, a religious education school in Canada.

Just last year, Vatican II completed its final session, and now its amazing, revolutionary documents are rippling through the Catholic Church, crying: Renew the Church, get back to the source—Christ. Take a fresh look at ancient creeds, doctrines, and moral teachings and reframe their meaning so that they illumine life as it is experienced by people today. Do Catholics still believe that only Catholics can be saved? Do Catholics still hold that the worst sins are sexual? What about war? What about racism? What does belief in God really mean? The Church needs radical new alignment—*Aggiornamento!* ("Updating!")

That was the mantra uttered by John XXIII. He was an old man of peasant stock, from whom little or nothing was expected when he was elected as pope in 1958, and yet he convened the Second Vatican Council—an event every bit as huge in its repercussions as the Reformation in the time of Martin

Luther. Curial officials in the Vatican, who wield huge power in papal elections, seemed to have thought Pope John would be an "interim" pope—a kind caretaker of the status quo, who would leave the Curia to continue running Church operations as they had always done. That a major church council did take place, with virtually every bishop from around the globe attending, was itself a first-class miracle.

Many of us nuns, working close to the people, felt that it was long past time for our church to join the modern world. Catholics in the United States, far more educated than in earlier days, could no longer be expected to obey blindly like children. Words spoken from the pulpit on Sundays would have to genuinely help people make connections between their faith and what was going on in their lives. Faith had to make *sense* to people.

But now Vatican II was opening new vistas on practically every major front of Catholic faith. The times were compelling us to come face-to-face with the modern world. That world had taught people how to ask questions, to question authority. And if the Church was going to enter into dialogue with this world—so long held at bay as a source of error and mortal danger—it was going to have to open the windows to doubt, uncertainty, and the possibility of change.

Looking back now, I realize that I entered the Congregation of St. Joseph not only with a Middle Ages mindset of blind obedience to superiors but with the coiffed headdress to boot. But, lest in my "enlightened" modernity I disdain too quickly that way of believing and living, let me contemplate for a moment the gifts of it, especially the mystical tradition that taught me to stay alert to God's mysterious presence in my own heart and the world.

What's good about belonging to a religious tradition is that it embeds us in a community, which sustains us in spiritual practice. For me spiritual practice is everything, and it's a blessed thing to inherit a religious tradition. Far better than having to create the meaning of my life from scratch. The Catholic tradition carried my Catholic mother and father and their parents and grandparents, and has carried me, shaping me, forming me, and pointing me into the future. Through these formative years I awakened to my calling, and I've been growing into that calling ever since, learning as I go along, awakening to the freedom of becoming more and more my own person, my own unique self. And all of it with the active support and encouragement of the Sisterhood.

But now it feels as if the structure of the traditional religious universe is cracking apart. Radical questions about life's meaning are being asked that have never been asked before. Authorities claiming definitive answers to inscrutable mysteries are in disrepute. Answers such as "Saints in sanctifying grace go to heaven," "Sinners in mortal sin go to hell," "Unbaptized babies go to limbo." It seems to me that agnostics sound a lot more honest. They just flat-out acknowledge that they know they don't know.

Out of this upheaval the Second Vatican Council had been born. In the four sessions and the documents they produced, the bishops took out the ancient loom of creeds and traditions, dusted it off, gathered rainbow skeins of experience from cultures across the world, and rewove the fabric of the Catholic faith. Here are some of the things that began to change:

• The way we think about God: A far more humble attitude, acknowledging that no name, no concept, can ever capture ineffable mystery, so that all we can do is name *toward* God.
• The way we think about Jesus Christ: Returning to the

source—the scriptures—to learn who He was (until Vatican II, Bible study had been uncharted territory for Catholics).

• The way we worship: The most intimate soul space, where we touch the sacred. The Mass is now celebrated in our native language.

• The way we approach the world: A confident tone of optimism toward the world is set first by Pope John XXIII's *Pacem in Terris* (1963), with its bold defense of freedom of conscience and human rights, followed by the council's "Pastoral Constitution on the Church in the Modern World" (1965), which invites us to discern the signs of the times and roll up our sleeves and enter the fray to address injustice and assaults on human dignity.

• The way we think about the Catholic Church, perhaps the most foundational change of all: The council defines the Church first of all as the People of God, not just as a pyramid with the hierarchy on top and the mass of laypeople somewhere down on the bottom shelf.

• The way we understand morality: No longer focusing on individual sins in a legalistic way and relying on fear of punishment for compliance, but instead realigning the moral life around Christ's mandate of love.

• The way we understand authority: Moving away from juridical authority, imposed from above, to moral, persuasive authority, which inspires by example, and which brings the laity into circles of decision-making.

The council documents urge a new balance. Right alongside the liberation of individuals to think and act is also the call to "think with the Church" by consulting church teachings and traditions, and by collaborating with local bishops and clergy.

But publishing the documents of Vatican II is one thing. Educating the people about their amazing new responsibilities in the Church is quite another. This is why I'm going to Divine Word in Canada. I'll be part of the new vanguard of teachers to bring this renewed way of being Catholic to the people in the pews. When I return to St. Frances Cabrini Parish in New Orleans, that will be my job. I will spend most of my time with adults, the laity of the Church, accompanying them in implementing the reforms of Vatican II.

I couldn't be happier. Along with the rest of my community, I've already been steeping myself in Vatican II teachings, and I know how liberating they are. Immediately upon the publication of the council's "Decree on the Appropriate Renewal of the Religious Life," our CSJ leadership team got copies and put them into each Sister's hands. We read. We prayed. Suddenly we were learning to distinguish between the essentials of our vocation and the traditions and historical accretions that had come to distinguish religious life—including the "maxims of perfection" and the religious garb that was originally intended to make us resemble ordinary people of the time. We studied—especially the council's triple mandate to go back to the Gospels, to the original inspiration of our founders, and to the needs of our time to light our path to renewal. We formed committees, we wrote position papers, we discussed and debated in meeting after meeting, with every Sister encouraged to have her say.

And so we became a microcosm of the Church as a whole. No more top-down decisions from superiors. No more blind obedience. We had new virtues to learn, new spiritual muscles to flex. Yes, every individual had freedom to think and freedom to choose, but always with the focus on service to the people and in communion with the wider Church. A new maxim floated in the air: Never do anything without taking the community into account. In many ways this was far more difficult than simply following orders. Now *everyone* had to think, pray, listen, search: *What needs in the world do I see? How shall I engage my life energies, my gifts, to help the new vision come alive?* We held meetings in the St. Joseph Academy gym. Microphones were set up on the floor. Every Sister was encouraged to speak. And the questions came:

- Do we have to do everything in lockstep? Is uniformity real unity? Can't each Sister be trusted to join in communal prayer but set her own time for personal prayer? Why do we continue to dress like widows of the seventeenth century?
- Instead of performing practices of humility and penance in our own cloistered world, why don't we get involved with abused women and children or black people in the projects to alleviate their suffering? Their suffering is real. Ours is self-imposed and artificial.

It was in this soil of open, give-and-take discussions that our individual selves, long dormant, began to flower. I dug in. I pored over the documents and recorded notes, and there I was at the microphone, saying my piece, and there I was writing a paper called "Unity in Diversity." There was open discussion about everything—it was challenging and at times scary, but mostly, at least for me, it was exhilarating. Maybe you would have had to have been embedded in that tight, closed terrarium of thought, which had muted intellectual inquiry and individual initiative, to fully grasp the delicious awakening of new life that came to us nuns through Vatican II. At the heart of the changes we made was the desire to connect with the people so we could be in touch with their needs and serve them.

So it was that in four short years—1964 to 1968—my CSJ religious community totally revamped our engagement with the world and our style of life: our way of praying and arriving at communal decisions, our dress, our style of community life around mission, our right to privacy (superiors no longer read our mail), and our freedom to form friendships. Every important aspect of our lives changed, with every bit of every change centered around the Gospel mandate of Jesus to serve the "dear neighbor."

And women began to leave religious life in droves.

In 1965 in the United States we were 180,000 nuns strong.

Today we number 60,000, with a median age of seventy-plus and only a tiny trickle of new members entering the community—all of them older now, no more eighteen-year-old "brides of Christ."

Some see Vatican II as the beginning of the end of religious orders. Some say we changed too much, too quickly—we became too much like the world. We lost our nunly *mystique*.

Am I sad about the downsizing?

Yes. It was heart-wrenching to see Sisters leave whom I loved and worked with. But, also no. It was time to shake out the vocation basket, and Vatican II did the shaking. I think one reason such large numbers of women in the past entered religious communities was because the then-monolithic Catholic Church offered a promising niche for women, and women responded. In the first half of the twentieth century, answering the needs of a burgeoning population of Catholic immigrants, we nuns built and ran Catholic schools, hospitals, and orphanages.

In those days the Catholic way of life was pretty much in its own contained world. In such a world, a vocation to the Sisterhood was, in a way, the main show in town for a Catholic girl who wanted to do something "extraordinary" with her life. True, it meant giving up sex and family, but there were definite benefits. Sisterhood brought with it education and a great deal of support and respect in Catholic circles—the only circles in which nuns usually moved. Then, you'd never see a nun in the public sphere—publishing a book, advocating at a court trial, or testifying before Congress or a state legislature. You'd meet a nun only if you ventured into a school or hospital or other Catholic institution.

I say it was good in its day. It's what was needed.

But the river keeps moving.

One of the truly great gifts of Vatican II was the way it reframed and widened Christian vocation—for everybody. Topnotch holiness was no longer only for nuns and priests. The council made clear that through baptism everyone in the Church is called to follow the way of Christ fully and radically. Everyone is called to be a saint. Everyone is called to pray deeply. Everyone is called to act boldly against injustice. No longer is there the "highest" vocation, to which only a chosen few aspire.

And, for me, the clincher—what really freed women to leave religious communities—was this: The fear was gone. No more terror that if you left the convent, you were deserting God and imperiling your immortal soul. No more stigma on those who chose to leave. In such a climate of freedom, many did choose to leave. I say, God bless them, Godspeed. I hope they have had happy, fulfilled, wonderful lives. I hope they've become mystics. I hope they have lived out bold, prophetic action against injustice. I have nothing but gratitude for the time they spent among us.

Meanwhile: Viva the Sisterhood!

It's a great life if you're called to it.

I predict that as long as there is a community of Christ followers in this world, there will always be nuns—few in number, perhaps—who choose to live a celibate, prayerful, nonmaterialistic community life in service to others. To be sure, a nun's life is not for everyone, maybe not for most, especially a life of celibacy, which is tricky because of the strong selfhood, spiritual depth, and ability to love in a wide circle it requires. Lord knows there are enough stories out there about "Sister Godzilla"—selfish and dried up and mean as all getout. But isn't it true that that can happen to *anybody* who never really learns to love?

So, HERE I am on this crisp September day, hurtling through the sky to London, Ontario—all because a few members of the St. Frances Cabrini Parish Council asked why all the nuns were always assigned to teach the children and why couldn't one nun work with them—the adults? My name came up, the pastor asked my superior to send me, and here I am, Canada bound. My life takes a dramatic turn, and it all happens with no initiative on my part, no self-direction from me—all of it simply part of my life as a nun, trying to do God's will by obeying my superiors.

But I'm deep-down excited about the move, pleased that I've been picked to go, thrilled to be trusted. I'm going to be living in an apartment with three Sisters from other communities, not in a convent, but out there in the world. We've modified our habits, and I'm no longer covered in black from head to toe. The veil has a white band on the front and is pushed back so my hair shows. Not only that, but—alleluia—the breastplate guimpe is gone, a simple black blouse in its place; the skirt is shortened to mid-calf; and the old-lady shoes are replaced with perky little black heels. ("Lord, I feel *naked*," lamented Sister Bernardine, an older nun, as she donned the new outfit.) Me, I don't feel naked. I feel like one mod, hip nun.

Don't laugh. You have no idea how mummy-wrapped we were in all that black serge. One time one of our Sisters in a fabric shop who had her back to the aisle felt someone fingering her veil and turned around to face one very amazed lady, who had mistaken her for a *bolt of black material*. It came with the territory. In a way we were indeed a walking bolt of material.

Trust me. Hair and fourteen inches of legs showing is a very big deal.

I come to school in Canada having navigated a few life experiences. I know I can teach in a dynamic way—learned in dialogue with my energetic seventh and eighth graders—they on the cusp of selfhood and me, just a few years older, on the cusp of mine. I'm learning the art of friendship with Sister Christopher. It's wrenching for her to watch me go to another country. It's only just across the border, I tell her—I'll write often, like I always do. I feel for her. I get to go on an adventure. She has to carry on with bone-numbing work.

As a teacher in middle school, I was always open about my life with the kids, except for one guarded, secret zone. When my eighth-grade girls would ask me if I dated boys before I became a nun, if I'd ever fallen in love, kissed, made out, had boyfriends, I would freeze, hope not to blush, fudge with generalities, try not to outright lie. I dated very little in high school, and then, only in my senior year. Augh . . . the man-woman thing—the most un-actualized part of me.

School dances were miserable. I knew I was popular with girls, but boys were another story, especially since the main way to meet them was at school dances, and I wasn't any better at dancing than I was at basketball. I could do only slow dances, which isn't saying a whole lot. *Anybody* can hold on to another body and sway and move their feet two inches to the right or left. It was the herd scene that was the worst: boys clutched on one side of the room, girls on the other, and the absolute worst, the trapped feeling of waiting to be selected, picked out of the crowd, the sheer enforced passivity was excruciating for me—a go-getter, used to taking initiative, used to people desiring my company, inviting me to things, enjoying me.

A girl wouldn't dare ask a boy to dance.

Things got a lot happier with boys when our family sailed to Europe, and Mary Ann and I met some boys on the boat. It was a very, very, very large ship—the *Queen Elizabeth*—with all kinds of fun things to do: shuffleboard, Ping-Pong, swimming, movies, and dancing—good, slow dancing, and with the ship rocking, we had a ready excuse if we stepped on each other's feet. And no curfew. Mama and Daddy knew we were safe on the ship, so Mary and I could stay up all night if we wanted to. A really nice guy named Patrick from Cleveland liked me and I liked him, and we did everything together, talked together a lot, and the night before we landed, we promised to keep in touch but never did. And in Sorrento, Italy, a cute elevator boy at the hotel kept coming to our floor so he could talk to me. He invited me to go to the neighborhood festival, but Mama nixed it, saying we didn't know this boy from Adam's cat, but it would be okay to sit on the hotel veranda and sip a lemonade. Which had to be the hottest date he ever had. But it surely did feel good—deliciously good—to feel my womanly powers at play, strong enough to attract one handsome Italian lad up and down an elevator shaft ten times a day.

But by any accounting, those few, fleeting experiences with men can only be called meager, and when at eighteen I joined the Sisterhood, men in my life were very much an unexplored field. So, now, as I make my way to school in Canada, I am twenty-seven years old, having just professed my final vows, which includes a lifetime vow of celibacy. And believe me, my vows are firm, not some flimflam, weak, anemic promise that I'll flip off as soon as something more promising comes along.

Going with me to Divine Word in London are two other nuns from New Orleans—Sister Judy "Ellie" Gomila and Sister Theresa Durepau. As we're sitting on the plane for the long ride from New Orleans, Ellie takes out the list of the ninety or so registered participants, and we look at who's from the States and who's from Canada and other countries, how many are women, how many men. And I am looking at the list, not noting anyone in particular, because I don't know anybody. If I had been in the least prepared for what was coming, I would have looked more closely at one name on the list, a priest named William, from Boston. His short bio noted that he was coming to Divine Word after recently completing graduate studies at Catholic University, and all I thought then was that if his diocese had sent him for higher studies, he must be pretty smart.

A Man from the East

Even the air feels different. It's early September and already the leaves are falling, and this is way, way up in Canada, so I know there's going to be real snow here which will stick and stay all winter—not like the rare flurries in Louisiana, which melt as soon as they hit the ground. There's an excited buzz of new people coming together at Divine Word Center, on Huron Street, as we're all pouring in to register and meet faculty and classmates. I love it—all the new people—and I'm meeting everyone, doing my Southern thing of warmly shaking hands and hugging those whose energetic welcome seems to match mine. I'm aware that they're almost all Yankees, as Mama would say, which means, by nature, they're more reserved, and you have to respect that.

My apartment mates and I quickly get nicknames. Judy's is Ellie (her name in religion is Sister Mary Ellen), Theresa becomes T-Mary, Sister Rachel from Arkansas becomes Rache, and I, Sister Louis Augustine, become Lou. For the first few days, we're bustling around, getting stuff for our apartment. We need practically everything but furniture: dishes, a mop and broom, curtains, cleaning detergent, groceries. All the incoming students are in the same boat. Everybody's settling in. We nuns, coming from institutional motherhouses, have never set up house, and many have never made coffee or cooked an egg. I come with one basic cooking skill: I know how to fix a good egg-in-the-hole—and I make good coffee. The Sisters in

New Orleans keep me supplied with New Orleans chicory coffee. And if we nuns are neophyte housekeepers, the priests and brothers are worse. They're coming from seminaries and rectories, where they had servants doing everything for them, even cleaning their rooms and doing their laundry. Some communities of nuns were founded just to take care of priests. That's over the top in my book.

The organizers of the program at the center, aware of the bishop's watchful eye on this new kind of co-ed school, have made arrangements for male students to be housed in apartments a mile or so away from where we women are housed.

Ellie, Rache, T-Mary, and I are wondering what we'll do for transportation. Most of the priests have cars (diocesan priests don't make a vow of poverty) but we don't, and the bus line looks to be pretty iffy, especially once winter comes. We're trying to see if we can carpool or maybe put together transportation money in our budgets to lease a car from somebody who knows somebody, so we can get it cheap. And sure enough, someone comes along who knows a farmer from the area with an old car he's willing to lease, and when we cobble our money together, it's enough for the lease. But making business transactions is off-limits for nuns. We have made a vow of poverty to forgo all material possessions, which means we can't buy, sell, or lease anything on our own. So it takes a few long-distance calls to our superiors to get permission to lease the car for the nine months we'll be here.

It's an interesting car. When we hit a pothole, small whiffs of hay or barley or some kind of grain puffs out of the back seat.

The feeling of independence is delicious. At the center we have meetings to pool our wisdom about setting up house. At one of the meetings, a priest named William stands up to say his piece. He's young, in his early thirties, and has a decided Boston accent, and he's saying that what we can do, since we all need cutlery, is just go ahead and buy a gross of the stuff, split the cost, and divvy out the forks and spoons. I notice that he's clean-cut, handsome, and lean like an athlete, and he seems to be one of those organized types, who says, *Hey, let's just buy a gross of flatware.* Not something I'd ever think of.

I know my congregation believes in me to send me away to school like this, trusting that, although I'm not protected by convent surroundings, I'm mature enough to tackle the studies and to handle whatever comes my way. I'm ready for the challenge, although my newly emerging self is still acutely dependent on approval from my superiors. On my own, I would never have had the gumption to request leaving the classroom to go away to study.

Life feels natural. No bells calling you to prayer in the morning. No meals served in the community dining room. No recreation schedule. No sacred silence rule at night. It's just me here in the apartment with Ellie, Rache, and T-Mary, going to class each day in the "wheat-puff" car and cooking our own meals at night. We take turns cooking and make a rule that anyone who cooks doesn't do dishes, and if you're not the cook, you are not allowed to utter a peep of complaint about what's served. The most you can say is, "Um, this is interesting."

Most of the time, after Mass on Sunday, I cook the brunch because I do a super job with eggs and good Southern grits—not too hard, not too runny, swimming in butter, but absolutely never—gag, gag—with sugar, like a lot of Yankees do. We have guests over, and, William, the cutlery purchase expert, who calls himself "the Wise Man from the East," obviously likes being with us, because he's always turning up at the "Southern Sisters'" apartment.

The principle of attraction that draws oxygen and hydrogen together to form molecules and the moon to orbit Earth is also at work among us at Divine Word as we form circles of friendship and eat together and have songfests and soon find ourselves making plans to attend the stage play of *Man of La Mancha* in Toronto. As soon as the idea surfaces, I'm on it and say, "Let's go, let's go," and William offers his car, and we circle the date on the calendar (Ellie makes our social calendar for each month with spiritual sayings for the season), and *Yahoo! We're going to Toronto!* The freedom to make plans and do things is pure joy. No endless permissions. Praise God from whom all blessings flow. I'm getting it back—being a free agent.

When the Wise Man from the East comes over to our apartment, he always comes bearing gifts—fruit, cheese, a bottle of wine, or a bottle of Canadian Club whisky. (Somehow, we from the South are more accustomed to drinking hard liquor than our Northern counterparts.) We sing together, and sometimes T-Mary and I play the guitar—badly, but with enthusiasm—but Doreen McGuire from Newfoundland can really play and sing, and she teaches us a bunch of Canadian folk songs and the national anthem, "O Canada," which we all learn with its solemn, haunting ending: "We stand on guard for thee." And sometimes as we're singing, I look over at William and feel that I'm standing on guard for him, that I want to be good for him.

On weekends our group of friends often gets together for dinner, and our close inner circle of friends begins to shape up: we Southerners and five priests—Irv, Reg, Coop, Paul, and

William. We sing all kinds of songs, a lot of religious ones, but love songs, too, such as "Lara's Theme" from *Dr. Zhivago:* "Somewhere my love, there will be songs to sing." Whenever we sing "Jamaica Farewell," I always lead and throw in a *ch-ch-ch* beat during the refrain. We sing fun songs that we get specific people to do, like Paul, who sings "Temperance Union" with its rousing chorus: "A-way-ay, a-way-ay with rum by gum, with rum by gum," and once while we're singing, I look up to see William looking at me and smiling and I smile back and my heart gives a little turn. It's no secret that we enjoy being together. At the center we always sit together for classes and films. He always seeks me out. People have begun to link us together. Will and Lou. That's sweet. I like it.

So, this is how it happens, I think—friendship between a man and a woman. How very natural it feels, and how real, how sure.

The energy between us feels more charged. Different from the energy Chris and I feel as friends, the way we express affection, encouraging each other when we sag and feel low and surprising each other with little gifts. My studying in Canada is tough for Chris. We got to visit the day before I left. Here I was going off for studies and she was being big-hearted about it, trying to be glad for the opportunity I was getting, but I knew things were rough for her. She always looked so tired. She was working so hard, and she had a vulnerable place about my going away for higher studies. She didn't even have a BA, just an RN.

She tried to say it in a teasing way: "Now, don't you go and get too smart and leave me behind. Let me know all the good stuff you learn." I promised I'd send a steady stream of letters, loaded with nuggets of knowledge, and I meant it, and I've been doing it, and she's writing, too. Our energies pretty much balance out, and often our letters cross in the mail. But with Will, most of the initiative comes from him. He calls. He comes over. He invites. He brings gifts. Being on the receiving end like this is different for me. I can see it's natural for him. Maybe it's a male thing—the hunter in him or something.

Last week I felt the first tension between us. Until now he's been great about it when I've said no to doing something with him because I have other plans. He's always left me free. But last week as the weekend approached he wanted to go to the park on Saturday afternoon, but I wanted badly to read a new book I just got, and he said, "No, no—you can always read a book—I want you to come with me," and he emphasized *me*. He was calling from his apartment and his speech sounded a little funny and he was insistent, and, for the first time, I felt uneasy. I held firm and he got quiet and then we hung up.

The next day at the center he met me as soon as I came in. "I was way out of bounds—I should not have pressured you." He was very contrite, very sincere. I smiled at him and repeated our pet mantra: "Freedom is the order of the day." He repeated it and said with a serious, almost grave tone, "Lou, you know I always want you to be free."

But, no doubt about it, we're spending more time together, just the two of us, and he's almost always the one who makes the plans to get away, which we can do because he has his own car. I'm not going overboard, though. I'm such a roaring extrovert and so spontaneous that I know I need quiet time or else I start zinging around on the surface of things, and I'm like a bird that can't light and all I'm doing is reacting instead of responding. Sort of like (bad joke) the woodpecker who got caught inside a tiled bathroom and ricocheted to death, the poor thing. I know myself and know I need to stay close to my soul center, the place where I can sort through what's happening to me and what arises within me, what I want to do. Ellie and I share a bedroom, and she values quiet time too, so we work it out that when we wake up, our mornings are silent, and we both sit up in our beds and pray.

But more and more often after classes at the center, even on weekdays, Will picks me up and we drive away from the city down country roads where there's a lot of farmland. We talk about everything. He tells me about his father, who had a successful furniture business, and his mother, who's so proud of him because he's a priest, and that his brother had gone to the seminary before him but left and how during summers in the seminary they had to go to a rustic camp in New Hampshire and there were plenty of funny stories about these proper Bostonians having to use an outhouse and getting poison ivy in the woods.

I can tell he's dedicated to serving the people, and he tells me about his first assignments and some of the crazy characters in the rectory and describes in detail when he was ordained a priest on a cold February day and how he prostrated himself in the sanctuary before the bishop and vowed obedience and arose an ordained priest of God forever. And he tells about his studies in moral theology at Catholic University, which introduced him to a new way of understanding morality, which at last was leaving behind the endless legalisms of mortal and venial sin, and that when he finishes at Divine Word he'll be working as a director of religious education in the diocese.

I tell him about growing up at Goodwood and the renewal in my religious community, and he loves my Cajun jokes and stories, and one time, very seriously, he confesses to me about how surprised he is at my . . . he stumbles a bit . . . well, my intelligence, the wide range of reading I've done, the way I probe and question, and he's embarrassed to admit that he thought Southerners were all rather dumb and uneducated, and I tell him he's seen too many films of potbellied Southern sheriffs, and he tells me that, of course, I must have heard that Boston is the absolute center of learning in the United States, the very hub of the universe, which, of course, I meet with a loud hoot of derision.

He likes my writing, my poetry, and he asks for copies of my papers and can quote lines and sections from them better than I can myself. His own writing is more fact filled and logical, more grounded in philosophy and scripture study. He has a prodigious memory and can recite in Greek the entire prologue of St. John's Gospel. He loves Irish poets and can reel off Padraic Pearce's "The Fool" in its entirety. He remembers geography of places and can give you directions to Alaska or the White Mountains of New Hampshire or wherever. I don't know squat about geography, even the places I've already visited, and I never know north from east or any of those things. I think it's a brain thing.

ON THE DAY Father Bernard Häring comes to the center to lecture, Rache and I arrive early with our tape recorders so we can catch every syllable that comes from this holy man's lips. His three-volume *Law of Christ* has just been published— a landmark work culled from twenty years of valiant efforts to reframe the way Catholics approach morality, guided by the way of love Christ taught and lived. Vatican II's effort to steer the Church in the direction of persuasive love rather than fear of punishment is due in no small part to Father Häring's faithful, courageous work. Pope John XXIII sought out his counsel and appointed him to serve as a *peritus* (adviser) at the council. When I tell you about the threats, intimidation, and persecution he endured at the hands of Curial officials who opposed reforms, you'll understand why I call him courageous.

But first, a story of the trauma wreaked on my young soul by the Church's pre–Vatican II moral code.

I'm in the fourth grade at St. Agnes School in Phoenix, Arizona (where our family lived for two years to help cure Louie's asthma). Sister Rosemona is my teacher, the sweetest nun who ever lived, and we're doing serious preparation for the sacrament of confirmation, which will mark our entry as committed believers of Christ. The bishop comes and it's a big deal and Sister Rosemona prepares us for the questions he might ask about our Catholic faith, questions that will be very public, because we're all going to be sitting there in the church with our parents there, and so Sister Rosemona is drilling us assiduously straight out of the Baltimore Catechism, but sweetly, as is her way.

We're supposed to choose a confirmation name, so I take Rose because it's the closest I can get to Rosemona, and I look it up in a saint book and find out my saint is St. Rose of Lima, but I leave off the Lima part and just say Rose because any kid who hears the Lima bit will start sing-songing, "Lima beans, lima beans, Helen's named for lima beans," and I don't want to invite that kind of silliness around a name that is supposed to be holy.

All is going swimmingly with the preparation, and Mama and Daddy have bought me a special mother-of-pearl-covered prayer book to mark the occasion.

Then one day an eighth-grade kid comes round to our class to hold up lost-and-found articles. "Anybody lose this?" he asks, as he holds up, in order, a sweater and a baseball hat and a sterling-silver rosary. My heart lifts because I had lost (yet another) rosary—a nice one. I'm always losing stuff—my purse, my sweater, whatever isn't downright duct-taped to my body, much to Mama's chagrin. So, when the kid holds up the rosary I can picture how it will please Mama that I got my rosary back, even though I can see right away that it's not exactly the one I lost, because the crucifix is different from mine. But I say it's mine and walk up to get it and enthuse about how happy I am to have my lost rosary back, which is the first lie, because I know it's not really mine, and I'm faking the enthusiasm (a sure sign I'm lying through my teeth), and I'm already rationalizing, telling myself that I had, in fact, lost a rosary very, very similar to this one and so what if the crucifix is a little different?

So every day in religion class we're learning about the sacrament of confirmation and how we must pray hard and make sacrifices to receive special graces on that day and pray that the Holy Spirit will descend upon us and make us brave soldiers of Christ, willing to suffer even death rather than deny our faith. We're learning that the sacrament will leave an "indelible" mark on our souls, which means that when we appear before God at death, God will recognize us right away as Catholic. Sister Rosemona explains that we will be receiving special graces, and it's a good time to pray for everyone in our family and for sinners, because it is a time when we'll be especially pleasing to God. She tells us to be sure to be in the state of grace, because if we're in mortal sin when we receive the sacrament, we add onto the mortal sin an even more terrible sin—the sin of sacrilege. Treating us as if we're midget canon lawyers (which is the way the Baltimore Catechism treats us), Sister writes the words *valid* and *licit* on the board and explains that if, God forbid, we should happen to be in mortal sin when we receive the sacrament, its reception would still be valid—we'd really receive it and get the indelible mark—but it wouldn't be licit or proper, because of the mortal sin, which would keep all the graces of the sacrament on hold until we went to confession and got the mortal sin wiped away. Then, after confession—this was comforting—all of the graces of the sacrament would immediately rush into our soul.

She explains it all so sweetly, and my soul begins to descend into a chamber of horrors. All because of the stolen sterling-silver rosary. I claimed it as my own, knowing full well it wasn't mine, and that set off the terrible sinning spree that follows. The second sin of lying came as soon as I got into the car after school and forced myself to cheerily say, "Look, Mama, I found my rosary," but there was my eagle-eyed sister, Mary Ann, who took one look and said it wasn't my rosary because she could tell the crucifix was different from mine.

"Look," she demonstrates, "this one has fancy curlicues on it and yours was plain."

My guilt-infused protest is vigorous—"No, no, no, this is mine, I'm totally, positively, absolutely sure this is mine" (lie number three, four, maybe five because I'm lying with enthusiasm).

Here was the crux of my ethical anguish: If the rosary is considered "valuable"—worth a lot of money—and I stole it, knowing it was valuable, then it's grave matter, the stuff of mortal sin. And like every Catholic child mini–canon lawyer, I well know the requirements for mortal sin: It's a grave matter, you know it's grave, and you give full consent of the will. So, it all hangs on what's a sterling-silver rosary worth. And my hand is up in class and I am asking question after question about how much would something you stole have to be worth for it to be a mortal sin. If you steal a yo-yo or a very tiny statue or somebody's marbles, that's just a venial sin, right? What about a vase? What if the vase has gold on it? (I'm thinking to myself: *Uh, what about a rosary that happens to be sterling silver?*) I hold my breath. My eternal salvation hangs on the answer to this one question. I know what's at stake, I can go to hell for one mortal sin. Okay, I stole a rosary, but what is it worth? Is it grave matter or not? Everything depends on that, because I know as well as I'm breathing that I took the rosary with full consent of the will.

Things get worse.

Saturday afternoon confession time rolls around, and I can't summon the courage to tell Father Donahue, our parish priest, that I stole the rosary and am in mortal sin, so I throw out some of the usual venial sins (not grave matters)— disobeying Mama, not doing my homework, fighting with Mary Ann, being mean to Louie. And I walk out of the confessional with another huge rock added to the sack on my back because I withheld a serious sin in confession, which means I've added yet another mortal sin. But, I tell myself, maybe one lousy little rosary made out of cheap silver—maybe it isn't even real silver—can't be a serious matter . . . not enough to send me to hell. Sister says that a mortal sin is really big, like having an elephant in your room, and you know you're in mortal sin just like you know when an elephant is in your room. Well, okay, since I'm having a lot of doubts, the sin must not be mortal because if an enormous elephant was in the living room I surely wouldn't miss it. How could I miss it? I must not be in mortal sin.

Then, to make things worse, when the family goes to Mass, I go to communion and commit yet another sacrilege because I'm most probably in mortal sin, so now I have a "bad" communion added to my growing heap of mortal sins.

While I'm in this terrible state, the bishop comes and I receive the sacrament of confirmation and we have a little party at home to celebrate and I eat the delicious cake and make like I'm happy but inside I keep telling myself it may not be licit but at least it's valid, at least I got the indelible mark.

I'm nine years old.

The ordeal lasts four weeks.

It feels like four lifetimes.

Finally, I pour everything out to Father Donahue in confession: the stolen rosary, all the lying to cover up—about fifty lies, the three bad confessions and four sacrilegious communions, and one illicit, though valid, sacrament of confirmation, all of it pouring out of my young soul through the lattice grill into Father Donahue's ear.

He listens quietly until I complete my epic, horrible list, and stuns me. Almost offhandedly he says that it's all okay now, that whatever sins were there God has forgiven, and everything's all right and I mustn't worry and for my penance—and, lo and behold, for this mother lode of terrible sins—he tells me to say three Hail Marys and an Act of Contrition, and I don't hear anything else. I come out of the confessional box liberated, the sack of heavy rocks gone, the dread and anguish lifted. Once again I'm in the state of sanctifying grace, and if I die tonight I'll go to heaven. *Thank you, Jesus. Thank you, Mary, and all you saints and angels, thank you, thank you.* And the next Sunday when I get into the communion line with my family, I am one happy nine-year-old, and I'm soaring inside, so light I'm afraid I'm going to lift up off the floor and float up to the top of the church.

When I was in the novitiate, I remember kneeling before Mary's statue to pray, and the thought came that maybe the reason I'm always asking Mary to intercede for me with God—even with Jesus, who is supposedly my merciful savior—is that I'm actually afraid of Jesus, too, savior or not, and that's why

I'm always going to Mary to run interference for me. And as I'm kneeling there, the fear lifts, and then, when Vatican II comes along, it finishes off the fear, and I've been past it ever since. Except for dying. I'm still scared of dying—faith or no faith.

So, imagine my happiness, all these years later, when I hear that Father Bernard Häring, credited with reforming moral theology in the Catholic Church, is going to teach us at Divine Word.

A short history of Catholic moral theology will help to give background. The early Church, closer to the time of Jesus, had as their only moral code Christ's command to love God and neighbor in a radical way: to return love for hate, to forgive injuries, to pray for persecutors, to never resort to violence to settle disputes (early Christians were forbidden to join the military), and even to be willing to give one's life for others.

But as the Church institutionalized and power was centralized, canon law codified into rigid rules what had been supple and spirit-sensitive, and everything got systematized, especially morality. Under the influence of Celtic monks in the eighth century, the practice of individual confession to a priest began to spread through the Church, and penitential books appeared to assist the clergy in determining appropriate penances for sins, according to their seriousness, and so the grading system of sins came to us, which gave us mortal and venial categories. Over the years, the moral code got more and more legalized, and amazingly complex moral questions—such as *Can unbaptized babies go to heaven?*—were given stunningly simplistic solutions by Church officials with no questioning allowed. According to this moral code, a teenage kid who masturbated always committed a mortal sin (sexual sins were almost always mortal, including using birth control methods, which were considered "unnatural"), yet killing in wartime was not only not a sin but a virtue if guidelines of the "just war" theory were followed (which were very difficult to interpret, almost always justified war, and never seriously questioned until nuclear weapons came on the scene). Over centuries, this legalistic moral code found its way into the Baltimore Catechism, which every Catholic kid memorized until the years of Vatican II.

Staunch traditionalists in the Vatican objected to the proposed reformed moral code with apoplectic fervor. In a spirit of compassion, let us interpret their resistance to the change as sincere: They simply could not conceive that reformulating the Church's longstanding, clearly spelled-out moral code, with priests at the helm of judgment in confessionals, could possibly be improved upon. Especially troubling to them was the reorienting of the entire moral code around something as indefinable and open to misinterpretation and flagrant abuse as—of all things—love. They were utterly convinced that the power of original sin would seduce the faithful to choose the easy, comfortable way rather than the way that is more demanding and sacrificial. Without the threat of mortal sin incurred by missing Mass on Sunday, do you really think the people will attend solely out of a motive of love? People need fear of consequences to help them do the right thing.

Father Bernard Häring is a good teacher. He tells stories about the real people in real situations that led him to question the old moral code. A man of the most gentle disposition, he recounts his experiences of threat and intimidation at the hands of Cardinal Alfredo Ottaviani, head of the Congregation for the Doctrine of the Faith (formerly the Sacred Roman and Universal Inquisition), who had little or no experience in his long church career of having his judgment questioned by an underling. In preparation for the council, at Pope John

XXIII's request, Häring served on the preparatory commission headed by Ottaviani. One of the moral questions before the group was whether babies who died without baptism could go to heaven. Ottaviani was adamant about maintaining the traditional position of the Church that such babies were excluded from heaven and sent to limbo. Häring countered that a loving God, who willed the salvation of all, would not levy unfulfillable conditions on souls. His questioning came from excruciating personal experience. When he was fourteen years old his mother gave birth to twin girls, both of whom died. One was born dead, but the other lived a few hours and was baptized. Following the traditional moral code, the parish priest refused to let the unbaptized child be buried in the church cemetery.

Ottaviani forbade Häring to question or debate the subject and ordered the traditional teaching to be presented unchanged to the council fathers. Häring replied that it was not within Ottaviani's authority to lay an order of silence on a commission named by the Pope. The council fathers, he said, should be the ones to decide the question. When it was time for discussion on the question before the council, Häring's position won hands down, but he had made a powerful enemy in Ottaviani, and for the rest of Häring's life, Ottaviani closely scrutinized his teaching and writings and repeatedly subjected him to formal investigations even in his old age, as he battled throat cancer.

Father Häring tells us a story of a woman's dilemma that helped him recognize how skewed the Church's moral framework was. The woman acknowledged that she was seriously considering having an abortion of what would be the sixth child in her marriage. She knew an abortion was a terrible mortal sin, but she found herself stressed to the breaking point with five children already, a husband who wanted sex often, and a church that forbade any method of birth control other than abstinence, which her husband adamantly refused. Better, she thought, to commit one mortal sin by having the abortion than to commit innumerable mortal sins night after night by practicing birth control.

"What would be Jesus's response to this suffering woman?" Häring asks us. "What does charity require?" He had begged the Pope (now Paul VI) to abide by the recommendations of a special commission that had urged the Church to adopt a more holistic approach to birth control. But in 1968, Pope Paul VI in *Humanae Vitae* reaffirmed the Church's traditional teaching that in marriage every act of sexual intercourse must aim toward the procreation of new life. No method other than "natural" methods (abstinence during fertile periods) would be sanctioned, and all "artificial" methods were condemned as "intrinsically immoral."

Fifty years later many theologians hold that no single teaching did more to erode confidence in the Catholic Church's moral teaching authority than this encyclical on birth control. Father Andrew Greeley, a sociologist who for thirty years tracked U.S. Catholic beliefs and practices, called the overwhelming rejection of *Humanae Vitae* by the vast majority of American Catholics as the "coming of age" of adult, educated Catholics, who weighed the encyclical's teaching but found guidance instead in the more holistic approach toward marriage implied by Vatican II, which urged couples to love generously and expansively while at the same time respecting their consciences and their competency to be the best judges about responsible parenting.

Sparrow Song

After the Christmas holidays we're all back at Divine Word, beginning the second and last semester of our nine-month program. As soon as we're back, we hear that we have to write a formal reflection paper, and we all give a deep communal groan. We thought that in this new kind of free-flowing lecture and discussion school we'd be spared time-consuming, labor-intensive academic papers. I hated them in college. Hours and hours of work and absolutely zero wattage of insight. And now that I've been entrusting to my journals what my own heart tells me to write, writing on demand to fulfill a requirement feels like a terrible intrusion. But obedience kicks in.

As I mull over what to write about, I get a big idea: Instead of writing the usual kind of paper, researching a topic and summarizing the ideas of scholars and experts, I'll summon my own voice and tap in to my experience to sound out the faith mystery. Hadn't Vatican II emphasized that the Holy Spirit is in *everyone*? I want to get past simply quoting doctrines and creeds, and, instead, crack open what they mean in my life, viscerally—the felt experience of translating these beliefs into my everyday life, the way I explore things in my journal. If faith is a living faith, shouldn't it generate insight, strength, and courage to question, to test the edges?

I've had more than my fill of dry, abstract, neo-scholastic theology, which has attempted to use esoteric philosophical categories to explain religious faith. For example, making a big deal over the distinction between "sanctifying grace" and "actual grace." Or defining Jesus's identity as God and human as a "hypostatic union." Or, talking about bread becoming "transubstantiated" into the body of Christ at the consecration of the Mass, the "substance" changed while the "accidents" remain the same. Early followers of Christ didn't express faith like this. The philosophical bent to explain theology began in the Middle Ages, when Aristotle was rediscovered and Thomas Aquinas in his *Summa Theologica* attempted to reconfigure the Christian faith in rational, Aristotelian terms. All kinds of dualisms sprouted up as a result: natural versus supernatural, nature versus grace, and so forth. This is why Vatican II was so needed.

In my paper I want to explore what *faith as it is lived* feels like, how it tastes, the way it illumines our path in daily life. Take the resurrection of Jesus from the dead. That's held as a rock-bottom, core belief of the Christian faith. So what does it mean? Is it a historical fact that can be demonstrated? If there had been a video camera recording Jesus's tomb on Easter morning, what would it reveal? Would it show a three-day-dead resuscitated, glowing body bursting out of the tomb? Was Jesus's overcoming of death a coup de grâce argument to "prove" Jesus must be divine? Is it a guarantee to believers that when we die, we, too, will come through death with our ego-selves intact—me, still quintessentially me, Helen—but now understanding everything and shining? Or are we talking about a more paradoxical kind of truth, as Jesus talked about the grain of wheat having to fall into the ground and die to produce its fruit, or when he said that each of us must lose our life in order to save it?

Maybe the mystery of life coming from death is not only about end-of-life-on-earth death but also part of our ordinary experiences of loving and losing, of feeling our life is taking shape, getting purpose, drive, zing, only to plummet, sometimes, into confusion, darkness, and despair. Soar and plummet, soar and plummet. Is life bipolar at its very core? How do we pull free of the grinding sadness that haunts us, creeping into our sleep, waiting to taunt us when we awaken? Always the voice . . . we can't stop the voice: *What does it all mean? My life is fake, hollow. Whom do I love? Who really loves me? Time is running out.*

We're talking resurrection? Meaning life *after* death?

What about life *before* death?

When I go back to the people in Frances Cabrini Parish, how will I help them understand and live their Christian faith if my own faith isn't real? It's a confusing, dark process. Much easier to let the "authorities" assign meaning and follow their directives. Much easier to obey than to create.

I entitle my paper "Sparrow Song," and in the introduction I write: "I came to realize that this paper would be of worth only if it expressed truth chiseled from my own life experiences—my truth—rather than a mere echo of the truths of other men."

Later, I'll learn that finding your voice and speaking out of personal experience was the heartbeat of women mystics in the Middle Ages. Cloistered in nunneries and barred from learning Latin, which in turn kept them from attending universities, they had only one field of exploration: inside themselves— their own interiority. And so they delved deeply into contemplation of divine mysteries and wrote down what they saw and felt in the earthy, colorful vernacular of the day. (The Latin root *verna* means "domestic, native.")

Not knowing Latin turned out to be a blessing. It saved

them from writing in the mold of staid Latinate treatises, which would be as boring as nails to read. Julian of Norwich, Catherine of Genoa, Clare of Assisi, Teresa of Ávila, Mechthild of Magdeburg—each took pains to make clear they were not speaking as theologians. Not in those heresy-obsessed times in which women, simply by being women, were already suspect. So it was standard fare for women to couch their writings in abject humility. St. Teresa of Ávila, writing her autobiography in Spain in the sixteenth century, when black-robed inquisitors were watching and sifting every word she uttered, adopted a shucks-I'm-only-a-woman style that steered well clear of the style of the *letrados*—the "learned ones"—who were thought to provide the only sure knowledge of God, and who, of course, wrote only in Latin.

"I should like to excuse myself from this since I am a woman," wrote wily Teresa. "Seeing so much stupidity will provide some recreation for your Reverence" (*Autobiography* 11.6).

I'm feeling nervous about using personal experience as the main content in my paper, so, just like Teresa, right from the start, I profess humility:

I write these reflections humbly. I am well aware that there are people holier and more intelligent than I, whose writings on the Christian life, far deeper and more scholarly, can make my own words pale. Pale or not, the words are my own, and only I can say them because they have been born of my own experience. . . . Kahlil Gibran in *The Prophet* says that you cannot command the skylark not to sing. Not that I think myself a skylark—a sparrow, perhaps. But Jesus has told us that in this world where God is Father there is worth even in a sparrow's song.

I can see that everyone else at Divine Word is going to the library and writing regular, footnoted papers, and when I hear my classmates talk about this or that theologian they're referencing, I don't say much. What I'm doing feels edgy, arrogant, even. But it's what St. Augustine did in his *Confessions*. He was the first Christian who drew on his own personal life story as the basis for theological reflection. He couldn't have made it more personal, writing about his childhood acts of vandalism, his struggles with lust and how he prayed "Give me chastity, but not yet!," and about how one day in a garden he heard a child's voice say, "Take and read," and he picked up a Bible and went right to one of St. Paul's epistles and it was a thunderbolt moment of revelation, and he changed his ways and realigned his entire life to follow Christ and never turned back. That's what I call a Jesus explosion, and that's what I'm hoping for, though it's not happening for me in one fell swoop as it did for Augustine. It's happening more in dribs and drabs.

At this point in my life, I am still pretty much smack-dab in a very enclosed world of personal, privatized religion. The suffering all around me in the larger world does not exist for me. It's not that I'm trying to block it out. I simply haven't awakened to it. But I guess when you're not awake, you're not awake. That's why when I do wake up to the call of the Gospel to resist injustice and get to work in the public square, I have to call it *grace*.

Cheeky or not, I'm doing it, writing my paper straight out of personal experience, and that carries me still. I've been keeping a journal for three years, and here in London my relationship with William fills a lot of pages. Sometimes, when the spirit moves me, I write down my conversations with God—which, I'm afraid, turn out to be mostly me talking and God just sort of nodding and going along. It's hard to know when exactly God is talking, or only me doing the talking for both of us.

In "Sparrow Song" I'm determined to write about what is real, so I write about getting past "shell reality," in which external forms substitute for the real: "We write a paper to meet a deadline, visit a person because social pressures demand it, work for the paycheck."

From Salinger's *Catcher in the Rye* I love Holden Caulfield's exquisite castigation of fake Christianity, where he said "old Jesus would've puked" if he could see what people are doing in his name. In "Sparrow," to illustrate "shell reality," I turn to Salinger's description of one character's concept of marriage in his *Raise High the Roof Beam, Carpenters*:

> My beloved has an undying, basically undeviating love for the institution of marriage itself. She has a primal urge to play house permanently. Her marital goals are so absurd and touching. She wants to get a very dark suntan and go up to the desk clerk in some very posh hotel and ask if her husband has picked up the mail yet. She wants to shop for curtains. She wants to shop for maternity clothes.

I write about how I'm learning to embrace the natural goodness of things, knowing that God is in the goodness, and I no longer have to practice a lot of penances and sacrifice to curry God's favor. Not as we had learned in the novitiate: "If something was good, it was always 'more perfect' to sacrifice it," I wrote. "I had in my mind that the more difficult a thing was for me, the happier it made God."

This attitude that pain pleases God has a long religious history. In the novitiate I remember picking up a book on asceticism (stripping away attachment to earthly things), which recommended that if something really delicious was served at a meal, *to counteract the pleasure,* one should quietly raise a leg under the table and continue to hold it in a strained position. *Keep that aching leg up. Don't you dare enjoy that fresh, sweet, succulent corn on the cob.*

In "Sparrow" I describe my old mindset:

> As for knowing what I was supposed to be doing with my life, that was determined by obedience to the rule and my superiors. I constantly hankered for their assurance that I was pleasing God. . . . My life was almost completely governed from without. My sense of initiative and vibrant aliveness seemed almost entirely dormant. The grain of wheat lay still in the dark earth without a hint of a green sprout anywhere.

But still, in this Catholic tidal pool at Divine Word, surrounded as I am by people just like me, it's all green hillsides and blue skies of self-discovery. No purple shadows of human suffering fall across my path. Not a single lecture or reading or film calls us to respond to the urgent social problems of our day. Among my classmates there is not one poor person or person of color. Poor people never seem to have the luxury to study theology.

I am almost totally unaware of the burning social issues: the nuclear arms race and the appalling injustices heaped upon African Americans. Other Christians are becoming engaged in these issues, but not I. I am not even aware of the passage of the Voting Rights Act by Congress, nor have I heard any of the stories coming from the "freedom schools" in Mississippi, in which white college-age students from the North have joined

African Americans in their struggle to secure the right to vote—some at the cost of their lives. Nor am I aware that at this very time that I am in London, Martin Luther King, Jr., is in the struggle of his life in Cicero, Illinois, as he leads a march to promote racial justice in the face of catcalls, screams of obscenity, spitting, and flying bottles and bricks from outraged whites. When I fly home for Christmas break, I'll meet him in the Chicago airport, standing right behind me at the ticket counter, and I look at him there and can't believe it's him and look again and step out of line and go to him: "Excuse me, sir, but are you Doctor King?" He looks so tired, so crestfallen, and he's just standing there in line with the rest of us, and he barely looks up at me as he takes my hand and says, "Sister, pray for us, we need a lot of prayers."

Later, when I wake up to justice and read about his life, I'll make the connection with the time, the airport, and his agonized conflict in Cicero. I wasn't yet lifting a finger to help in the battle for racial equality. I thought that all I had to do was to be charitable to those around me and maybe make a contribution to the missions. I thought that praying was enough.

A year after I meet Dr. King, he'll be shot dead in Memphis as he joins with sanitation workers in their "I am a man" long slog for a barely minimum wage. I don't think my encounter with him in the Chicago airport is what you would call a real meeting. That would come only later, when, after encountering Jesus of the poor through my black brothers and sisters in New Orleans, I was set free to join the movement for justice for which Dr. King gave his life. Only then did I really meet him. What I still remember about the airport encounter is how very tired he looked.

As you can perhaps guess, if I'm oblivious to civil rights struggles being waged on my own doorstep, you can imagine the depth of my oblivion to much larger—global—issues, such as the buildup of nuclear weapons in the Cold War. I will be shocked to the roots of my being when I find out how during the Cuban Missile Crisis in 1962, a few years before, we came so breathtakingly close to nuclear war. When I do find out, I'll get on my knees and thank God that John F. Kennedy had the sanity to communicate directly with Nikita Khrushchev and the courage to resist the pressures of hard-liners among the Joint Chiefs of Staff and the CIA, determined to launch a pre-emptive nuclear attack on Russia. Only much later did the chilling facts of our close call become public knowledge, but news about the buildup of nuclear weapons had long been public knowledge, which I could have easily accessed had I cared enough to investigate and get involved.

As it turns out, even my hero, Thomas Merton, the cloistered Trappist monk who had written *The Seven Storey Mountain,* awakened to the nuclear threat long before I did and raised his voice in resistance in the only way a cloistered monk could in those days: He wrote a poem and had it published. It was entitled "Chant to Be Used in Processions Around a Site with Furnaces." The speaker in the poem is a commandant of a Nazi death camp, who concludes: "Do not think yourself better because you burn up friends and enemies with long-range missiles without ever seeing what you have done." Merton's poem, published without permission of his superiors, caused a storm of protest from both inside and outside cloister walls: *What was he, a monk, with a vocation to pray for the world, thinking he was doing, getting involved in politics?*

WHILE AT DIVINE Word, I, along with 140,000 other nuns, participate in a Sisters' Survey, sponsored by the Conference of

Major Superiors of Women Religious, intent on assessing the impact of Vatican II on our ideas about our faith and our mission in the world. Who among us embraced a pre–Vatican II mindset, which sees our vocation as "called out of the world" to seek "God alone," and who among us saw God as present in the world and guiding us to become agents of social change? The sociologist chosen to design the questions on the Sisters' Survey was Sister Marie Augusta Neal, a Sister of Notre Dame de Namur. Remember her. You'll meet her farther down this river. She's the one who will explode my spiritual consciousness and change the trajectory of my life.

"I wake to sleep, and take my waking slow . . . I learn by going where I have to go," said the poet Theodore Roethke. And in my awakening to new worlds in London, I am thoroughly engaged as I set out to write theology out of my personal experiences in "Sparrow Song." And then there's this interesting, blossoming relationship that is happening with this man, William. Our classmates at the center expect to see us together. We're not the only nun-priest friendship happening. A number of duos have been springing up. For almost all of us, strictly kept apart during our novice training, this coed experience is a first. And in the new spirit of freedom and experimentation, a new kind of man-woman relationship called "the third way" is being widely discussed among us: A man (priest) and woman (nun) commit to love each other with a "preferential love" but stay in their vocation and remain celibate. Rumor has it that some exchange rings as a sign of their "spiritual marriage." And if this sounds confusing and tricky in the extreme, that's because that's exactly what it is.

William and I are nowhere near that kind of relationship, but I like being linked to him, and I've welcomed him into my life. I'm glad to round out in my life an unfinished part of me that only a male relationship can complete. He is attractive, yes. Very masculine, yes. Smart and spiritual, yes. Just what I like in a man, yes. Our relationship is deepening, and when he says he loves me, it's like breathing, and I say I love him, too. I like the way we talk about everything, and I feel comfortable telling him about the absence of men in my life—until he came along. He likes that. He likes being the first. He went out with girls in high school, like going to the prom and ballgames, but it was all pretty lightweight, and, like me, he entered the seminary right after high school. I tell him all about my friend Chris, and show him her picture, and talk about the fun we had at Grand Isle, and he says he wants to meet her. We're a good match, William and I.

So, it's William at the door to take us all out sledding and William calling me on the phone and the two of us talking for a long, long time, and Rache trying to get through on the line and teasing, saying we're just like a couple of moony teenagers.

William and I are out for a drive one day in April. Spring is poking its sticky green leaves out of the dark, skeletal trees, and we're aware of the time, the season, the winding down of our last semester. By mid-May classes will end and we'll both be home. We drive and talk and then he stops the car out by a farmer's field, and he moves over close and puts his arms around me and kisses me—a sweet kiss and gentle—and I'm not at all surprised and I kiss him back. It's all so natural. It's all so good.

Later, when I'm back at the apartment and lights are out and I'm lying there in the dark, I think about the kiss. I know things with William are taking a more serious turn. Here he is, a man in my life, a wonderful man, who obviously is growing more serious in his love for me. But there's a shadow. It's not that I'm afraid of sinning. I'm not afraid of God's displeasure. I know I'm truly free to fulfill my life in a way that makes me happy. So what's the worry? Can I name it? Maybe this— maybe his growing need to be exclusively just with me. He is talking about wanting to spend the rest of his life with me. Is he looking to me to fill his loneliness? I like a lot of streams feeding my river. I can't picture settling into life with just one person. I'd shrivel, trying to focus most of my soul's energies on one man. And I know I need hunks of solitude the way I need sleep and food. I'd lose a sense of who I am without it.

I've heard from a friend in the men's apartment complex that my friend William drinks too much. But, then, a lot of priests I know drink, and everybody at some time or other drinks too much. In my French family, I started drinking good Bordeaux on Sundays when I was six, and Daddy and Mama had great parties with Daddy serving his prize martinis and everybody having an uproarious, wonderful time. At the center, we had a session on pastoral care of alcoholics and attended an Alcoholics Anonymous conference at the civic center here in London. I hadn't noticed the "Anonymous" part of the name, and as I met people in the lobby, I was immediately struck that one family in particular had been hit especially hard by the disease. I met Bob London and Mary London and Louise and Dick—every one of them in AA. Imagine what a suffering that must be for that poor family! Finally, inductive reason kicked in.

So, okay, I tell myself—sometimes William drinks too much. Maybe when he's in his groove, back at work in Boston he'll be all right.

The words of E. E. Cummings spring up, words I've written in my journal, words I try to live by:

> be of love (a little)
> More careful
> Than of everything

When Rache and I board the train to go home, William is there to see us off, and I'm there at the window with Rache to wave goodbye. I've promised to call often, and write, and he says he'll come to New Orleans soon—very soon. He's standing there in the station alone, moving from foot to foot, and looking forlorn and miserable. He's been telling me about how plans for his life are very unsettled. He hasn't heard from priest personnel about his assignment or even where he'll be living. I feel for him, I want him to be okay, but I'm excited to be going home—I can't help it. My community is waiting and Chris is waiting, and I'm champing at the bit to take on Cabrini Parish as the new director of religious education.

As the train begins to pull away, I wave and wave until I can't see him anymore, and Rache whispers, "Lou, that guy is smitten *bad*," and I say, "I know, Rache, I know."

What that means for William and for me will take seven years to figure out.

PART IV

~~~

BECOMING
AN ADULT
CHURCH

Cabrini Parish

no time ago
or else a life
walking in the dark
i met christ

jesus)my heart
flopped over
and lay still
while he passed(as

close as i'm to you
yes closer
made of nothing
except loneliness
—E. E. Cummings

I'm home at our convent in New Orleans. It's the fall of 1967.
Everything feels the same.

Everything feels different.

Back from my studies in Canada, I'm set to become the
director of religious education (DRE) at St. Frances Cabrini
Parish. So, who am I now? How am I going to tackle this new
job? All I know is that I'm hot in the saddle to put Vatican II's
teachings into practice: the idea that truth can be found everywhere, not only in the Catholic Church, and there's no secular
world over there and sacred world over here, because for those
who have spiritual insight, nothing is profane, the holy is ev-

erywhere, and it's high time to start translating the message of Jesus into terms people can understand and—you know— *connect with.*

In the chapel for morning meditation, I'm listening for the voice within. Sitting still until I sense what I'm feeling—dark and brooding or light and bubbling up. *I'll have to go in slow, do a lot of listening. . . . I'm the new kid on the block. . . . I'll be working with the priests and mostly with adults.* It's scary— and exciting.

Chris managed to get off the weekend after my return and will arrive Friday night from Houma by Greyhound bus. She says she'll have to walk with her suitcase from the convent to the bus station, but she doesn't care. It's not that long a walk, she says. Anything to get away from the gulag. Just last week, she had to work three sixteen-hour shifts back-to-back.

We wrote regularly while I was in London, but during the last couple of months my letters were pretty much aimed at encouraging her, pumping her up. "Hang in there, I'm coming home soon. Wait until you hear about the new Dutch Cate-chism. By hook or crook I'll get a copy for you." I send it within the first couple of weeks that I'm home. Inside the cover I write: "To our nursing sisters, who have borne the heat of the day."

In my letters to Chris I didn't say much about William. I sensed she'd feel threatened. She's not as sure as I am that rela-tionships endure.

But I'm the one inside myself, and I know what I think, what I feel, and what I intend, and I'm figuring that there's room inside my soul for both her and William—and the com-munity. Maybe I'm like a carbon atom with valency to form bonds with a lot of other atoms. Different people spark differ-ent parts of me—humor, curiosity, spirituality. (Doesn't every interaction between two people have a unique "chemistry"?) Maybe Chris is more like a hydrogen atom with just one portal open for close relationships. Maybe, when it comes to relationships, different people are just configured differently.

High valency or not, I know I need Chris. I need the way she slows me down, the way she quiets me. Everything she says comes from her soul. She seems incapable of duplicity. Me, in my spontaneous, extroverted thrust, I can be pretty showy and glitzy. Not Chris. She doesn't trust surface sparkle, and she can spot a fake a mile away. Once at a meeting, after a Sister was exceedingly verbose, spouting one half-baked idea on top of another, Chris said, "I have absolutely no idea what that lady was talking about." I need that. True-blue Chris. When she stands up to speak at our community assemblies, everybody listens, because she does it so seldom. She's not good at spinning stuff off the top of her head. She knew right off the bat she could never be a teacher. She couldn't stand the thought of having to stand in front of a room full of people—kids or not—and talk all day long. The thought made her soul shrivel.

We've been friends now for four years. Enough time for the contours of our relationship to take shape. I guess, over time, every close relationship has a way of settling into its natural contours. Maybe like the way a house takes shape. In a blueprint, there seem to be endless possibilities: a deck, a great big room, a large kitchen with plenty of cabinets, a skylight. Then the house is built and the deck has to go (too costly) and the kitchen is more compact than plans originally called for. Like houses, relationships in real life take on actual shape, but with far more fluid contours. Relationships are always in a state of becoming, always flowing, always freshly created—like those lava lamps in the sixties, but more open-ended. Over the course of four years, Chris and I have invested a lot of ourselves in each other. We've built trust. And we keep seeing that we're good for each other. Our friendship tree keeps sprouting fresh green leaves.

Now, here comes William, upsetting the balance. I can tell Chris feels tense about my closeness with him. The tension hasn't hit the air—it's unspoken—but it's there, and it makes me feel tense as well. In her last letters to me in London, I could sense Chris was pulling back, and instinctively I pulled back, too. My notes were just as frequent but shorter, and newsy about everything but William. But I'm home now and sure that once Chris and I can talk things through, we'll be okay. Mama and Daddy always talked things out. That's what people do who care about each other. Besides, it's not like Chris and I are married—as if we're linked solely to each other for our happiness. We're part of a community, and in our vocation our two boats will never nestle in a snug, domestic harbor. We'll always be out on the open sea. Maybe that's true for all of us.

On one life front for sure, it's true: dying. Every soul passes over into death alone. No matter how others hover closely and try to accompany us, it's very much a solitary journey. We're alone in a lot of other ways, too. Behind our eyes, inside ourselves, we're always teeming with thoughts and feelings nobody else can see. We're such *interior* creatures. We carry universes of thoughts, imaginings, and emotion inside ourselves. The tiny revelations that emanate from us, the tiny glimpses others get of us, are so minuscule when compared to the teeming galaxies swirling around inside ourselves, to which we alone are privy. Or, maybe not as privy as we think. I mean, the dark realms inside us that heave and recede without any agency from us, that move us to feel and think and act sometimes in ways that surprise us and leave us clueless. Here we are walking around—movable mysteries. Maybe we're like the universe itself, which scientists say is made up almost entirely of dark matter and dark energy. Only about 4 percent is visible. Maybe we're like that. Chris and I are always quoting the wise fox in Saint-Exupéry's *The Little Prince:* "It is only with the heart that one sees rightly; what is essential is invisible to the eye."

So, with this man, William, weaving himself into my life, who am I now? And what will happen to my friendship with Chris? When Chris and I talk about this, I know two things are going to be important: that I'm open and candid about my friendship with William, saying what it is and what it isn't, and that all the words in the world telling Chris what she means to me will never cut it—only my actions, showing her how much I prize her, will do. So we'll do what we always do—cordon off space and time on our calendars to spend time together. (*Spend* time, as if we pay it out like currency.) I once heard a friend described as someone with whom we're willing to *waste* time. Sounds profligate. But it's true that when I love somebody, no matter how busy I am, I can feel time opening right up, and suddenly the calendar becomes porous, brimming with openings.

For Chris and me, a bright spot arises: rules about family visits are easing up, and one of the first things we put on our calendars is my visit with Chris's mama and family in Houma. Chris has told me that her mama can *really* cook, and no town in Louisiana has better fresh seafood than Houma—fish, crabs, shrimp, oysters, right off the boats. The town teems with Cajun fishermen who trawl for shrimp in the early morning and deliver straight to restaurants or sell their catch in their trucks there on the highway right out of a cooler. In Houma there are all these hole-in-the-wall eating places where you can get boiled crabs and shrimp (everybody uses cayenne-peppered

Zatarain's seasoning) or an oyster or shrimp po'boy. Po'boys, a Louisiana staple, have been around ever since the first *poor* kid jammed some baloney into a loaf of French bread and washed it down with a soda. I can't help but talk about food. I'm Cajun.

So I get to go with Chris to her family home and eat her mama's cooking. What better way to seal a friendship? It's said that the Last Supper was called the "last" because Jesus was always eating with his friends, and one of those meals just happened to be the last one. The Gospels are filled with stories that include meals. Even after Jesus was killed by the Romans, the way his disciples recognized him as alive again was at meals— breaking bread, or cooking fish on the beach. Maybe Jesus had a little Cajun in him.

William is telephoning and writing often: "I'm coming to see you, Lou, as soon as I can come." Which sets me scurrying inside myself.

"I can't wait for you to come." I tell him that I'm just starting a new job and moving into a new community of Sisters and will need to be present there and settle in. I try to explain that it's not like when we were in Canada, when I was freer to chart my own time.

I feel the stretch. As I've said, priests have a lot more freedom to travel than nuns do, and they have more money at their disposal. In a heartbeat William can jump on a plane and come to New Orleans. He also doesn't have a community in the rectory to whom he needs to be accountable. When he leaves, all he has to say is that he'll be "out" and when he expects to get back. So, here he is on the phone: *When, Lou, when? How about next weekend? How about today, tonight, right now?*

One day the convent doorbell rings and the local florist is delivering a dozen red roses—to me. I try to take it in stride and say, "Well, isn't that sweet? Father William is sending us flowers," and take them right to the chapel. But already, there they go, twenty sets of eyebrows arching upward.

I've barely been home two weeks.

The Great Balancing Act begins.

ALMOST AS SOON as I arrive back home, the big news is that we Sisters who work at Cabrini will soon move into two houses in the parish. The pastor, Father Paul Raymond Moore, my new boss, has leased two houses for nine of us—one on Mendez Street, where I'll be, and one on Paris Avenue. Both are in the Lakeview suburb, just a few blocks away from the CSJ motherhouse, where I made my novitiate. Both houses are also close to the church, so we can go to daily Mass and share evening meals. Sister William Matthews is going to be the new principal of the school, and she will be living at Mendez, too. I'm glad about that. I like Willie. Like me, she grew up in Baton Rouge and attended SJA. Unlike me, she was an excellent basketball player with a deadeye for the basket. We called her Billie in high school. She was named after her father, who died before she was born. So, it was an easy switch: Billie to Willie. A lot easier than Helen to Louis Augustine.

Nuns' living in the neighborhood close to the people is one more change in religious life inspired by Vatican II. We'll gather in the living room morning and evening for prayer and attend Mass together, but there will be no chapel, no bells calling us to assemble. Making time for personal meditation is up to us, and we'll decide together about times for daily common prayer. I'm sharing a bedroom with Sister Bernardine, an older Sister, so, to pray in solitude, I usually head for a chair way over in the backyard behind the garage, where there's an awning, so I can be there even when it rains.

My new job as parish director of religious education brings some big changes into my life. I'll no longer be part of the school staff (a little heart wrench here) but part of the parish team with the priests, and I'll have an office in the parish center with the pastor as my boss. *That's* different. All the other women employed by the parish do secretarial work, cooking, or housekeeping. I'll be in charge of my own time management and I'll have funds to buy books and other educational materials, and *wheels*—I'll have use of a car. Did I say car? No longer having to plan weeks ahead to sign up for use of the community car? And maybe the biggest change of all: After only four years of teaching kids I'll be educating adults.

The terrain's opened up. I think of Psalm 18: "He freed me, set me at large." DREs on the parish scene are entirely new entities. I'm being handed an empty drawing board on which to design and carry out programs, and I'm in charge. That's what I call *executive agency,* and, for the first time, I'm going to partner with men and women colleagues outside the circle of Sisterhood. (Good training for the day when I'll be thrown outside the pale of "nuns' work" into roiling public debate, but we'll be coming to that.)

In a Catholic parish, the pastor and his priest associates are in complete charge of just about everything: what is preached from the pulpit and who does the preaching, which hymns may be sung at Mass and what musical instruments can be used, which textbooks will be used in religion classes, who is acceptable to serve as acolytes (boys, yes; girls, no), and, most serious of all—the hiring and firing of every parish employee, from the principal of the school all the way to the guy who cuts the grass.

If a pastor arrives at a parish that happens to have a fully functioning lay parish council and school board and decides to dismantle them and take complete charge of everything himself, he has the power to do it. The people can write letters and make phone calls in protest, or even picket in front of the church and call out the media, but to no avail. Almost invariably, they get word back from the bishop: *The Catholic Church is not a democracy.* And unless there's been a flagrant, scandalous abuse, you can bank on the bishop's backing up the pastor. We nuns are in there somewhere with the laity, though we're supposed to have a kind of honorific status as "consecrated brides of Christ." But honorifics don't count for beans when it comes to decision-making power.

We're definitely *not* clergy—that's for sure. Canon law, the Church's legal code, categorically states that only baptized *males* can be ordained priests. I don't question this. I didn't want to be a priest, anyway. I just wanted to be a teacher. Priests, it seemed, were always saying Mass and baptizing babies and hearing confessions, paying utility bills, or having fundraising drives for a new organ or altar or . . . *something*. Besides, their lives in rectories seemed so lonely. They don't have community like we do in the Sisterhood.

I TRY TO sound casual, but inside I'm nervous as all get-out when at supper with the community I announce that my priest friend William is coming for a visit. I've been talking about him, that he's from Boston and in charge of religious education in the diocese, that we studied together in London, and that he's very spiritual, very dedicated. I want them to know he's rock-solid in his priestly vocation (as I hope they know I am in mine) because we're really pushing the edge here—a priest-and-nun friendship—with all the stories going around of priests, and nuns, running off to get married.

I tell about Will's coming visit pretty much all in one breath, carrying them along in the gushing current of words—a good way to forestall questions. I'm the only one who knows how very, very much depends on their being okay with his visit. Will has been so overwrought, pressing me so hard to be able to visit soon. So, if there's a snag, some kind of scheduling problem, a community event going on I had forgotten about, or, worst of all, if even one member of the community has a real problem with his visit—I mean, so upset she feels bound by conscience to report it to the provincial superior, to prevent scandal—that's a *real* problem. I'm banking on Sisterly trust. With so many nuns leaving and all the changes happening in religious life—realizing we don't all have to always be doing every single thing together to have unity—we're being stretched to trust one another in ways we never have before. Okay—that's the theory. But seeing Will and me living out our friendship right in front of their eyes is something else.

The Sisters seem fine with the visit. No questions. These days priests traveling to visit Sisters is not exactly common, but just a few weeks ago Sister Alice Marie's priest friend came all the way from Canada to see her. There's a guest room for priests at the motherhouse, and the academy right next door has a makeshift guest room in the counseling office. At the end of the meal at which I announced William's coming, I finish by saying that I've been telling Father William all about them and he can't wait to meet them, and he'd like very much to say Mass in the chapel at the motherhouse if we'd like that. There's some talk about when he'll arrive and where he'll stay, all of which I have worked out in fine detail—Swiss-watch detail.

So, it's done. William's coming and the Sisters are okay. Afterward, I go to my private praying place and take some deep breaths. This tension about William is like no other I've ever known. What I didn't say out loud to the Sisters, what I kept tucked inside and couldn't say, are the feelings I have for William, the commitment I've made to love him through thick and thin. Not marry. But love in this new way—the "third" way—which we are forging together.

Will's a manly guy. He says what he thinks and goes for what he wants. He's really smart and logical and must have a photographic memory. He can digest reams of information, organize it, and write about it or teach it in such a way that it comes out all coherent and organized. Unlike me—no fuzzy-feeling-amorphous stuff for him. I'm always kind of feeling my way into what I'm thinking. I almost never just talk about bare facts or historic data. I constantly try to make connections, to relate facts to experiences, to ask about significance, personal implications, teasing out metaphors, trying to see what things point toward. Maybe William is like prose and I'm like poetry.

William is the first man I've ever been really close to. He has awakened me deep inside, and when I'm with him, I'm far more in a receiving mode than I usually am. He's the initiator, he woos, he pursues. I respond, I receive. He tells me over and over how beautiful I am, how desirable, and he showers me with presents. And his energies are all so charged, so like a current, pulling me in. There's one thing about a current, whether it's water or electric or sexual: It courses through you, it catches you up in its power. When you're in it, you're in it, and with William I know I'm *in it*.

But there's this countercurrent, too—this holding him off—because he's coming on so strong. And he's telephoning constantly, and writing so often that I make it a point to get the mail first, to intercept the letters so the Sisters don't see the bombardment, and with no privacy on the community phone in the hallway, I'm always finding excuses to go over to the parish office so I can talk to him. It's not that I want to be sneaky, but I know we need privacy. Every close relationship needs privacy. I want to let William in—he brings vibrancy and aliveness and a sense of completeness—but he's *so* forceful.

As old Sister Tharcilla used to say: "The Lord in his mercy, help Lady Percy," and this Lady Percy knows she needs a lot of help. I pray, *Lord, help me be authentic.* I know that with my commitment to my vows and the community, it's going to be all about balance. I've watched some of our Sisters get involved in close relationships with outsiders ("seculars," we used to call them) and drift right on out of community. They might show up every now and then for community events, but even when they were present, they weren't really there. As for me, I'm going all in. I can do this. I *will* do this. I'm going to be William's friend and still remain a bona fide, wholehearted nun. It's not going to be either-or. It's going to be this-and. Anyway, that's the theory, that's the plan.

Will knows I'm happy as a nun, and we banter about how I could never be "domesticated." He admits that marriage would hem me in, and I say, laughing, "No, h-i-m me in," and he gives a little laugh, but it's kind of weak and his heart's not in it. Whenever we discuss this subject, he always comes away sad. He struggles with loneliness, and he is always telling me how much he misses me, how much he can't wait until we're together again. He has this hole in his heart, he says—a hole only I can fill. When he tells me this I feel sad—and anxious. I hate not being able to make him happy. When all is well between us, Will says that he wants from me only love that I can freely give, that he'll never force me into giving what I don't want to give, and it's enough for him to know he has a special place in my heart.

He likes being a priest. He prays, he has deep faith, and he loves to tell me again about the frigid day in February in Boston when he was ordained in the great cathedral and how his hand trembled as he held the long white candle during the procession up the long aisle, the choir in full voice singing *"Tu es sacerdos . . . in aeternum"*—"You are a priest . . . forever"—and in his heart it was indeed forever, a promise he had made to God as a young man, his mother and father in full support and so very proud of their son, who would have the power to forgive sin and anoint the dying and at Mass to summon Christ himself to be present when he bends over the bread and wine and whispers: "This is my body, this is my blood"—the awe of it.

William gets into a kind of reverie as he takes me through the ordination ceremony, his voice low and reverent, remembering every detail of how he and his forty-six classmates, clothed in long white albs, had lain face down in the sanctuary, prostrate before the bishop, to profess celibacy and obedience as they would to Christ himself. The bishop, summoning them to rise, laid his hands on them and anointed them with the holy oils, imprinting on their souls forever the indelible seal of holy orders, which nothing in heaven or earth could ever erase. Even if they faltered and left the priesthood, even then the seal would still be there, even at death: *You are a priest forever.*

After the ordination ceremony, he tells me, the most humbling part of all were the lines and lines of people passing slowly before him to receive his first priestly blessing, pressing

envelopes into his hand and murmuring adulation, full of respect and awe, "Pray for me, Father—you're close to God
now." Then, there before him, were his own mother and father,
in line with all the rest, bowing their heads to receive his blessing. He says that it was humbling and exhilarating at the same
time, to know you were just like them, a human being, but
chosen to put your hands on their heads and draw down divine blessings.

My own religious community relies heavily on the service
of priests. Priests come to the motherhouse to celebrate Eucha-
rist and teach us theology in our junior college and preach at
our annual six-day retreat. Priests can bank on nuns' unquestioned affirmation of every syllable they utter and expect that
even the most threadbare attempt at humor or cleverness will
be met with outsized laughter or giggling.

But, hands down, the single most challenging service priests
rendered nuns has to be canon law–mandated weekly confession. Weekly. A formidable challenge for both sides: we nuns
to drum up a week's worth of sins or semi-sins or maybe-
might-be-sins, and they, poor souls, to open their priestly ears
to the mind-numbing experience. No wonder a priest once
compared nuns' confessions to being pelted to death by popcorn. But ah, the deference—the over-the-top hospitality
priests receive the minute they step into the motherhouse. We
serve them on our best china in the special *priests'* dining
room, and during weeklong retreats we clean and tidy their
rooms and do their laundry—even ironing their *undershorts*.

So, here comes my new priest friend, William, to visit, and
I am ready. I am so ready. We'll be in New Orleans for two
days—Chris is coming in, so she can meet him—and we'll visit
in Baton Rouge, so Will can meet my family. I take Sister Rita
with me to meet him at the airport. When we were in London,

priest-nun rules were a lot looser, but here in Catholic New Orleans, the rule is that it's not considered proper for nuns even to sit in the front seat of a car with a man, lest scandal arise.

William's visit will be very much a community affair—I'm making sure of that. Every event will send the strong signal: He's my friend, but *we're not going to run off and get married.* William will share a meal with the Sisters in my community and say Mass at the motherhouse. He's good about going with the program, and he remembers names and teases the older Sisters, drawing them out. He's charming, and he really knows his theology, so his homilies have heft and make people think.

Priests always know theology better than nuns do. Their seminary training is more rigorous than our highly devotional studies, and they're grounded not only in philosophy and theology but in canon law as well. As for canon law—no big loss there for me. I never did have much desire to learn the legal code of the Church. But Vatican II shifted the balance dramatically, and nuns began relentlessly pursuing studies in scripture, theology, and spirituality.

Sadly, parish priests always have one foot nailed to the ground of administration of the parish along with their pastoral duties: saying daily Mass and maybe six Masses on Sunday, and hearing confessions, visiting and anointing the sick, and all their other sacramental duties. We nuns are freer to study. And study we do, getting BAs and MAs and PhDs in our professional fields as educators, and taking advantage of local classes, workshops, seminars, and symposia in theology on weekends and summers. We're all over the study thing. (We still are.) Talk about a turnaround. When, in the late fifties, a member of our community, Sister Jane Aucoin, went to study at Notre Dame University, she was talking to a priest, and he asked her what she was studying, and when she said theology, he said, *No, nuns study religious education—only priests study theology.*

So, now in 1968, I'm excited to hear that leadership has selected me to study for a master's in theology at Notre Dame. My community has worked it out with Cabrini Parish for me to study in the summer. This will be rigorous, disciplined study with first-rate scholars, which I *know* I need, and I'm keen as all get-out to study scripture, with all its varied literary genres: mythology (Garden of Eden), history (never straight-out history, always from the point of view of faith), and, of course, the four Gospels. I've been praying with the scriptures my whole life, but in a pious, not scholarly way, ferreting out personal inspiration wherever I can find it.

I read commentaries when I can, but that's catch-as-catch-can. I want to know how the different parts of the Bible got composed and who the different authors were, the situations they were up against, and to whom they were pitching their message. You can be sure, for instance, that the last book in the Bible, the Book of Revelation—which sounds, in some parts, like a bad drug trip, filled as it is with fierce dragons, and, in other parts, like a war manual, with Jesus in the final battle coming back to earth with a sword in his mouth to cut unbelievers to ribbons—just had to be written by somebody or some community engulfed in a terrible persecution or war. I want to know how to interpret these writings.

One thing about William—he has a disciplined mind. He loves learning, knows how to do systematic research, and is good at presenting information crisply and cleanly. He knows a hundred times more about theology and history than I do, and that's a big part of my attraction to him. He has great respect for the "scripture men," and says that they've "paid their dues," meaning the long, long years they spend learning Latin, Greek, Hebrew, Ugaritic, Aramaic. I'm such a lightweight. I barely know a little French. Everything I read has to be in English.

HERE IN CABRINI Parish, an all-white suburb near Lake Pontchartrain, everything is neat and clean—houses with trimmed lawns, fathers with good jobs, wives busy with children, generous contributions in the packed Cabrini church on Sunday mornings, most children in Catholic schools.

If I were to venture six blocks south down St. Bernard Avenue and take a quick left, I'd be in the St. Bernard housing project, where African Americans live. But that's a world away from my life now. What's happening to African Americans in the ten major housing projects of New Orleans is not my concern. They're not "my people." My people are the parishioners of Cabrini Parish, and all I want to do is get in there with some good religious education so we can revitalize our Catholic faith.

I put a notice in the Cabrini bulletin and issue an open invitation to people to join an adult discussion group. Pretty mild stuff—a group of grown-ups meeting to discuss religious beliefs. Not exactly a revolutionary cadre. But for the Catholic Church it's going to be revolutionary, all right. The axis of teaching authority is about to undergo a radical turn. For the first time, regular folks, the laity, are going to dig into the faith in light of their own life experiences, weighing, discerning: *Yes, this rings true,* or, *No, that can't possibly be right—that doesn't make any sense.*

A new form of authenticity is being born. It's not that we're becoming a loose conglomerate of fierce individualists, each going his or her own way. Not that. Belonging to the Catholic family means taking seriously what has been handed down in the tradition. But there's no denying the fresh spirit of inquiry rippling through us all. At last, there's respect for individual conscience. It has another name: *religious liberty.* Vatican II was the first Catholic council ever to unequivocally affirm religious liberty for other faiths. So, how could it affirm this freedom for other religions while not also affirming freedom of conscience for its own members?

This, of course, means an *educated* conscience, and that's where I come in—that's my job. Once adults in the Church come into their own and begin taking personal responsibility for their faith, a top-down authoritarian church is bound to lose traction. Simple juridical pronouncements about faith or moral behavior will no longer be enough to ensure compliance, to say nothing of threats of censorship or punishment. Something more will be required: moral authority—which persuades rather than dictates.

The Dutch Catechism that I gave to Chris is something new in the Catholic Church—new because it didn't come from Catholic central headquarters (the Vatican), but from a local gathering of Catholic bishops—in this case, from the Netherlands. As a result of their experience at the council, these bishops felt empowered to be pastors to their people in a whole new way, and here's their catechism to prove it. Before Vatican II, a bishop tended to see himself solely as a delegate or vicar of the pope. But the experience of collaboration with the global body of two thousand bishops from around the world changed all that. The publication of the catechism in 1966, just one year after the council ended, put the Dutch bishops in the forefront of pastoral leadership. The dust jacket of the catechism states:

The greatest overall achievement of the Second Vatican Council was its conscious proclamation that Christianity is an adult religion. It is the child who leads a submissive, compliant existence. . . . In controversial areas, rather than supply a traditional though unsatisfactory solution, it is frankly acknowledged that a great many problems remain unsolved, and that only time and candor in the face of reality will provide answers.

Candor in the face of reality? How about *this* rambunctious reality: College students taking to the streets, occupying buildings, burning draft cards to protest U.S. involvement in the Vietnam War. And not only young people, but two priests—Daniel and Philip Berrigan—burning draft files, getting arrested, going to trial, where they make impassioned speeches, quoting Jesus's own words: "Blessed are the peacemakers, blessed are those who mourn, who hunger for justice."

Everywhere, every place you look, young people are questioning church, government, educational institutions. Bumper stickers are popping up with the words "Question Authority," and at our own St. Joseph Academy in New Orleans, a small group of African American students are refusing to pledge allegiance to the flag. There's sex, drugs, and rock and roll, and right here in the Cabrini neighborhood, a few African Americans are moving into the previously all-white Parkchester Apartments, which unleashes a firestorm of fears: *"Property values will plummet; the neighborhood's going to go to the dogs!"* Then, there's the cataclysmic assassination of Martin Luther King, which sets off rioting in D.C. and Detroit, Harlem, and Watts. The lid, it seems, is coming off the whole blooming country, everything busting wide open, kids with long, shaggy hair and beards and beads around their necks, demonstrating and singing protest songs.

These bristling realities will be a large part of the subjects I'll be dealing with in Cabrini Parish. I'm thinking of what Bob Dylan says: "The times they are a-changing." And that other line: "It's a hard rain's a-gonna fall." It's a good time, a wonderful time, to be a young nun.

An Evening at the Garveys'

SUNDAY SCHOOL, CIRCA 1950

"Who made you?" was always
The question
The answer was always
"God."
Well, there we stood
Three feet high
Heads bowed
Leaning into
Bosoms.
Now
I no longer recall
The Catechism
Or brood on the Genesis
Of life
No.
I ponder the exchange
Itself
And salvage mostly
The leaning.

—Alice Walker

It's fall, 1968. People are streaming through the door of Joan and Walter Garvey's spacious home at 7:30 P.M., right on time—ten or so people, some couples, some single—for our first adult discussion group. I had put a notice in the parish bulletin inviting adults to gather to discuss the changes brought about by Vatican II, and right off the bat here they come. Everybody a practicing Catholic: church every Sunday, weekly offering in the collection, kids in Catholic schools. (The Garveys have seven of them.) It feels like suppers and parties at Goodwood, when Mama and Daddy's friends would come over, talking a mile a minute as soon as they came through the door. Joan Garvey and I became friends when I was teaching her oldest daughter, Peggy, at Cabrini. If ever there was a poster child for a creative, test-the-edges teenager, it was Peggy Garvey. I loved the kid, and she wrote the most amazing things in her Creative Journal.

Joan and Walter greet people at the door, their bevy of kids assigned to their rooms to do their homework and the little girls, Eileen and Mary, firmly encouraged to "play nicely and to stay upstairs." This proves to be effective for most of the evening, give or take a couple of quick sorties downstairs by two nightgowned, giggling nymphs.

When kids are present at any adult gathering, you can be sure that conversation is guaranteed not to get lofty or ethereal for very long. A fellow DRE told me about his first religion teachers' training session, which he was holding in his home, to be—you know—folksy and warm, not institutional. He was prepared to the hilt—with teachers' guides in neat packets on TV trays in front of each chair, the coffee made, muffins set out, name tags printed—and things were proceeding marvelously, splendidly, the teachers engaged in riveting discussion, pertinent questions. Until his three-year-old son comes down the stairs, clad only in his shirt, and shouts over the bannister: "Hey, Dad, can you wipe my bum?"

I'm alive with it all. How better to grow than to be with such down-to-earth people, my peers, not out to become levitating mystics or anything like that—just people trying to make it through the day with a modicum of sanity, perhaps even a little serenity.

Until now, learning the faith for Catholics meant rote memorization of questions and answers on Church doctrine. Scripture, and even the teachings of Jesus, were never central. And, of course, all doctrines were unquestioned. In contrast, the open-ended questioning approach of the council is down-right refreshing, and there's no denying the new spirit of curi-osity, the desire to explore, discover: *Hey, what's out there?* The world with all its teeming possibilities is no longer the secular enemy, to be shunned, but the site of action—the place where life itself unfurls and where God is to be found. I love to scribble on postcards: *Hey! God is alive and hiding in New Orleans.* Or *Mamou, Louisiana.* Or *The bathroom.* Or in *Bob Dylan's songs.* "It's time to open the windows of this musty old church," Pope John XXIII had said in summoning the council. Goodbye to fortress thinking. *Hello, world, what have you got to teach me?*

Hands down, Vatican II's best gifts were its call to get back to Jesus and the Gospels and its strong affirmation of personal conscience—each person's "secret core and sanctuary." In the Catholic Church the affirmation of religious liberty was a long time coming. In all of the Church's long history, Vatican II was the *first* Church council ever to affirm unequivocally people's freedom of conscience—not only for Catholics but for every-one. (Even if it's going to take some doing to live this out in practice.) And as for Catholic dialogue with people of other faiths, the conviction that "outside the Catholic Church there is no salvation" hasn't exactly been a great conversation starter: *Okay, honey, we know your faith tradition is flawed and heretical, but let's talk anyway. And I'll look for openings to see where I might steer you right.*

But here we have a Copernican-sized revolution under way that is going to change forever the authority structure of the Catholic Church. With the affirmation by the council that regular folks, the faithful, are guided by the Holy Spirit as much as any bishop is, and with their now becoming educated and empowered to tackle social problems head-on, Church officials will no longer be able simply to issue juridical pronouncements and expect to be obeyed.

Not all Catholics desire this new kind of church. Some lament the prospects of a "people's church" and see any move toward democratization as a loss of Catholic identity, with pure anarchy in its wake. How, they ask, can there be "one, holy, catholic, and apostolic church" without close scrutiny from the Pope and the Congregation of the Doctrine of the Faith to assure orthodoxy?

Their concern is legitimate. In every institutional body, there has to be a balance between preservation of tradition and staying open to the needs of people in an ever-changing, fluid world. On the one hand, without tradition, the identifying characteristics of the Church would become so fluid that the name *Catholic* would have no meaning. On the other hand, too much emphasis on an immutable "deposit of faith," codified in unchangeable language, kills the spirit and freezes the creative power of the Gospel in its tracks.

Vatican II introduces innovations that are felt by every Catholic, such as the mandate to change the language of the Mass from Latin to the vernacular language of the people. There is the encouragement of laypeople to study scripture and the acknowledgment that God's salvation is offered to all people—not just Catholics. And then there is the proclamation that holiness is the calling of all Christians—not just of priests, monks, and nuns, who have supposedly chosen the more "perfect" path. This is something I am particularly excited about sharing with the adults in our parish.

But beneath all these changes, the most astonishing revelation from the council is simply that the Church can, *and should,* change. One of the documents draws on Jesus's reference to reading "the signs of the times." Could God be speaking to us through the changes in history and culture—such as young people all over the country speaking out against U.S. military involvement in Vietnam? Might Simon and Garfunkel be right—that all those scribblings on subway walls could possibly be, not mere graffiti vandalism, but, rather, "the words of the prophets," calling on us in the United States to change our ways?

Of course, these changes in the Church come as a disturbing jolt for many Catholics, especially for those whose whole sense of what it means to be a Catholic has been defined by dos and don'ts enforced by fear of eternal punishment: Catholics don't eat meat on Fridays; they go to confession before receiving communion; they don't enter Protestant churches; and they sure as shooting don't use artificial birth control. Pope John tried to move the conversation away from guilt and fear as the motivating markers of Catholic identity. And he made it clear that the purpose of the Second Vatican Council was pastoral—to help Catholics live more authentic, Christian lives—rather than simply to denounce errors or heresies. In his opening speech he set forth his hopes for the Church:

> The Spouse of Christ . . . meets the needs of the present day by demonstrating the validity of her teaching rather than by condemnations. . . . The "prophets of doom" say that our era, in comparison with past eras, is getting worse.

Everyone had a pretty good idea of who those "prophets of doom" were. They included many of the prefects of his own Vatican Curia. But it was astonishing to hear a pope talking about "opening up the windows" of the Catholic Church, moving it away from its legalistic way of enforcing doctrine and rules to a more human church bent on following the way of compassion of its Nazarene founder.

Pope John's approachable, humble personality, which welcomed candid conversation and varied viewpoints—a skill no doubt honed as a child with *thirteen* brothers and sisters— quickly spilled over into the council fathers, freeing them to talk to one another openly and frankly about the issues facing the Church.

Sociologists might call Vatican II's surprising reforms the result of grassroots, democratic power rising up and asserting leadership at a time that was ripe for change. Maybe that was the historical groundwork, but Christian believers, myself included, have another take. As Pope John put it: "When we believe that an inspiration comes to us from the Holy Spirit, we must follow it. What happens after that is not our responsibility."

In 1963, Pope John issued his encyclical *Pacem in Terris,* completed just two months before he died of stomach cancer. In it, words ring clear and true for freedom of conscience and staunch affirmation of the United Nations' Universal Declaration of Human Rights, which he called a "beacon" that would light the road for all of us. His words about human rights would sit in the soil of my soul for years, until the time when my consciousness and determination came together, allowing the seeds to sprout.

.   .   .

As THE GROUP at the Garveys' settles in, I stand before them holding up the Dutch Catechism. They're an assorted group of housewives, college professors, lawyers, teachers, businessmen. Some are champing at the bit for change in the Church. Others, dead set against it. Some, not so sure.

I read straight from the Dutch Bishops' introduction, the line that says, "The greatest overall achievement of the Second Vatican Council was its conscious proclamation that Christianity is an adult religion." What does that mean for them?

Right out of the box we're off and running, everybody either saying their piece or itching to get in the conversation, opinions all over the lot:

"Father Moore had the nerve to say from the pulpit that people who had roof damage from the hurricane might well have sinned and were being punished by God."

"Kids will never go to Mass on Sunday unless they're told it's a mortal sin to miss Mass. They need the fear of God in them. What kid wants to go to Mass?"

"There's too much questioning. What I love about being Catholic is that we have the answers our faith gives us."

"The Church ought to be run like the Marines: Shut up and obey."

"Kids don't know their prayers anymore. Why are we paying tuition for them to get a Catholic education?"

"My kids say that in religion class they're listening to Beatles music, like 'All You Need Is Love.' They need to be learning the Ten Commandments."

"I think Vatican II is a first-class miracle. Our church drastically needs changing."

"At Mass, why do the priests always talk about sex like it's the only sin? What about Vietnam? What about poverty?"

"I heard a theologian say that if the United States were dropping condoms over Vietnam instead of napalm, the bishops would be out there opposing the war in a heartbeat."

Laughter from some, scowls from others. A fierce argument breaks out and two men rise to their feet. Walter Garvey intercedes and calls for a coffee break, and Joan points out sweetly that there are brownies, cookies, punch. . . .

I lie low during the break. Let tempers cool. I notice that the wives of the two arguers have made their way over to calm their red-faced husbands. Ahhh, women—always the peacemakers.

The break over, we're back. Nobody misses a beat:

"Did y'all hear about the blacks moving into the Parkchester Apartments right there on Mirabeau Avenue? Next thing you know our property values are going to hit the toilet."

"Can you get your kids to go to confession? Our kids say they just talk to God directly and God forgives them."

"All this 'Let love guide you' morality scares me. This loosey-goosey morality is going to get our daughters pregnant." (Big group hubbub for a while on this one.)

"Using rhythm for birth control is a joke; three of our four children are 'rhythm babies.' " (Loud guffaws.)

"Why can't girls be altar servers? Why can't women be priests?"

"My daughter says she doesn't buy into purgatory and limbo anymore. I'm not sure she believes in hell, either."

For over an hour it's been popping like corn kernels in hot grease.

Whew! It's lively, that's for sure. *Hold back, hold back, Prejean—let them talk. Hold your horses. They're not kids—they surely don't need "Teacher Nun" guiding them as if I'm some sort of authority and not in the swim, searching, like everyone else.*

The Dutch bishops are challenging us to confront the "complex new realities" emerging in the world. This is a far cry from years-on-end of papal declarations insisting that the faithful be fed only the "simple truths of the faith" and "protected" from "too much knowledge," which will only "confuse" them.

Back again in the Garvey group, we're winding things down, giving out Dutch Catechisms to everybody, setting place and time for the next gathering, when a man named Carl explodes. Maybe I should have seen it coming, maybe not—this is such a new ballgame—but, reflecting later, I realize I could have seen a few warning signals. Carl was keeping his eyes down, with his face in a constant scowl. But with so much going on in the group, Carl's subtle under-his-breath grumbling paled in contrast to the verbal slug-out of the two guys who got into it over Vietnam. Now, suddenly, Carl rises to his feet, pushing away the Dutch Catechism Joan is trying to hand him, and starts yelling. He is really loud.

"I've had it! I want my church back! I'm so sick of all this. I could throw up. Everything is not just one damn question after another. We Catholics *do* have answers. God speaks to us through Mother Church. I say ditch this heretical trash of these Dutch bishops. And you, YOU! It's you nuns who are ruining our church. Where's your habit? You don't even look like a nun. Where's your obedience to Mother Church? No wonder our kids are so confused." (He's jabbing his finger at me.) "It's you nuns, throwing the baby out with the bathwater. I'm outta here!"

And "outta here" he is, all right. He leaves the Garvey

house and goes straight to Father Moore to inform him that he has a renegade, radical nun on his hands who needs to be fired. He has a daughter at our high school academy, and the more she comes home with reports of what's happening in religion class, the more upset he gets. During a parent-teacher meeting in the gym, Carl took hold of the microphone and made an impassioned speech imploring the teachers to hold strong to traditional Church teaching, especially that missing Mass on Sunday and sex outside marriage are always—always without exception—mortal sins that can land them straight in hell. "Our daughters' souls are in peril!"

May I say, as you read these orderly lines of print, that in the present day, the conflicts I'm describing here might seem to have been settled long ago. Maybe even solved. (*I get it, the Catholic Church went through some changes.*) But believe me, for those of us who lived through this tumultuous period, the days right after Vatican II felt like Old Faithful Upper Basin in Yellowstone National Park. Sometimes I felt like we were all drowning, going down, down, down in the sea of change. And many times I found myself sitting with Father Moore in his office to sort things out.

I feel for Father Moore, the poor guy, in his fifties, thinking he was moving toward serene retirement. What's he going to do with this out-of-control Church he has loved and served since he was twelve years old? (He entered a minor seminary in eighth grade.) He's trying hard to be obedient to the directives of the Second Vatican Council, but he hasn't studied scripture or theology since seminary, and that was thirty years ago. Why aren't the age-old teachings of the Church enough? Christ, Alpha and Omega, today, yesterday, forever the same? His homilies at Sunday Mass are amazingly out of touch, his words droning on and on in his deep, sepulchral voice, floating just above the heads of his captive parishioners, lulling them into semiconsciousness or outright sleep. As the drone goes on, there goes head after head dropping to chests. *Plop. Plop. Plop.* Thank goodness liturgical protocol mandates that after the homily everybody's got to stand up to recite the Nicene Creed. It's one surefire way to wake everybody up. (Protestants are always wondering why Catholics sit, kneel, and stand so much in church. Now you know.) But I have to say that all that Father Moore way of being pastor was perfectly fine with many parishioners, maybe most. Comfortable. Familiar. Ballast in the Bark of Peter on a tumultuous sea.

It's sad, really. Father Moore is achingly sincere, so very pious, so wanting people to love their Catholic faith. I feel for him, pressured from every side, and now having me to contend with, me—a woman, God help him—at close range within the inner sanctum of the priests' house, a sort of free-range chicken version of a nun (maybe not the chicken part but definitely the free agent). At a loss because he's not in control the way he's used to, and I make sure to meet with him faithfully every Monday morning to share what's happening in my classes. But here I am, driving around the parish and setting up gatherings with parishioners in their own homes, and stirring up God-knows-what, and leaving him to handle the malcontents.

What's he supposed to do? He well knows that as an ecumenical council, Vatican II ranks way up there as an authoritative body, and its teachings must be obeyed. Who's he, a lowly servant of God, to oppose an ecumenical council? But, oh, Lord, the confusion. Even the once quiet, contemplative Mass, when it would just be you and God, is lost now with all the "laity participation," which has made once reverent worship turn really *busy,* with twangy guitars replacing the organ, and sing-along hymns edging out solemn, mystical Gregorian chant—and maybe most intrusive of all, people greeting each other with the "kiss of peace," which leads to chatter and noise.

He quietly counsels people upset by the new Mass to find a place apart in the church, where they can quietly say their rosary. The daily rosary is *the* traditional Catholic prayer of all time, and Father Moore's never-failing standby—his lifeline, he says. You can hold tight to the beads, feel them with your fingers as you pray your way: *Hail Mary . . . pray for us sinners.*

He never dreamed Mother Church, his church, would take such a turn. And to top it all off, here now, in close proximity, *me,* encountering him day in and day out. In the seminary he was taught never to look a woman directly in the eye—a rule of chastity he scrupulously obeys. I can vouch for it. In all my conversations with him during his years as pastor at Cabrini, our eyes never meet—not once.

It does not help at all that my fellow nuns and I have shed our religious garb. No more swaddling reams of black to hide our womanly forms. In seminary he had been taught a strategic way to shake hands with a woman that would prevent her from coming too close. What you'd do (I learned this from William) is take the proffered feminine hand, and as you grasp it, you bend the wrist slightly outward, just enough of an awkward angle to steer her away from coming in too close, which might turn into—God help us—a full-frontal embrace.

In the course of time, I find out Father Moore has never had a birthday party—I guess because he entered the seminary at such a young age. I find it hard to believe. Never once had a cake and candles and presents and friends around him singing "Happy Birthday"? Never? I suppose that as a baby priest in training, heaven-bound as God's anointed one, birthday parties must have been considered too mundane, too merely human. Even in strict convent days, we sang "Happy Birthday" to one another, though a few super-pious ones wanted to sing "Happy Baptismal Day to you," which, thankfully, enough of us were able to nip in the bud.

When I hear this about Father Moore, I call Charlotte Schully, whose husband, Denny, is one of Father Moore's brandy-drinking, cigar-smoking consultants, and we pull a party off without a hitch. And what a full-blown, no-holds-barred, super-surprise birthday party it is. We have it at our house on Paris Avenue, complete with a happy hour and bar-becue and a cake with candles and singing and presents—the whole affair, surprising him utterly—and he is very, very touched and stands up at the end to thank us in his low, rum-bling voice, close to tears, words halting and jumbled: "Well . . . quite the occasion, us here together . . . all the changes we're going through . . . the Sisters not in habits anymore, and the guitars and hootenanny singing at Mass and so on down the line"—his pet saying, added to the end of practically every sentence, even during homilies. "As you know, very difficult for me, personally, all the changes . . . but tonight . . . even a cake . . . all of us together . . . tonight . . . everything is looking . . . looking"—he searches for the word "rosy," but what comes out instead: "Tonight everything is looking ro-sary."

We rise to our feet and clap and cheer, and it's one shining moment of hearts in harmony in this riptide of change. I en-case the words in my heart and summon them when argu-ments flare and the path seems dark. We can do this, we can make it if we keep "leaning" (à la Alice Walker) toward each other and keep talking things through. Pope John XXIII has his own "looking rosary" mantra to guide us as we launch this new way of being Catholic into the world. "Unity in essentials, freedom in nonessentials, and in everything, charity."

Jesus at Notre Dame

It's the late sixties, summer, and I'm in a community car with three other nuns for a two-day drive from New Orleans to South Bend, Indiana, home of the University of Notre Dame, where we are going to be studying theology. I hear that for its summer sessions ND gets top-notch scripture and theology scholars to teach in its master's program. I am so ready for serious study. In undergrad studies, I just went along and took courses that were required, and all I wanted was to hurry up and finish and take the exams so I could get out there and teach. No desire to dig deeply, no fired-up intellectual curiosity. There was the sporadic wow-that's-interesting spark as I listened to a lecture or read an article, but my study schedule didn't allow for much free reading. It was all about covering the subject matter so I could be ready for tests and exams, which were always looming. And always I absolutely had to get a top grade. My superiors, who believed in me enough to send me to school, expected the best. Now, looking back, I realize that I earned my BA degree in what's called a "banking" model of education. Professors "deposit" subject matter into students' heads, and the trick was to cram the stuff in the night before, then rush into the exam room and spill it out as quickly as you could. Then, forget it. Sometimes before you even leave the building. Easy come, easy go.

When it came to learning, even in my major field of study, English, I read and learned with a divided heart. After all, it was the spiritual life I was after—the eternal mysteries, not transient worldly knowledge. Theology alone was considered "queen" of the sciences because its object of study was as holy as you could get: God's own divine Self. Holy, holy, holy . . . Piddling "secular" subjects like history, science, and mathematics? Well, you had to study these things for a profession, but you couldn't sink your deepest soul into such things. Hadn't St. Paul said "the world as we know it is passing away?"

I'm not yet cohesive in my intellectual and spiritual life, and I'm still very much motivated by outside forces—like making a good grade to please my superiors. And, Lord help me, I'd flat-out die if I flunked out at ND. I've heard of a religious brother who flunked. Getting a master's degree at this first-rate university is not a shoo-in. And some of the exams are oral. The pressure is on. But so is a great, wonderful opportunity to learn what my soul desires, but this time in a disciplined way. I need the rein of scholarly, disciplined study to gather in my loose and lurching soul.

Among the professors scheduled to talk at ND is Charles Curran, who taught William moral theology at Catholic University a few years back. He has been critical of Pope Paul VI's birth control encyclical, *Humanae Vitae,* and I hope to learn from him how to critique Church teachings in an intellectually honest way: a new skill for us Catholics. This encyclical, which condemns every form of "artificial" birth control seems so . . . off—so patently out of kilter with science and actual human experience. Can a faithful Catholic disagree with a pope and still be considered Catholic? William says Curran's a smart guy, devoted to his faith, but also intellectually honest. He refuses to "pretzel" a line of argument so that its conclusion "fits in" with official Church teachings. I can't wait to hear him.

Hans Küng, one of the stellar theologians at Vatican II, is

also coming to ND. Almost more than anyone else he has opened a new vision of the Gospel-inspired way that Church authority ought to be practiced: "servant leadership," he calls it—genuine listening to the people, who, as a body (like homing pigeons), have a deep, lived sense of faith. But for some (perhaps many) Church officials, the act of listening to the faithful seems a redundant exercise—a matter of being polite, but hardly necessary—not for authorities absolutely convinced that they are, after all, God's appointed shepherds with the sole authority to hand down sacred tradition.

Here's a story that's going around. Patty Crowley, one of the few laypeople allowed to participate in the birth control commission during Vatican II, tells of a monsignor on the commission who got extremely upset when it looked like the commission was moving toward recommending that the Church modify its teaching on birth control (which it did—only to be overruled by Pope Paul VI). He asked in great perplexity: "For hundreds of years the Church has taught that the use of artificial methods of birth control is a mortal sin, punishable in the fires of hell. If we change Church teaching now, what will happen to the millions we have sent to hell?"

Crowley replied: "Monsignor, do you really believe that God has obeyed all your orders?"

Meanwhile, as our car makes its way to Notre Dame, I have two more personal concerns weighing on my heart: One, Chris; the other, William.

William, once I tell him I'll be studying at Notre Dame, hurries and registers, and tells me, all excited, how he can't wait to be with me, that we'll be together for six whole weeks, seeing each other every day and taking classes together again just like in London. Meanwhile, the worry wells up without my summoning: *I hope he doesn't drink too much*. During his last visits in New Orleans, a couple of hair-raising incidents happened around his drinking. Bad, bad scenes of desperate weeping and pleas that tear at me and leave me racked with guilt. How can I not assuage his suffering? Thus far—thank you, Jesus—none of the incidents have happened in front of the Sisters. What a full-fledged nightmare that would be. My community has begun to elect me to offices of leadership. The word I get from Sister Lydia Champagne, one of our top leaders, is that my "star is rising" among the Sisters. I'm invited to give presentations in our assemblies. Being trusted and admired by the community of people with whom you've invested your life has to be one of the most satisfying feelings in the world.

After the drunken meltdowns, Will is always so apologetic and full of remorse and promises: "Never, never again. . . . I respect you and want to love you as you deserve." He's so sincere, I have to believe him; get a grip, tamp down my fears, move on. But it keeps happening, and I can't help worrying that at Notre Dame we have six whole weeks of days and nights ahead of us. I'm hoping the thirst for study is as strong in him as it is in me. Unlike me, he's already had a chance to do graduate studies, and he knows how excited I am to have this opportunity.

Okay, I steady myself. This summer is going to be one great big balancing act. And here it is once again, tension from the underlying fault line in our relationship: He wants to marry me, and I don't want to marry him. It makes me feel sad and heavy and guilty. Maybe I've been leading him on. Maybe I ought to be totally honest and make a clean break of it. End it. Why can't I do it? Augh. My stomach tightens. I'm a coward. Out. Out. I need to put him out of my mind. I need to be present to where I am now, here in this car with my Sisters on our way to study at Notre Dame. Everything's going to be fine. Besides, Will truly is smart, and maybe when he settles into the classes he'll be fired up enough to plunge into his studies and not get fixated on me. Maybe . . .

My concern about Chris goes deeper. I hate to leave her behind. I get all the breaks. As a teacher, I go off to a university for graduate studies, and Chris has to slog it out day and night at the hospital. She tries to be happy for me, to wish me well, glad I am getting to study. Here I'm going for a graduate degree and she doesn't even have a BA—only an RN in a crash course at Mercy Hospital so she could be on the hall working as soon as possible. She dreams of one day getting six whole weeks to do nothing but study theology. She's not just a nurse. She's a nun. How can she help but long for a chance to deepen her spiritual knowledge? We don't have money for long-distance phone calls, but I'll be sure to write her often to share the new stuff I learn. I promise to take detailed notes "like a medieval monk." I know it's not enough. Secondhand learning can never be enough.

It's sad. It's not fair. I feel for her. But Chris is being obedient to her superiors by working, just as I'm being obedient by studying. Our selfhood isn't actualized enough yet to assert to the community what we feel is vitally essential for our lives. Nor is the community yet developed enough to fully respect the individual aspirations of all its members. Not yet able to recognize the preferential treatment for its teachers, even as it enlists its nursing Sisters, who earn decent salaries in state-funded hospitals, to be year-round worker bees for the rest of us. Economic necessity drove this thinking. The truth was that teachers in diocesan and parish Catholic schools received pittance stipends. Where else could the community hope for decent salaries except from our nurses?

Then, too, our life of faith tells us that God's grace will be there to sustain us. True as far as it goes. But isn't it equally God's spark that drives us toward fulfilling our unique potential—becoming our true selves? Thomas Merton said that's what a saint is—that's what makes us holy: shucking off our shriveled, ego-centered selves and becoming our true selves. It's what led Merton to call the little yellow flower on the side of the road a saint. The way Merton saw it, that perky little flower, simply being itself, was being true to its purpose in creation.

As our car approaches South Bend, we strain to see the golden dome of the Fighting Irish stadium. We're here. We unload the car and settle in our dorm, Stanford Hall, which has been set aside for women—99 percent nuns. (To ready the male bathrooms in a way proper to our nunly dignity, sensitive souls have draped sheets over the urinals.) I register for class and check out the large dining halls with their long rows of wooden tables and chairs. I can't wait to call Daddy. Good Catholic that he is, he's always hoped his children would attend Notre Dame. I'll describe everything to him. He'll be so proud.

I DIG RIGHT into the studies. I take careful notes in class and head directly to the library—my favorite haunt with its seven-story outside mosaic of "touchdown Jesus," his arms uplifted in victory.

Of all the courses at Notre Dame, what I most want to learn about are the Gospel accounts about Jesus of Nazareth. I hope not just to study Christ with my mind intellectually, but to also encounter him mystically through prayerful meditation on his life. I want to know him in his humanness—how he grew into his vocation and practiced his Jewish faith, stretching its assumed boundaries to reach out to the "foreigners" of his day, and thereby coming to understand compassion as the heart of religious practice, especially for the "least of these."

In my courses at Notre Dame I'm learning that the Gospels are *faith* testimonies, not historical accounts. When I read the Gospels, I'm learning to become an amateur literary archeologist, doing the "digs" through textual layers to get to the human Jesus.

I already know from personal experience that an ongoing encounter with Christ can transform the way I think and live my life (a long, slow process, believe me). But my image of Jesus is still gauzed over with pious images of him shining so brightly with divinity that I lose a sense of his humanness and find it hard to relate to him. So I jump at the chance to take Seán Freyne's course on Mark, the earliest of the Gospels, written around 60 c.e., and closest in time to Jesus. It's fresher and more unvarnished and shows Jesus as truly human: losing his temper at hypocritical religious authorities, weeping and terrified, pleading "aloud and in silent tears" to God to spare him from the terrible death coming down on him, hurt to the core when, on the night before his death, his closest friends desert him, and shunning attempts of people to attribute divine power to him. When someone calls him "good master," Jesus responds, "Why do you call me good? No one is good but God." Mark also shows Jesus frustrated out of his mind by his dull-witted disciples, who, even to the end, never get his true message. Pitching his Gospel to the Gentile community, Mark even goes so far as to portray a pagan Roman soldier, a member of the execution squad killing Jesus, as the only one who recognizes who Jesus is: "Truly this man is the son of God."

Mark is also quick to notice Jesus's need to withdraw from hectic activities and pressing crowds to steal away into desert solitude to pray. In fact, all of the evangelists say this about Jesus. I get that. In my own life I struggle to cordon off hunks of solitude to be attuned to the depths of my own soul so I can attend to the inner voice that steers my life: "Be still, and know that I am God" (Psalm 46).

Learning about the human Jesus means learning about the socioeconomic situation of Jesus's life, and that leads me to reflect on my own. I'm proud that my daddy pulled himself out of poverty and educated himself to become a successful lawyer and businessman in Baton Rouge. And I'm happy that our family is devoutly Catholic. And, thinking back on it, I have to admit that I'm rather pleased to be a nun. "Many are called, but few are chosen," the Gospel saying goes. I guess that at least in the Catholic universe, having nun status puts me somewhat up there with the religious elite. Actually, I guess I pretty much take for granted the respect I get as a nun, the way lay Catholics are always seeking my advice and asking me to pray for someone who's sick or needs a job.

And yet whatever you can say about Jesus, it seems clear that he was not part of the religious elite of his day. He had enough education to be able to read from the scroll of Torah in the synagogue, but the question will be put to him over and over again by the experts and religious elite: *By whose authority do you do this?* When it comes to Jesus's religious credentials, and I realize that he was not a priest but simply a member of the laity, it plumb knocks my religious socks off. Jesus Christ not a priest? I'm so used to the heavy preponderance of clerics and bishops as authorities in the Catholic Church. *Jesus, a layman, an ordinary believer, a simple practitioner of Judaism?* I picture him, unnoticed in the crowd, attending synagogue, arms uplifted in prayer, singing hymns, and there in his house, fashioning wooden cabinets and door frames and perhaps a yoke for oxen. I picture him celebrating the holy days, dancing at weddings, and relishing the wine. Unlike his ascetic cousin John the Baptist and his followers, who scrupulously refrained from alcohol, Jesus clearly enjoyed the fruit of the vine, and his disciples (I imagine) were only too happy to follow suit. Jesus's critics accused him of being a drunk and a glutton.

If, within the Jewish community of his day, Jesus emerged as a holy rabbi and teacher and healer of the sick, and if, as the people said of him, he taught "with authority" and "not as the Scribes and Pharisees," this had to be super threatening and upsetting to the institutional religious authorities, used to being revered by the people as having the last word.

So who was Jesus Christ? For starters, *Christ* isn't Jesus's last name as *Prejean* is mine. The title *Christ* means "the anointed one," a title the Jews applied to other sages and heroes, such as King David. It's probably better expressed as: Jesus who *became* the Christ. That's how the theologians put it. Because Jesus was truly human, from childhood into adulthood, he must have evolved and matured in consciousness, personality, sexuality, intellectual ability, religious belief, and a sense of vocation.

Many thought Jesus was the Messiah, come to lead them to military victory over their Roman oppressors. But if there is one truth that shines through the entire New Testament, that truth is the radical nonviolence of Jesus. Not only did he say—and exemplify—that his way of loving means that we must not seek revenge on those who hurt us, but he goes further, urging us to forgive our enemies. Then Jesus really pushes it over the edge. He says that if someone hits us on one cheek, instead of hitting them back, we should turn the other cheek. If someone takes our shirt, we should hold out our jacket and say, *Hey, you want this, too?* It seems so over-the-top, maybe even psy-

chologically unhealthy. But people like Mahatma Gandhi and
Martin Luther King discovered a way to actively resist social
injustice by harnessing a positive, nonviolent force that Gandhi called *satyagraha,* or "truth force."

Until I learned the positive force of nonviolence, I always
shied away from it. It sounded so passive, so like becoming a
doormat and inviting your attackers to walk all over you. And
as little sister to Mary Ann, I had a six-year-old's experience
that turning the other cheek wasn't such a hot idea. I was fresh
out of Sister Mary Lawrence's religion class one day, and Mary
Ann and I were playing and she slapped me. To her great surprise (I can still see her amazed, gleeful look), I turned my
other cheek, announcing that I was doing what Jesus said to
do. Mary Ann was happy to oblige and she popped me again.
I couldn't believe it. Wasn't my sister supposed to be a Christian, too? Crying, I ran to Mama, and I remember that Mama
kind of smiled and said something like not taking Jesus's words
too literally—at least, not around Mary Ann.

So, early on I didn't take too kindly to the turning-the-
other-cheek bit, and being a nun didn't change the way I *felt*
about it. With my seventh- and eighth-grade boys in religion
class, I equivocated a bit. I taught them what Jesus said to do,
not what I felt. That would have been one sorry religion class
at St. Frances Cabrini School: *Okay, class, Jesus said to turn
the other cheek, but I say when you get that bully out on the
playground, get your buddies and knock the tar out of him.*
Not pretty: nonviolence turned into nun-violence.

Interestingly, Jesus never used the word *savior* to refer to
himself. He spoke instead of inviting people to leave behind
"half-dead" lives and to become "born again" into a vibrant
life in union with the divine. This makes me curious about

what *savior* actually means. The shorthand theological formula that I was taught goes: "Jesus died on the cross to save us from our sins." But what does that really mean? I get it that someone can actually save a person from drowning by pulling him or her from a river. But one thing I absolutely know cannot be true is that Jesus saved us by offering his life as a substitutionary sacrifice to appease God's wrath.

What kind of God would demand such a thing? As a Christian, I do believe that Jesus is my *savior*. I don't doubt that I need "saving" from my self-centered, ego-driven, adulation-seeking self. Okay, I get that, but how exactly does Jesus save me? I have to search deeper. This desire in me to learn things in a fresh way—is this what Zen Buddhists call having a "beginner's mind"? Is it, perhaps, what Jesus meant when he told us that unless we become like little children, the portals of the Kingdom of Heaven will remain closed to us?

In the first sermon that Jesus gave in the synagogue in his hometown in Nazareth, Jesus picked up the Torah and read from the prophet Isaiah: "The Spirit of the Lord is upon me, because he has anointed me to preach good news to the poor. He has sent me to proclaim release to the captives and recovery of sight to the blind, to set at liberty those who are oppressed, to proclaim the acceptable year of the Lord." And then, before sitting down, he simply said: "Today this scripture has been fulfilled in your hearing."

Isaiah has always been my favorite prophet, and Chris's as well. Wait until she hears about everything I am learning. She'll want to read more about all this, and she'll ask where she can find articles and books. When she and I have been able to steal away to a private place of quiet for a few days of prayer in preparation for Christmas, we always take Isaiah with us for meditation. Frederick Handel's *Messiah* opens with Isaiah's words: "Comfort ye, my people." And now Handel's music moves through me as I write, catching me in its current the way music does: *Then shall the eyes of the blind be opened, and the ears of the deaf unstopped; then shall the lame leap like a hart.*

In the tragic aftermath of Jesus's abrupt, terrifying, shameful crucifixion, it was to Isaiah that the disciples of Jesus turned, meditating on Isaiah's portrayal of the Messiah as Suffering Servant, who takes the betrayals and beatings and death without threat of retaliation, letting himself be led to slaughter like a sheep, who does not cry out. In fact, the Gospel accounts of Jesus's passion, death, and resurrection are one extended meditation on the Hebrew scriptures by Jesus's followers, trying to make sense out of the horrifying catastrophe. It is faith addressing inscrutable mysteries, turning to God, who receives and vindicates his faithful servants. "Comfort ye, comfort ye, my people." The scripture as revelatory text. Like flint striking rock. Read it with faith, and it can set your soul ablaze. Or, in the face of inscrutable mysteries such as death, it can provide the strength to abide in darkness, to breathe, to wait, to hover . . . until life and hope flow once again. No wonder ancient monks used to ponder scripture on their knees.

I've been praying the scriptures for years, but now to be able to learn the historical context and literary structure of biblical texts at Notre Dame is soul satisfying in the extreme.

IN WRITING A reflection paper, I'm learning better how to write what's real. I go over my class notes to let ideas swirl around until something big, a key idea, starts glowing. Then (always painstakingly) I begin to etch out first thoughts, trying out words, at first blah words, wooden and clichéd words, then, ever so gradually, erasing, scratching out, chucking out

swaths of empty patter, then losing the thread, until, until . . .
all whole it comes out, the energy rushes in, and I write it
down before I lose it.

The happy part of having William here is that I can tell he's
as excited as I am to be studying. His recall is almost perfect,
and from the probing questions he asks in class you can tell
he's done graduate studies before. In a study group with some
of our Sisters, Will is terrific—insightful, funny. I begin to relax
inside. We do a few things together, just us, but he's not all bent
out of shape just wanting to be with me. Why was I so worried? In the Huddle, the student hangout where we often gather
for lunch, songs pump out of the jukebox: *"I've looked at life
from both sides now."* . . . *"Good morning, starshine, the earth
says hello."* . . . *"Like a bridge over troubled water."*

I'm writing lively accounts to Chris, always feeling a little
guilty when I mail the letters, knowing she's working so hard.
Her letters back to me are brave, upbeat, squeezing in every
splinter of sunshine she can think of: "We got to go fishing
with Mildred Pellegrin in Montegut last weekend. . . . The husband of one of the nurses brought us two huge ice chests of
boiled crabs and shrimp, perfectly seasoned—nice with good,
cold beer. . . . We got to see the musical 'The Fantasticks' on
TV the other night. Wonderful! . . . Sister Johanna managed to
get permission from Mother Blanche for us to see it by telling
her it was a morally uplifting opera."

One small cultural victory for our worker-bee nurses and a
highly creative coup for Johanna Pellegrin, who managed the
permission. But an opera? *The Fantasticks* is an off-the-wall
musical, replete with witty lyrics and hilarious scenes, like the
satirical "Rape Ballet." Chris goes on to tell me how everyone
froze when Mother Blanche happened to walk through the
community room just as the "Rape Ballet" was at fever pitch—

loud, loud singing: "Raaaape! Raaape!" But, Johnny-on-the-spot Johanna, quick as a flash, comes rushing to Mother's side, deftly blocking the TV from her view and talking loudly right in her ear as she walks her across the room.

I'm right back to Chris with a letter and I tell her about Charles Curran coming for a lecture on the birth control encyclical and how we're all looking forward to it, and that one of the issues in the encyclical he's supposed to tackle head-on is the long-held Church position that sexual sins of all kinds are always seriously sinful. I put it in Church-speak for Chris, because I know she's interested. Get this, I tell her: When it comes to sex, there is no "parvity of matter." *Parvity!* Now there's a fun word to know and use. In other words, in the Church's view, when it comes to sex, there are no lightweight (non-"parvous"—my coined word) sins. I end the letter by promising to take careful notes at Curran's lecture to share with her. Which I faithfully do. I know I'm her main pipeline to knowledge about theology. I owe it to her.

I'VE BEEN PRETTY happy with how William and I are handling six whole weeks in such close proximity to each other. He's been mostly okay about respecting my need to study, not phoning me every night, not pressuring me to leave campus to be alone with him. Maybe his own desire for study and learning has kicked in. The professors are challenging, the reading lists formidable, the exams exacting. A graduate in theology from Catholic University or not, he has to have his nose in the books like the rest of us. Maybe the thought of doing badly—or maybe not so much doing *badly* as coming off less than stellar as a scholar up against a bunch of schoolteacher nuns—maybe that's in there, too, prodding him on. Or maybe it's just that he and I have a decent hunk of time together under the same sky each day, not like the rushed, pent-up three- or four-day visits with separation always hovering.

It helps that we're engaging in hefty intellectual work, our minds charged by new knowledge and stimulating conversations. On Sundays and some weekdays, we attend Mass together in small chapels that dot the campus. William is happy to attend Mass without having to preside. It gets old fast, he says, always to be the one up front, the one who (some people believe) singlehandedly has the power to draw down the presence of Christ. He's all on board with Vatican II's emphasis that, at Mass, Christ is present through the faith of the entire community, not just through the priest. He's happy, he says, just to be there with everybody else. He says, hands down, it's the constant pressure on the priest to get up in the pulpit every Sunday to deliver a decent homily that's the hardest.

I like praying with William. We both like to sing, and it's sweet hearing our voices blending. After Sunday Mass a bunch of us often go to the dining hall for brunch. Lots to talk about. Lots of teasing. Everybody grateful to be in this rich oasis of learning. "Praise God from Whom all blessings flow," somebody chirps, the first line of a hymn we nuns like to belt out when good things are happening. And if someone's in the mood, we might even get the next line: "Praise Him all creatures here below."

Nuns know a whole lot of hymns. We sang all through the novitiate. Sometimes I think that singing saved my life during those long three years with everything so silent and solitary and no close friends. Whenever my soul is in equilibrium and I'm not worried and tense, I'm humming, singing, or whistling. It's a family thing—Mama, Daddy, all of us; it's like my default mode. William is a first-rate music man. In his first parish assignment, fresh out of the seminary, he directed a young people's choir. There he is in a group photograph looking seriously priestly in his solemn black cassock. Until you get to his face: He looks like he's twelve years old.

Did you notice that qualifying word *pretty,* right before the word *happy* in the opening sentence about how Will and I are doing? That is so me, always trying to put the most positive spin I can on my relationship with William. *Pretty* happy? Not outright, blue-sky happy? Here's an image of the ambivalence always present in my relationship with William. Picture a wave, its topside all green and sparkling and pacific as it pulses toward shore. But below the surface, the undercurrent is roiling with sand and sucking the wave back into the sea. That's the tension of us, trying our best to make this "third way" priest-nun relationship work.

And it's not just with William that I'm bent on giving things an overly positive spin. When I really want something to work out, I emphasize every positive thing I can think of, no matter the negatives. And on the positive side with William, there's plenty to celebrate. He's truly a good man, and at times insightful and inspiring. One gift I've received from him is that I now feel much freer and at ease relating to men and enjoying their company. But more and more, spontaneous delight in Will is giving way, almost every day, to worry and nervous effort to keep him on an even keel. More and more I'm having to handle his upsets over the smallest things, and I find myself having to dig down and summon up commitment to our relationship, saying to myself, *I do love him, I do,* and a line from *Oliver!* wells up, a woman singing: "As long as he needs me, I know where I must be, I'll cling on steadfastly."

Maybe I have to work so hard on my relationship with Will because I'm so flat-out inexperienced with men. In my onward and upward bent toward the positive, I've downplayed the time earlier this summer at a student picnic when Will erupted in fury about a priest at the picnic who anchored himself at my side and kept talking to me all afternoon. Afterward, as Will and I walked back to campus, he exploded, saying the guy had "claimed" me. I say to myself: *Nobody claims me, bud, including you.* But I say it only to myself. Better not get into a huge argument in public. (When Will and I argue, we get really loud.)

It's hard for me to face Will's deficits. I so want to make our relationship work. If you really commit yourself to love someone, aren't you supposed to stick it out through thick and thin? There's this nagging guilt (and I suspect I'm hardly the only woman who's felt like this) that I'm the one who must be doing something wrong. Maybe the guilt comes because I lack the courage to just call it quits and end the relationship. But something's building. Within the confines of my own mind I'm starting to make rebellious little speeches. Not yet out loud. Not to him.

To put it mildly, William and I are not the only close priest-nun relationship on campus. All through the seventies, Notre Dame summer school would be a major lodestone for priest-nun romantic encounters. On weekends there are cookouts and parties with sing-alongs, led by sincere-if-untalented souls strumming guitars and singing their hearts out, often with beer and wine to juice things up. Most of us in this crowd, having entered seminary and novitiate at tender young ages, are piously naïve about the strong undercurrents at play beneath our bobbing boats. I remember one party where a young woman student played the guitar and sang a song that some of us knew was aimed at only one person in the room: her priest professor. I still remember the words, and the hushed feeling in the room: "This love of mine had no beginning; it has no end. I was an oak, now I'm a willow. Now I can bend."

The strumming singer wasn't alone. Willows are bending all over the place. Later we hear of outcomes. As it turns out, Willow and her professor do not marry. The word is that he left the priesthood and they were engaged to be married, but the wedding never took place. Others do leave and marry— some happily, others disastrously. Though, in some ways, when you think of it, committing your intimate life to one person for the rest of your earthly life has to be one of the biggest crap- shoots of all time. Not that people aren't totally sincere, not that some couples, like Mama and Daddy, don't pull it off beautifully for forty, fifty years. It's just that the life river keeps moving, and we humans move and change with it. Unless we're stuck—and boring.

As William and I listen together to the young woman's song, we're going into the seventh year of our relationship. How savvy are we, really, about just how far willows can bend? A couple times, feeling for William's tortured soul (and my own as well), I have talked to him about our maybe sepa- rating for a while to get perspective. But every time I broach the subject, he gets really, really, really upset. He says that no matter the cost, he cannot think of his life without me, he can- not live without me. It's scary. He's willing to put all of his eggs in one basket: me. He's content to drink from one fountain- head. I like to drink from many springs. Here it is again, the familiar leitmotif of tension in our relationship.

Two weeks before Will and I are to leave ND for home, *"pretty* happy" gets blown to smithereens. It happens on a Saturday night when I'm working late at the library on a re- flection paper for my scripture class. I'm all into the paper.

Words are flowing, and in the flow there's the surge of excitement. The paper is due Monday, and here it is only Saturday, so I'll have all day tomorrow after Mass to put on the finishing touches. Perfect.

One worry: William wanted us to get away this weekend, just us. *Badly* wanted. It's the second to last weekend before we leave for home, and he pleads with me to be done with the paper. "You don't have to always write papers like poetry," he says. "It's only a class assignment." He has a cut-and-dried way of writing, and he always gets papers done ahead of me. For him it's straightforward: Do the research, organize the notes, and chop-chop (his expression), type it onto paper. "I just pump out plain prose, but incisive," he says. "That's the correct way to write theology."

"I can't do that—it's not the way I write," I tell him. We argue. I stand firm. He raises his voice. To calm him, I lower mine. I turn to leave. He grabs my arm. I break away. That was last night.

But all day today I'm hoping for the best. All in all, William has balanced things *pretty* well this summer. He'll be okay. Maybe he'll relax and do something with the guys—maybe watch a game on TV. He has good priest friends here for the summer, and he hasn't come by all day, even for lunch. I know he's stretching, trying to be generous, respecting my need to be alone to work. It's close to eleven P.M. Time to call it a day. I collect my papers and books and start to head back to the dorm. I press the elevator call button, the door opens, and there he is, hunched in the corner, roaring drunk.

When William is drunk, his face is distorted, his speech is slurred, and he yells real loud. To hide the scene I close the elevator doors quickly, but already Will's grabbing at me. He's all over me. *No!* I tell him, pushing him away. As soon as the elevator gets to the ground floor I rush out and head for the front door of the library. *Thank God it's late, not many around, and—Thank you, JESUS!—none of my Sisters is here to see him like this.* I head out walking fast, half running toward my dorm, out past Mestrovic's colossal statue of Moses, with his uplifted arm pointing heavenward. William's coming behind me, swaying and lurching and yelling at me, saying mean things like he always does when he's had too much to drink: "Lou! Lou! You coward. Don't run away. You've never loved me, not like I love you."

The strap on one of my sandals breaks, flapping and slowing me down. I reach down and grab it. Easier to run barefoot. *No use stopping and trying to talk to him. Not when he's like this. Maybe I should, just to calm him down. No—not good. Better to end this night as quickly as I can. If I can just get to the dorm, shut the door, it'll lock, he can't get in. No, he'll yell to me outside the window and wake everybody up. Too bad. Take my chances. Maybe he's too drunk to make it that far. Maybe he'll drop off before he gets there.*

So here I am running barefooted across campus and praying like mad that I can make it to the dorm. Somewhere along the way Will drops off. All I know is he's not here. *Thanks again, Jesus.* The dorm door locks behind me. Safe. And on-my-knees-grateful that no one in my community witnessed the nightmare.

A Fork in the Road

~⌒~

Riding back to New Orleans with the Sisters, I realize a shift has happened within me about William. Talk in the community is gathering steam that my name is at the top of the list of recommendations to become the new director of novices. In some ways it's the most responsible leadership position within the community, since it involves the formation of new members, the community's future. It means I will live in community with the novices on a daily basis in the motherhouse in New Orleans.

I can't even imagine how I could arrange for Will's phone calls at exact times and deal with his emotional tirades when there's a glitch in the plan. Besides, in the novitiate the community phone is out in the hall and couldn't be more public. My stomach muscles tense from just picturing my having to walk over to the professed side of the large motherhouse to a private phone every time Will and I talk. No way. It'll never work. How can my relationship with William continue if I say yes to this new job? And by now I know that William does not have it in him to change the way he feels about me. Fork in the road.

The car is heading home. Our conversation is all about what we learned in classes, questions we fielded on exams, what awaits us at home. Summer at ND melts away. I did solid work, passed all my exams, and even had one of my papers read aloud in class by a professor. But if there is one thing learning does, it opens up the vast realms of everything you don't know. I promise myself to set up a firm schedule of study, along with daily meditation. It may mean getting up earlier in the morning, a resolution I have made many times but seldom succeeded in doing for more than a couple of days. It's hard to carve out time for study in the thick of busy activities.

As we ride along, my mind is awash with the huge decision awaiting me. The community vote on director of novices is imminent. Thankfully, Chris and I will soon get away to Grand Isle for a few days of retreat. We build solitude into the days, so that we'll have time to meditate. In the evening we'll cook a meal and share where our souls have been. Caught in the crosshairs I decide Psalm 139 will guide me in my prayer: *Yahweh, you examine me and know me, you know if I am standing or sitting*.

The community vote comes through. I'm asked to become the director of novices. I tell the community *yes* and head for our retreat.

CHRIS AND I are driving down Louisiana Highway 1 through all the tiny Cajun fishing towns to Grand Isle: Larose, Cut Off, Golden Meadow. . . . She's alive with questions about my classes at Notre Dame. She drives; I read from my notes. She's especially interested in the scripture classes and how ordinary people experienced Jesus of Nazareth in a way that transformed their lives. She'd give her eyeteeth for the chance for the two of us to get away to study. A little community affirmation of her intelligence surely wouldn't hurt, either. Old story. Old tensions. Chris, the nurse workhorse. Me, the teacher scholar. Chris, the indistinguishable, lost-in-the-crowd member of the community. Me, chosen to be the director of novices.

She holds off talking about William. He's a source of tension between us. She respects my continued choice to remain close to him, but I know it costs her, and until now I've kept my fierce ambivalence toward him hidden. But now as we're driving toward open days of quiet and prayer on our favorite island, I settle into her presence. Who better than Chris to entrust with my crisis?

I tell her about the scene in the library. I realize as I say the words out loud just how bad my struggles with William are. She's surprised. She had no idea. She says that on the outside my friendship with William looked so smooth. (*Why do I always want to appear in control? What is it about me that makes me hide vulnerability so fiercely, even from my best friend?*) She couldn't agree more that by my accepting the role of director of novices, William's frequent visits and phone calls will need to be drastically curtailed. What would the novices think? They are not deeply rooted in their vocations yet—just learning to live a celibate life, and not nearly spiritually mature enough to handle my having such a close relationship with a man.

I get it. The truth is, I'm not doing so hot, either—at least, not with *this* man.

It feels good to get everything out to Chris. I'm praying for the grace of what we nuns call a "good retreat." Which means being truthful, allowing hidden layers to be uncovered, shucking off inauthentic ways. In classical theology, St. Paul described this as "putting aside the *old man* to put on the *new man*"—Christ. The patriarchal metaphor doesn't carry much punch these days, though it makes the point of calling for personal transformation. I translate *old man* as the small, selfish, ego-centered self that's in all of us, certainly in me. It's been at work in me: *Save face—above all put a good spin on this bal-*

*anced, mature nun who stays true to her vows yet maintains a
close relationship with a priest . . .*

On the first day of retreat I pack a little bag for the beach:
my Bible and journal, a folding chair, and a bottle of water. At
first, I stroll awhile on the beach to become present to the lap-
ping waves, the puffy clouds, the light breeze on my face. Very
hard to do. Very. I'm churning inside like the spin cycle on a
washing machine. Here I am on the beach of my childhood.
And who am I now? And what am I going to choose at this
fork in the road?

*Come, Holy Spirit, help me to open up to your liberating
grace. I feel so trapped.* The day is clear, the sun out in full
force. The fall chill hasn't hit Louisiana yet, but it's brisk
enough for a sweatshirt. Mine is gray with a hood. I've con-
sciously chosen to wear a wooden cross around my neck. From
habit, I kissed the cross as I put it on. *Come, Holy Spirit.* I'm
in a tight spot, facing what up to now is the most critical choice
of my adult life. I pray for illuminating grace. I do my best to
stand poised. *Behold, I come to do your will, O God*—a prayer
Jesus must have uttered many times. It comes from Isaiah, perhaps his favorite spiritual mentor. Now it's my prayer, too.

As I walk, I open the Bible to Psalm 139 and I'm stopped
in my tracks. I don't make it past the very first verb in the very
first sentence: "Yahweh, you *examine* me." When I see the
word *examine* I think *probe,* and that makes me think of
X-rays and CAT scans—machines that can see inside and tell
the truth about what's really going on, and how scary it is
when you've been having a pain in your belly that won't go
away and you say it's nothing, just a passing thing, and you
don't tell anyone about it and try to treat it yourself with vari-
ous remedies, but the pain stays and gets worse and you

awaken in the night worried out of your mind that maybe it's something really bad, like cancer, maybe it's terminal. Finally, you can't stand it anymore and you go to the doctor. It's real information—reality—that you need: the *truth*. Do I have cancer or not? *Yahweh, you examine me.* The turmoil inside has to be fierce and close to the surface for one word to stun me like this.

With the Bible in hand, I stop walking on the beach. God is truth. When God looks at me my true self is known. Like a divine CAT scan. After all the worrying, the days and nights of wondering, fearing (*please don't let it be cancer*), the scrutinizing scan is going to tell the actual, real truth. Everything will be revealed, nothing will be hidden. But what is the truth I need to face in my relationship with William?

He is going to be so very upset when I tell him about this new responsibility in the community. He has never been able to be away from the sound of my voice for even a few days. Face it, Helen. Truth. The truth is that this job is going to mean the end of our relationship. Face it. I've never been able to love him the way he wants me to. From the very beginning our needs, our desires, have never matched. Have I fooled myself into thinking I truly love him? True, I've written reams and reams of words professing my love. But I need to face that I'm always in tension, always anxious not to upset him. I try to picture the phone call I'll make to break off the relationship. I'll say: "Look, I chose to take on this new responsibility in my community. It's who I am, and if I'd said no to it I would have betrayed my own soul. I need distance. I feel entrapped by you. Mostly now it's fear of your being upset that's behind my phone calls and visits. It's fear, not love."

That's it, my speech—the exact words I'll say.

I am pacing at a clip up and down the beach, my head down. I don't see anything, just the sand strip ahead of me. I've put the Bible on my chair. The words of the psalm are already at work in my soul.

I'm afraid of him. Afraid? Why? Is it guilt? Am I the cause of his dependence on me? Have I offered him false hopes I can never fulfill? Have I been untrue in my vow of celibacy? Have I been untruthful by pretending to be in a relationship that from the start has never been whole?

Yahweh, you examine me. . . . Descending into my fear, I hear Will's anguished voice: *Lou, if I ever lose you, I can't go on living.* Suicide. He's threatening suicide. Without me he says he'll take his life. I can't picture pills or a rope or a gun. He'll probably drink himself to death. I'm being held hostage by the scariest of all fears: *I could cause this man to end his life.* After pledging love to him through thick and thin, how dare I withdraw from him a source of life he's come to rely on? There it is: the terrible fear unmasked.

But a flash of grace comes . . . and liberation. I'm talking to myself, sorting out the pieces. *I can't be his God. I can't be the outside force that animates his life and holds him together. He needs to find the resilience to live within himself. His life is false if he needs someone like me to be his life plasma. For his own sake I need to withdraw. When I do, yes, he'll grieve and fall apart, but I can't assume personal responsibility for that. His life, his choice.*

Who knows? Maybe by my withdrawing, Will just might have the chance to meet someone who will respond to his love in a way that is truly reciprocal. As long as he's so invested in me, this can never happen. I need to face up to his drinking. Alcohol is already his main prop, his way to numb the pain of his loneliness. Maybe if he crashes and succumbs to the alcohol, his fellow priests will intervene and get him the help he needs. I'm surely not the one to do it.

Sweet, blessed grace. I walk into a circle of light. The huge, terrible tension drops away. I feel calm, steady, solid. I can let Will go. Turn him over to God. Like the lady whose husband always came home drunk and one night fell down in a stupor on the front lawn and a neighbor gave spiritual counsel to the aggrieved woman, telling her: "Don't you go out there. You just let him lay where Jesus flang him."

I am very clear about the boundaries I want to set: for six months no visits, phone calls, or letters. If he calls or writes, I won't respond. After six months, if he's willing, we'll talk by phone about how we've each fared. I've never been firm like this with Will before, and I have no doubt that he is going to get wickedly drunk and scream at me, probably blame me. But I'm free and clear now. He can't persuade me differently. Even if he drinks himself to death, it's his life, his choice, not mine.

I walk back to the camp where Chris is, and in one steady, unbroken stream of words I tell her everything that happened.

Oh, Helen, this is momentous. Are you sure?

Never surer in my life.

We pray together. Chris lights a candle and we read aloud Psalm 139. We read the words slowly so we can let them sink in. This time, though, I can get past the first sentence. To this very day I cannot so much as glance at this psalm without entering the soul space of that day on the beach when grace opened up a circle of light for me.

Where could I go to escape your spirit?
Where could I flee from your presence?
. . . If I flew to the point of sunrise,

or westward across the sea,
your hand would still be guiding me,
your right hand holding me.
If I asked darkness to cover me,
and light to become night around me,
that darkness would not be dark to you,
night would be as light as day.

AFTER MY RETREAT, even before I unpack, I head to the private phone at the convent in New Orleans to talk to William. This is it. The line in the sand. I tell him word for word what I came to realize on retreat. I don't hold anything back. For six months: no communication between us. Non-negotiable.

I feel the awful power of my words. At first, silence. He brings up all the beautiful moments we've had, says that we don't want to throw it all away and this is one more challenge that will help us to grow. He admits his mistakes; he truly loves me for who I am and doesn't want to change me. We just need to give it a greater try. . . .

Now *I'm* silent. Then I feel his anger. He accuses me of never having loved him. I have lied to him, I have faked a love I never really felt, I'm a fraud. It continues for some time, but I feel like I have a protective cloak around me. He can't upset me anymore. My soul horizon has opened. Maybe that's another way to talk about "doing God's will," a phrase we have always bandied about, sometimes to refer to something we feel we have to do, not necessarily what we would have chosen. But now I'm wondering if it isn't a matter of becoming more authentic, more attuned to the clear-sighted, natural goodness in every heart that learns to shed the delusions of arrogance and pride. Maybe at the center of it all is the surge of grace that breaks us free of our tight, narcissistic egos. Maybe.

Human dynamics are exceedingly complex. And when it comes to the human-divine mix, words fail.

For weeks after this conversation, Will writes letters, which I don't open; he makes phone calls, which I don't answer. Then he goes dark. I hold him in prayer, hoping that if he does crash, his breaking apart will usher in some healing in his life. I feel sad for him. But inside myself I feel new energy and joy. It's not unalloyed. It's always tinged with an ache for Will, and I can't completely shake the guilt of knowing that my break from him leaves him empty and disconsolate. I hate that he's hurting. Yet the new freedom I feel is stunning. Until breaking free of fear I haven't realized how trapped and scared I had become.

A poem by G. K. Chesterton about liberated slaves rises within me.

> Breaking of the hatches up and bursting of the holds,
> Thronging of the thousands up that labour under sea,
> White for bliss and blind for sun and stunned for liberty.

So many of the Sisters, especially in leadership, even though they have respected my freedom, have been worried out of their minds about me and William. It has been quite a stretch for them to give me latitude, trusting that my commitment to the vow of celibacy would hold fast. I feel I owe leadership a personal account of my decision to end the relationship with Will, so I go to see a few of those whose trust I treasure most. As I recount my retreat experience to Sister Kathleen Babin, our regional superior, she gets up out of her chair to hug me. Sister Jane Louise Arbour, my high school English teacher, who knows my limited experience with men before I entered the convent, tells me that she's happy William happened in my life. What were her words to me exactly? Something about my being "rounded out" as a person.

It was risky business for them not to rein me in. Especially with so many Sisters leaving. They blessed my freedom and trusted me. I love them for that. I'm grateful I didn't betray their trust. I feel a surge of joy to be home again and ready to throw myself wholeheartedly into community life.

As for my vow of celibacy, I've come to understand its meaning in a deeper way. *Virginity* has come to be super-identified with biology. For women, one question: Is the hymen intact or not? Not so clear for men. After all, in sex, males are the penetrators, not the penetrated. But while the spiritual meaning of *virgin* lies deeper than biology, bodily integrity does matter. For me it certainly does. And, to say the least, it would be highly hypocritical to engage in casual sex with one person after another while staking the claim, "Inside my deepest self I'm pure virgin." But, finally, it is the virginal spirit that crowns everything.

As Jean S. Bolen puts it in her book *Goddesses in Every Woman: A New Psychology of Woman,* the core meaning of the Virgin Archetype is integrity in one's being, "the 'one-in-herself' character," who is owned by no one and does not act out of the desire to be approved of or even to control. "She does what she does . . . because what she does is true." Thus, in its core meaning, *virginal* can be understood as a quality of single-heartedness, purity of intent: the *virginal* artist, the *virginal* husband, author, architect, teacher, lawyer, and, yes, politician (although in the United States, the brokering of money and power in politics sets the "purity bar" pretty high).

It is the single-heartedness at the core of a virginal heart that has been the struggle in my relationship with William. My energies began to feel more and more divided between him and my life as a nun. Attention to his emotional needs consumed more and more of my time and attention. And to avoid scandal, I began to keep our visits secret—the sure signal of something amiss, the telltale sign of a split-level life.

So here I am now, emerging from my William experience more real and more grounded—that's for sure. And a lot more humble. I'm learning that not every relationship I set my sights on and invest in necessarily turns out successfully. Yet I don't feel Will and I are a complete failure. In our good moments we soared, and I miss the special aliveness I experienced with him. I learned firsthand a cardinal rule of love: to never let fear manipulate me into giving what I do not freely desire to give. There you have it: the delicate balance of loving well. Simple to say. A good hunk of lifetime to achieve.

As I move on in my life without William, I hear from his friends that he's having a terrible time of it. Several months after our separation, he got drunk and did not come out of his room for three days and nights. His fellow priests found him lying on the floor, unbathed, dehydrated, and drunk. They did for their brother what brothers do—they rushed him into the detox unit of a hospital. He lost his teaching position at a prestigious university, and, perhaps hardest of all, lost the standing he held among the clergy and people of the diocese. He made his poor mother weep—and, as he later told me, he lost me.

PART V

RIVER RAPIDS

Director of Novices

After an eight-year drought without any new members, our community will once again welcome four young women into our refurbished novitiate. Not eighteen-year-olds fresh out of high school. That was the fifties. This is the midseventies. During the years after Vatican II, when the community was in flux, we stopped admitting novices until we sorted ourselves out. And we're not finished, that's for sure. Our renewed image of ourselves as Sisters of St. Joseph is that of a people journeying, not settled, making our way alongside the rest of humanity. No more are we the elite "God Squad" set apart from ordinary Catholics. Indeed, "Pilgrim People" is Vatican II's image of the entire Catholic Church. People seeking the light, muddling through the fog like everybody else. Gone the Triumphant Church in command of Truth and ready to "give orders" for God to follow. Also gone is nun-on-a-pedestal. Gone the comfort of nuns in the habit, nuns who teach our kids in Catholic schools and nurse our sick in Catholic hospitals.

The novices coming to join us reflect the flux. None of them come from "solid" Catholic families, and none have done much "praying" in the traditional sense, including praying the rosary or even being able to recite the creed. Hopefully, they know all the words to the "Our Father." A few are coming to us fresh out of college retreats in which they've experienced a "touch from God" and felt a call to give themselves to our way of life.

We're a mixed bag—that's for sure. With all the changes that have happened in religious life, older Sisters are wary in general, but especially of the "new" novitiate, which, after their own ultra-strict training, must seem downright free-wheeling and hopelessly slack. I'm not picking up the responsibility for the novices alone. A formation team joins me, and we shoulder the task together—good women with plenty of experience in religious life under their belts, willing to accompany the neophytes through two and a half years of training.

We're naming the new novitiate Joseph House. A rough-hewn, wooden sign with the name hangs at the top of the stairs of what was once our postulant dormitory. The spacious room that once held twenty head-to-head metal-framed beds with curtains pulled around them at night has been transformed into a living room, dining room, and kitchen.

And here, in a few ticks, pass seven years of experience as novice director, some of the most pioneering, migraine-producing years of my life. A roller-coaster ride if ever there was one. What guaranteed the ups and downs of the experience for us on the team was, hands down, the fluidity of soul, the mercurial unsteadiness of the women trying out our life. On Monday, feeling joyful, close to God, purposeful, heading toward vowed commitment. On Thursday—or even by Monday evening—doubt, tears, spats with the other novices, complaining about kitchen duty: *Why doesn't* she *ever do her share? She just stands around. . . . I want to go home. . . . I miss my car. I miss my freedom. My prayer is crap. I don't believe in God anymore. What kind of intimacy can I possibly have if I don't have sex?* A few days later: *Okay, I prayed and God was as close as my own breath; I made it through the crisis. More than ever I want to be a nun. I always knew this was the life for me—ever since I saw* The Sound of Music.

And that's just the novice side of things. On the professed Sisters' side, signals of dissatisfaction drift in—mostly rumors: *Too much freedom . . . a boisterous, drinking party at Joseph House the other night . . . You need to clamp down. . . . Discipline! They need discipline!*

Lord help me. I never in my entire life had a migraine headache until I took on Joseph House. (I'm probably too empathetic. When a novice seems to be settling in, I feel happy with her. When she falls into doubt and anxiety, I feel anxious, too. Maybe too much. And I'm terribly sensitive about professed Sisters' criticisms of the novitiate. *Yeah?* I say to myself. *Armchair criticism from afar is always easy; let's see you do this job for even two weeks.*)

Of course, we do have a serious, structured novitiate program of studies, prayer, psychological counseling, and personal spiritual guidance, but ours is a way of life that cannot be imposed by harsh discipline. It must be freely embraced from within. Learning to discern God's will in prayer and loving others generously are the main values I stress. I do try to embody these in my own life, but I'm tested, all right. Sometimes I feel that if I could just wring a few necks, all would be well. And often enough—heartbreak. A novice whom I get to know and treasure, who seems to have just the gifts to be a great nun, decides to leave us. And I have to force myself not to summon every ploy I know to plead-persuade-badger her into staying.

Thank God Chris, who is finally attending Louisiana State University School of Medicine, is living close by at the motherhouse during these years. She befriends the novices, who seek her out, pouring out their woes. Unofficially, she's a vital part of our team, doing her share of staving off a couple of "bolters" who were secretly plotting to leave the novitiate in the dead of night. I'm so grateful to have her near. She helps me learn to be a take-charge leader—something she learned early on as a young nun when she was head nurse of her hall at the hospital. She tells me that I'm too understanding, that I let troublemakers go too long, spreading negative spirit in the community, before I stop it in its tracks. Chris becomes a lifeline of sanity for me. Sometimes we pack up and leave for a weekend at her sister's getaway house across Lake Pontchartrain— a peaceful lagoon.

A RIFT IS developing in our community, with "social justice" Sisters advocating for us to become engaged with the struggles of poor people (in Louisiana, overwhelmingly African Americans), and in the other camp, the "spiritual" Sisters, who emphasize prayer and the practice of charity. No surprise: I'm solidly in the "spiritual" camp.

And I'm up at the microphone at our meetings arguing that we're nuns, first of all, not social workers, and our main job, our only real mission, is to help people find God, and if people have God in their hearts, they'll be able to conquer whatever oppresses them. *What do you mean, "poor" people? Even Jesus said the poor would always be with us.* I make these speeches with a whole lot of enthusiasm and sincerity. And defensiveness. I do a lot of vociferous arguing, hammering home my point.

Awakening to the real struggles of desperate people on the margins in a way that ignites compassion and concrete action is a grace, a precious gift—which at this point in my life I clearly don't have. I just don't get the Sisters going on and on about all this justice-for-the-poor stuff. As if affluent and middle-class people don't have spiritual struggles, too?

It's not that I'm doing anything wrong. I'm not being mean-spirited, and there's surely nothing the matter with praying for people who are suffering. What I take from these arguments in the Sisterhood is that I have to pray even harder for God to help poor people in the world—and I definitely need to work harder at being charitable toward our in-your-face activist nuns, who are quickly becoming my nemeses. Even at wakes in a funeral home, when we're supposed to be quietly consoling the bereaved, there's that agitator Sister Alice Marie—once my shining spiritual ideal in high school—sitting off to the side, plotting revolution. (True, she already did express her condolences.) In her clarion calls for social change, Alice Marie likes to quote the canticle of Jesus's mother, Mary, in which she praised God for pulling the rich down from their thrones and exalting the lowly.

"The Gospels are not neutral," says Alice Marie. "Jesus clearly sides with the poor."

Yeah, yeah, yeah, I think. *What about Christ's words to Pilate that his kingdom is a spiritual one, not of this world? What about that?*

This roiling controversy begins to seep into Joseph House, as well. Because I'm conflicted myself about social justice, I do zilch to spur the novices in that direction. Instead, I emphasize prayerfulness and charity, especially toward those we dislike. I say "we" dislike, since we on the formation team have our own share of personal conflicts, especially about how to deal with high-octane novices whose antics can suck all the oxygen out of the room. Or, on the opposite end of the spectrum, overly quiet, docile novices who don't utter a peep. The Loud Peeps on one side, the Peepless on the other.

So that the novitiate experience will include service to others and not become totally inward focused, we—team members and novices together—conduct weekend retreats for young women at Joseph House. The retreats require generous expenditures of energy. Besides giving talks and taking part in group prayer and conversations, the retreat team hauls mattresses out of storage to set up sleeping quarters, cooks and serves all the meals, and cleans up afterward. All's fine when everybody's getting along, but a real challenge occurs when intense conflicts among the novices continue right up to the time we are set to open the doors to a new batch of young women.

I don't see Alice Marie much. As the foremost leader of the social-justice nuns, she's not in my inner circle of friendship. I still have a deep soul connection to her from high school days, and I have nothing but admiration for the way she recruited young black women to integrate St. Joseph Academy. I also admire the way she not only studies activists such as Saul Alinsky but puts into practice what she learns—publicly. I enjoy reading about the spiritual journeys of Catholic social activists, including Dorothy Day and the Jesuit Daniel Berrigan, but I am nowhere near ready to engage in public protest or civil disobedience, much less get arrested and go to jail. Wow, I think—what's *that* like? To be so inspired by the biblical prophets and Jesus Himself that you're willing to go to prison? Not me. Not this nun. Not in this lifetime.

Alice Marie has a poster of a person in a jail cell with these words by Thoreau: "Under a government which imprisons any unjustly, the true place for a just man is also a prison." She also loves quoting Martin Luther King. Her spiritual diet is filled with such push-the-envelope people. She feeds off them, claiming that Jesus's "social gospel" lies at the very center of his message. I'm on a more "spiritual" track, the latest of which is meditation on St. Ignatius's "Rules of Spiritual Discernment," which he appended to his *Spiritual Exercises*.

I hate arguing with Alice Marie. I hate that we occupy opposite viewpoints about our mission as nuns. One day, we bump into each other at our motherhouse in New Orleans. She has come in from her ministry in rural New Iberia to shop. She and Sister Francine moved there several years ago to teach literacy to African American plantation workers who plant and harvest sugarcane, still live in primitive shacks much like the ones their ancestors occupied seventy-five years ago, use special vouchers instead of money at the plantation store, and who can barely make their way through a fifth-grade reader.

There are no "Dick and Jane" reading primers in Alice and Frannie's program. Following Brazilian Paulo Freire's pedagogical method, they believe education should empower people to take charge of their lives. How much more respectful of adults, Alice Marie says, it is to learn to read words from daily life: nouns such as *work, sugarcane, church, God, jail, citizen*; and verbs such as *study, speak out, struggle, budget, pray*, and *organize*. Freire named his activating educational method "Pedagogy of the Oppressed." Are underserved, uneducated, isolated, indigent African American plantation workers in Louisiana oppressed? You better believe it, says Alice Marie. That's why Jesus says they deserve preferential care.

Almost immediately, Alice and Franny, the "socialist, revolutionary" nuns, have set off a storm cloud of controversy involving the bishop, their parish priest, and, above all, the plantation owner, who tells them they're not welcome—that his workers are happy and have everything they need right there on his plantation. Anne Curtis Rigby, a former student of Alice Marie, comes to visit her in New Iberia and drives up to her house just in time to witness Alice coming out to meet armed sheriff's deputies, who are telling her to leave immediately, that she and the other nun are trespassing on private property, and there's Alice standing up to them, telling them that she's been invited by the residents and she has no intention of leaving.

I admire what Alice is doing, and I tell her so. That's not what we argue about. Well, maybe what we do is not really argue. It's more like she raises questions about our formation program, and I get defensive and feel she's attacking me. The particular question that gets my hackles up is about the retreats we're doing for young women at Joseph House. *Do the retreats ever deal with questions of social justice in the real world?* Alice wants to know. *Is the novitiate like a protected hothouse from which novices never venture out to meet people stuck on the lower rungs of our society?*

I tell her that for novices, social activism will come later—that our priority is to make sure they have a firm spiritual foundation. But Alice sees passion for social justice as an integral part of a solid spiritual foundation. Augh! I always leave her feeling like we're on separate, grinding tectonic plates.

At one of our community gatherings, we're invited to participate in a justice orientation program to "cross over" from our suburban neighborhoods into places of poverty. One of the choices is Mexico City. It appeals to me because Margie Navarro, a good friend, is a missionary there. I've heard how terribly poor the people are in Mexico, how dirty their living conditions, and how easy it is to get amoebas and parasites, and I know only a few words in Spanish—not exactly religious words (though, at least at a biological level, they do seem to be linked): *cerveza* (beer) and *baño* (bathroom).

Two whole weeks among desperately poor people? Something I've never done. Maybe by immersing myself in the lives of such people I'll catch the fire for social justice. Something deep in me is hoping for that. I figure that staying with Margie in her little house will help me get through it. The argument with Alice Marie is still simmering. As director of novices, I need to set a good example. My going to Mexico will maybe encourage our new members to venture out to new Gospel territory. The time commitment—only two weeks—seems manageable enough.

Here's the long and short of it. In a slum area outside Mexico City I do in fact witness unbelievable poverty. People's houses are made of cardboard and tin, the unpaved streets turn to mud whenever it rains (which also makes the electricity go out), most of the people have parasites of some kind, their crops and gardens are fertilized with human waste, water needs to be boiled before you can drink it, little kids as well as adults are out in traffic trying to sell things, children die young. It's desperate. Yet here's Margie, welcoming us, cooking for us, bringing us to meet the people and justice workers in the neighborhood. Margie has to translate every syllable for us.

I'm bumping along with the program of field trips and talks on Mexican history and culture until the last night, when one of Margie's coworkers, Fernando, comes to her apartment with his guitar and a bottle of tequila. We eat tacos and enchiladas. (Margie washes the lettuce from the market, first with a little bleach, then with water, to kill the parasites.) After we eat, Fernando brings out the guitar and the tequila, a new drink for me.

The way you drink tequila is from these thimble-like cups with a bit of salt and lemon as a chaser. Sing and drink, sing and drink, sing and laugh and drink, salt and lemon, sing and drink. I have no way of knowing how many of those tiny thimbles I'm imbibing. In the gusto of the moment, there's no way to keep track, and I'm all in the moment. We're coming to the end of the two weeks and I'm feeling satisfied with myself. I've done it. I've immersed myself in desperate poverty and survived.

After a while, Fernando puts the guitar down and launches into a full-blown jeremiad against U.S. capitalist policies that hurt poor countries. He also takes aim at the hypocrisy of Christian churches, who do nothing but preach sexual morality—forbidding birth control and promising eternal bliss in an afterlife—while not lifting a finger to join the people in their struggle for justice. I don't know beans about U.S. capitalism, but I feel I know a thing or two about Christianity, and I jump in four-square to defend Jesus, the Gospels, and Christianity.

It gets pretty heated, me and Fernando, going at it with poor Margie as translator. What's not so good about revved-up tequila arguments is that while heat and passion may run at fever pitch, memory the next day of insightful points is close to zero. But I do remember well the argument I kept making— that the kingdom Jesus preached was spiritual, not political, not achievable on this earth. This succeeds in making Fernando apoplectic, rattling off Spanish so fast he sounds like an AK-47. Nor do I improve the effectiveness of our exchange by throwing in my take on the American way of life, which I call the best democracy in the world: "Just look at our high standard of living and the huge number of our middle class, Señor Fernando."

Mercifully for Margie, the evening eventually comes to an end, and Fernando leaves and we go to bed. Well, Margie goes to bed. I try to go to bed, but the bed keeps moving. Every time I lie down, the bed starts spinning. I can't stop the bed. It's impossible to sleep when your bed's whirling around like a merry-go-round. Anyone reading this who has ever had a "tequila experience" knows what I'm talking about. It's a very busy night, mostly spent in the bathroom. Thank God Margie has indoor plumbing. To this very day I can't get near tequila.

My two-weeks-immersion experience with "the poor" having concluded, I return to New Orleans, never in my life happier to get home. Along with the unease I still feel inside from my contentious argument with Fernando, I also carry home an amoeba in my gut that will soon manifest itself in a most intense and inconvenient manner. Once again, thank God for Chris, who just happens to be studying tropical medicine at the Louisiana State University School of Medicine. I'm running to the bathroom and she's poring over her textbook and talking to her professors and getting me to the Tulane tropical medicine department for tests.

I'm home, but nothing has shifted in my views about my life work as a nun. The currents of my spiritual life continue to flow smoothly as they always have: *We're nuns, not social workers.*

Until, at last, my boat hits the rapids and grace breaks through.

Lightning in Terre Haute

Hidden in the storm, you answered me in thunder.

—Psalm 81

Lightning strikes are startling, loud, and last only about one-quarter of a second. At temperatures up to 50,000 degrees F, five times hotter than the surface of the sun, the 3 or 4 discharges of each flash travel up and down an ionized path at speeds going down to the ground at 500 miles per hour and return along the same path to the cloud at ten times that speed. The superheated air along the ionized path of the strike expands drastically and produces a shock wave of thunder.

—A Yellowstone Journal by Tom Murphy

In nature it's called lightning.

In philosophy, insight.

In the spiritual realm, enlightenment.

When it happens to me, the way I know it's real is it jolts me out of the way I used to see and do things. It permanently alters the trajectory of my life.

The jolt happens in June 1980, at a community gathering in Terre Haute, Indiana.

En route to the conference from New Orleans, novices in tow, I'm hardly enthused. The chief presenter will be Sister Marie Augusta Neal, SNDdeN (nun-speak for Sisters of Notre Dame de Namur), a full-throttled advocate of social justice. It'll be three whole days and nights of nothing but social justice and no chance of escape, with all of us housed in college dorm rooms out in the middle of the woods. (The college is not called St. Mary-of-the-Woods for nothing.) Augh. Brainwashing to get us all to be social revolutionaries.

I dread the arguments that will surely erupt in the small group discussions following each presentation. Discuss. Discuss. Endlessly discuss. That seems to be all we nuns do. I know the predictable questions: "What new insight struck you, challenged you? What part of the presentation stirred emotions—positive or negative?" (How we *feel* about things is always paramount.)

Group discussions are where I have the least control over my runaway mouth. I'm such an arguer, so impulsive, and afterward, I say to myself, *What was that all about?* So, on the bus trip up to Indiana, I'm steadying my soul: *Okay, okay, it's just one more conference. I will try to pry open a tiny crack of openness. Holy Spirit, help me.* But that wisp of sentiment is quickly crowded out by the overriding passion that has dominated my soul for months: I must stand guard to preserve Christ's spiritual message and our spiritual vocation as nuns.

The first day of the conference, I manage to come through unscathed. Sister Marie Augusta, who teaches sociology and the New Testament, lays out the sad statistics of how unfairly the resources of the world are distributed—the bountiful gross national product of rich countries such as the United States, and poor countries with all their misery statistics. I'm listening and saying to myself: *I know that; I know that life isn't fair. I know children are starving and women and girls aren't educated and are being abused. I get it. All bad, sad stuff. But what, tell me—just what is one lone person like me supposed to do about such gigantic world problems?*

Sorry, but misery statistics, even about little kids starving in droves, roll right over me. I feel bad for them but in a sort of general way. I don't personally know anyone starving to death. I figure the big problems of the world are where God comes in. Planetary problems are God's problem. Way too big for us mortals. Besides, tackling economic and social injustices involves political action, and as a spiritual person I'm above cantankerous, corrupt politics. I'm apolitical. Politics brings out the worst in people. The only time I ever heard my good Catholic daddy cuss was when he argued about Louisiana politics.

So the first night of the conference I sleep like a baby. As the day was ending Marie Augusta had announced that tomorrow she'd be talking about Jesus's Gospel message. *Yes!* I say to myself. *Bring on Jesus!* I love learning about Jesus. Not to brag, but I do know a thing or two about his Gospel message, which I happen to have studied and meditated on almost every day of my entire earthly life. A refrain from an African American spiritual wells up: "Ride on, King Jesus!" My sentiments exactly. After a full day of nothing but global statistics, finally we're going to get to Jesus. I am so ready.

When the bolt comes, it comes in a mere twenty-two words.

In the first part of the sentence, Marie Augusta says: "Jesus preached good news to the poor." And I'm thinking, *Yeah, yeah, yeah, I know those words by heart,* and I'm waiting, I'm sure about what's coming next, what the good news of eternal salvation must be for poor people. Isn't the best of Gospel good news that God, like a kind daddy, personally loves each of us, including the poor, and watches over every intimate detail of our lives, down to knowing the exact number of hairs on our heads? Jesus said that: *Every hair of your head is numbered.* And the psalms about how God's ear is especially attentive to hear the cry of the poor.

Surely, certainly, the next words announcing good news to

the poor will be the great, shining, glorious reward that will be theirs in heaven. At the heavenly banquet, their place will be right next to God at the head table. Of all the bejeweled crowns, theirs will be the shiniest. One day, by and by, when all the suffering, the struggle, the hurt and loss and grief and pain are done . . .

But that's not what Marie Augusta says.

She says, "Integral to that good news is that the poor are to be poor no longer."

Poor no longer?

What Jesus was telling them, Marie Augusta says, is that, far from accepting lives of oppression and misery as God's will, they have God's blessing to resist the injustices that make their lives wretched. Their very dignity as sons and daughters of God calls them to strive for what is rightfully theirs. Justice, not charity. Active struggle, not passive compliance.

I'm stunned.

Poor no longer. So that's what our community's social-justice debate has been about. But if this is true, being pious and charitable is never going to cut it.

And as I consider that thought, I begin to get it. Something deep within me must have been waiting for it. How can I claim to be a follower of Jesus if I'm not aligned with poor people in their struggle for simple human dignity? Where have I been? Why have I been so resistant to the Gospel call to work for justice?

I realize that in all the theology courses I've studied, there has been a subtext that fed the conviction that if some people were poor, then somehow that historical reality must be God's will—a fate in life that poor people must simply accept, relying on God's merciful grace to help them, even as global corporations steal their land, tax their crops, and destroy their natural resources. I thought this was what Jesus meant when he said "Blessed are the meek." Accept God's will. Endure. Don't resist.

Then I realize that I don't personally know one single person or family on this earth who is poor. I'm always hanging out with middle-class or affluent *white* people like me.

Marie Augusta has one more zinger. She explains that working for justice necessarily means working for just policies, which means getting involved in the political process. Simply praying for people is not enough. Marie Augusta further explains that in a democracy like the United States, there's no such thing as being *apolitical*. If we sit back and do nothing, leaving all the policy making to others, that is, in fact, a position of support for the status quo, which is a very political stance to take.

Bam! Bam!

Twice the lightning strikes. There in the auditorium, I stay sitting still, I don't move, I don't say a thing. Something in me must have been poised and waiting for these words to catch fire as soon as I heard them. I think of the opposition I had put up in the community debates. Yes, Alice Marie has been on the right side of this all along. She is still in New Iberia, teaching African American plantation workers how to read. My childhood friend Sister Kathleen Bahlinger is living in the St. Thomas housing project in New Orleans. Margie Navarro is now serving in Nicaragua.

After Marie Augusta's talk, feeling stricken, I follow her into the elevator and blurt out, "I'm the director of novices." I feel a need to confess, to acknowledge how slow I've been to understand the heart of what Jesus was about. What took me so long?

What I remember most is Marie Augusta's kindness as she

looked at me. Evidently, I'm not the first shuttered soul she's helped to understand the challenge of Jesus's message. Nor am I the only soul whose life purpose has been ignited by hearing a cluster of words. There are similar moments of awakening in the lives of the saints.

For St. Francis of Assisi, the crucial moment came as he was gazing at a crucifix in a dilapidated chapel. He saw the lips of Christ move as the command came: "Francis, rebuild my church, which has fallen into ruin."

St. Clare, a rich, young noblewoman, heard St. Francis preach the invitation of Jesus: "Sell what you own and give to the poor and come follow me." She became Francis's most devoted follower.

For Edith Stein, a Jewish philosopher, a moment of awakening came when she stayed up all night reading the autobiography of St. Teresa of Ávila. As the sun rose the following morning, she said to herself, "This is the truth." It was the beginning of a path that led to her conversion and becoming a Carmelite nun (and ultimately dying in a Nazi death camp).

For Father Thomas Berry, it was a childhood view of a meadow filled with yellow flowers that sparked his passion to care for our planet: *Whatever is good for the meadow is good; whatever harms the meadow is bad.*

What gets me the most in Marie Augusta's interpretation of Jesus's message to the poor is the realization of how passive I've been. *All these twenty years living in New Orleans and I've never once ventured into a single neighborhood of struggling people. The only African American people I know are those who serve in our schools and hospitals and our motherhouse as cooks, gardeners, or maintenance workers.*

I'm in disequilibrium, free fall.

I think of St. Paul's question when he was still Saul, lying there on the ground after being jolted by his vision of Christ: "Who are you, Lord? What do you want me to do?"

The bus trip from Terre Haute back home to New Orleans feels mighty different from the ride up.

FUNNY, BUT IF I were to rely on my memory to describe the transformative effect of Marie Augusta on my life, it would go like this: Marie Augusta's words about Jesus and poor people shook me out of the way I used to see and do things and forever altered the trajectory of my life. As if—*kaboom!*—I returned to New Orleans enlightened and immediately moved to the inner city and began working with poor people.

Not quite.

My journal tells a different tale—a chronicle of unreal plans, false starts, and a lurching soul still living far too much in my head.

As it turns out, it's going to take me a whole year to catch up with the new understanding of the Gospel that Marie Augusta has opened up. But the journals record an even more startling surprise, at striking variance with my recollection that I reached the decision to move to the inner city entirely on my own. The reality is that my religious community had to take me by the hand and lead me every step of the way. That included steering me clear of a pie-in-the-sky plan I proposed to establish a Catholic training program out in the countryside for young adults (suburban white kids, naturally) who, through prayer, living in community, and a bit of inspired teaching, would become impassioned to roar out of the woods into the slums of America as champions of justice.

Getting inspired by Marie Augusta's words is one thing. Translating those words into flesh-and-blood action is quite something else.

Back from Terre Haute at Joseph House, I continue my work with the novices and retreats for young people. For a few years the dream to develop some kind of training center for young Catholics has been brewing in my soul. Through encounters with young people in retreats, I feel the intensity of their spiritual thirst, and I'm looking for a way to respond to that need more comprehensively than weekend experiences can offer. Somehow there must be a way that such young people could be a part of a faith community that would sustain them in their spiritual quest.

Now, looking back at my journals, I realize that the way I always framed everything was around forming community: a movie-star club in school, a Blessed Mother club, an acrobatic club (okay, that was just two of us, Harriet Jacob and me, but, hey, you've got two people? you've got yourself a club). These clubs came into existence quickly and disappeared just as quickly, and I never seemed able to imagine any kind of action to better the world that these clubs might address. That's always been the fuzzy part. So many needs in the world, so many hurting people, so very close by here in New Orleans. But where to start? (Maybe the lack of focus has something to do with the fact that I was still living out in the suburbs with all my needs cared for, sincere as all get-out and pious as ever, but . . . isolated.)

To help me get real about my proposed training center for young people, it's going to take an open forum of all the Sisters in the region gathered together to discuss the proposal. I seem to have a special talent for building fantastical plans in my head, convinced that they come straight from God's mouth to my ear. All I can say is, thank God for my community. They are the ones who finally help me translate inspiration into action.

Here's what happened at the open forum.

First though, a little background. My way of praying and discerning God's will at the time are recorded in my journals, cast in revelatory language like that of the Old Testament prophets.

Jesus: *The young people are drowning in materialism. Who will gather them into community and teach them my Gospel?*

Me (à la Isaiah): *Here I am, send me.*

I am drawn to journal writing because words take away fuzziness and make things explicit (maybe drop-dead deluded but at least *explicit*). I can see on the page what I'm thinking, feeling, and imagining as well as what I feel in my heart that God is telling me. It is probably a holdover from my wannabe mystic days. Mystics like Hildegard of Bingen and Teresa of Ávila were always writing down their visions and revelations from God.

Along with prayerful discernment, I have for several years been consulting with different Sisters in the congregation about my idea for this training center (which I sometimes call a Christian Leadership Boot Camp—not for the fainthearted). When Scotty Scardina, whose daughter, Leigh, is one of our novices, purchased a tract of undeveloped land in the country seventy miles out of New Orleans and offered us ten acres for our use, the idea blossomed to locate our center on this land; that is what led to the proposal that I am presenting to the community. Of course, locating the center on undeveloped land would mean having to do virtually everything: dig a well, erect buildings from scratch, plant a garden, install electricity (though I am toying with the idea of going natural with kerosene lanterns)—all this before we could begin to hire staff, plan programs, and recruit participants.

You can *imagine* what's going to happen when Sisters start raising even the most basic practical questions:

Where will you live while buildings are erected?

Will the buildings have indoor plumbing, electricity?

If novices are part of the project, where will they study theology? Isn't it a long commute from the country to Loyola University in the city?

Way out in the country, how will young people even meet poor people?

And here comes the hardest part. When Sister Barbara Miller, whom I could count on to question me at community meetings, stands up to speak, I brace myself. I know it's going to be a critique, and I wait, standing there at the microphone in front of the group. What surprises me is not Barbara's critique of the egregious impracticality of the plan, which, by the third or fourth question, has already been devastatingly exposed as a Prejean-feet-firmly-planted-in-midair *Mission Impossible,* but her stinging judgment about my credibility.

Journal entry:

> *Barbara Miller stood up and challenged me to live and work among poor people myself before I try to inspire young people to work for justice. How can I teach them what I don't live?*

What hurts the most is that I know it's true. I'm all talk, all glowing, spiritual-sounding ideas and no action. All preach. No practice. The forum on my proposal happens fully six months after the conference in Terre Haute, which reveals just how long business-as-usual has been going on in my life. If I hadn't consulted my journals, right now I'd probably be writing this: *After Sister Marie Augusta Neal awakened me to Jesus's call to serve the poor, I came home, packed my bags, and moved in with poor people in the inner city.*

With my airy dream shattered at the forum, my life begins to move forward on a more solid path, a path I still walk. A month later I meet with Sisters Lucy Silvio and Cynthia Sabathier on our leadership team. The open forum with the Sisters had been such a disaster and they feel for me, a compassion I welcome clean down to the marrow of my bones. They too see the need for more challenging Christian formation for young people, and commission me to continue to create a justice-oriented program (not in the bloomin' woods, but no need to utter a syllable of those words). They confirm my decision to begin a new ministry at Hope House, a Catholic service ministry in the inner city here in New Orleans. For the last several months I've been volunteering there on Tuesdays, a small first step to getting to know poor people that I had put into practice as soon as I returned from Terra Haute, where the Jesus lightning struck. (Good news to the poor: you will be poor no longer. Translated: There's no authentic following of Christ if I don't work for justice.)

Hearing God's voice and recording it in the pages of my journal has proved to be exceedingly tricky business. God talking, me talking, all mixed up together. Responding to a summons to serve poor people in my own backyard is shocking in its ordinariness. Not to mention humbling. My untethered spirituality is crashing.

I guess the sheer grace of it is that I woke up at all.

In June 1981, one year almost to the day after hearing Marie Augusta at Terre Haute, I walk into the St. Thomas housing project to begin work at Hope House.

St. Thomas Project

Stony the road we trod,
Bitter the chastening rod,
Felt in the days when hope unborn had died;
Yet with a steady beat,
Have not our weary feet,
Come to the place for which our fathers sighed?
—James Weldon Johnson, the Black National Anthem

With all our belongings packed in a little truck, Therese St. Pierre and I drive up to Hope House—an old green house on the edge of the St. Thomas housing project in New Orleans. Sister Kathleen Bahlinger and Lory Schaff, a Mercy Sister and founder of Hope House, come out to welcome us. A year earlier Lory had started an Adult Learning Center in St. Thomas—a way for high school dropouts to earn a high school diploma. Therese and I will be volunteering there. The first thing I notice is that we're the only white faces around. In fact, some of the staff at Hope House are the only white folks in the neighborhood, period. A totally new experience for me.

It's June in semitropical, humid New Orleans. A lot of the residents carry sweat rags, dabbing at foreheads, necks, and arms. Summer. Sweat time. Most residents of the project can't afford air-conditioning. Even if they could pull off buying an AC unit, the utility bills would kill them. After fourteen hours of sun beating down on the three-story brick buildings, the housing units are like ovens, and by dusk people are heading out to front stoops, hoping for a merciful afternoon breeze off the nearby Mississippi River. Otherwise, they rely on cardboard fans, the kind the funeral homes give out with a pretty scene and a Bible quote.

Okay, it's hot. People sweat, and we sweat with them. One time, sweating our buns off as we're lugging piles of clothes out of a van for a rummage sale, Kathleen says, "Whooee, y'all, I know I don't smell too good," and Lory says, "It's okay, we all stink together." I haven't heard the word *stink* since I entered the community. In our Southern, genteel culture the saying goes "Horses sweat, men perspire, women glow." Well, we're glowing, all right, like thousand-watt incandescent lightbulbs.

For the first time in my life, I have a chance to enjoy the close company of black people and begin to realize how much more varied and interesting and, well, *colorful,* life is: the laid-back, drawly talk in black dialect; the home cooking that forms the hub of every gathering, with plenty of extras for folks to take home; and the humor bubbling up, never far away, sandwiched into the bluesy tales and drop-dead, break-your-heart (endless, unstoppable) tales of justice betrayed, beatings wreaked upon bowed backs, and, O God, faith that rises, faith in God, in Jesus as a friend who plodded the path of suffering, the brother who "makes a way out of no way," Jesus humiliated, scorned, nailed to two pieces of wood, Jesus, with ear bent, as close as a cry, a moan, a turn of the heart crying, *Mercy, Lord, mercy.*

I don't know all I'll be doing here. I'm one unseasoned, raw recruit. But I'm determined to learn all I can so I can be of service. Or, at least, as in the medical profession, to "do no harm." In my journal I'm writing, *"Be open, let go of precon-*

ceived ideas, everyone can teach me something." God, save me from being a "do-gooder" nun, here to save poor, helpless people.

When I was growing up in the days of strict racial segregation, I never mixed socially with black people—not in school or church or restaurants or anywhere. And, as I've said, I never thought twice about it, just like it never crossed my mind to notice that when black men passed us white teenage girls on the street, they never looked us in the eye. For eons in the South, white women—especially young white women—have meant nothing but trouble for black men, and the savage murder of Emmett Till for supposedly flirting with a white woman is still writ large in every black man's memory.

Lory points out that she has noticed that even to this day a black man approaching her on the street will lower his eyes. She makes it a habit to be the first to greet people when she meets them in public, and I make it my practice as well. Almost everyone responds with a nod, and many seem surprised. I have never actually thought about any of this. Maybe culture is like air you breathe, or glasses you wear that screen out what you see and what you don't, with us whites justifying segregation by saying such things as, "Black folks like to be with their own kind, just like we do. There's trouble if we try to mix the races in a way God never intended." And you're just a kid and you take it all in and don't question. Even in Sacred Heart Church, "God's house," where I made my First Communion in my little white dress, black people had to sit in pews way over to the side of the church and had to wait to receive Holy Communion after whites.

Now, somewhat awakened, I look back in amazement at how ignorant I was. But I guess when you're not awake, you're not awake. Waking up to the suffering of people who are different from us is a long process, and has a whole lot to do with what community we belong to and whose consciousness and life experiences impact our own on a daily basis. I have a hunch I'm going to be waking up till the moment I die.

FROM DAY ONE at Hope House, I watch Lory. She's my model. She taught at an upscale Catholic high school for white girls, and she was awakened to racial injustice in her own school when she tried to invite black girls from St. Mary's Academy to come to the Mercy school for a religious project. It turned into a battle royal with administration and parents stringently protesting against "mixing the races."

"Don't we believe in the 'one body' of Christ?" Lory asked. "Why are we separating ourselves?"

The incident pushed her past boundaries that had always contained her. With permission of her leadership, she left her white, uptown convent, moved into one of the apartments in St. Thomas with another Sister, and launched Hope House. There they were, the only white folks in a sea of black faces. By the time I arrive here, ten years later, I get the benefit of the people's trust that Lory earned. The kids call every white person "Sistah," even men. *You white? You a Sistah*.

I'm drawn to Lory's spirituality. She has found a way for her prayer and meditation on the Gospels to inspire and energize every dimension of work at Hope House: a food pantry for the hungry; used, clean clothes at rummage sales (every piece 25 cents, whether a coat or a pair of shoes); emergency funds for rent and utilities, especially at the end of the month when welfare checks run low; sometimes simply a safe place to unburden your heart with someone who listens and cares; and a meeting place for community organizers to gather and strategize action plans.

Every staff meeting begins with prayer, aimed at opening our hearts to the cry of the people, to feel their suffering as our own, and to push past rushing in with Band-Aid solutions to the harder work of asking systemic questions. Who among the power brokers in the federal and Louisiana political and so-called free-market systems stand to benefit from policies that keep poor people poor? Budgets and tax codes make it clear who is valued in society and who is not. No wonder Martin Luther King was fond of calling a budget a "moral document." This is all new learning for me, sparking my curiosity to learn how these systems operate. Because now I know people who get kicked to the curb when hurtful policies are enacted. And now as a Catholic I know that the "Real Presence" of Christ isn't only in the tabernacle in church with the little red sanctuary candle burning that says Jesus is "in."

I find that after all my years of religious life and studies at Notre Dame I'm also learning to know Jesus in a new way. His big theme was about how we show love for God through love for the neighbor, and he roundly rejected the super-religious types who prayed, *Lord, Lord* all the time and adhered strictly to ritual prescriptions of the law but ignored those suffering around them. I used to think prayer was about persuading God to intervene to correct things that were wrong with the world. (Now that I'm awake . . . no wonder honest people feel they must reject that kind of Super-God.) Now I'm learning that real praying means taking on other people's suffering as my own, and letting the experience rouse me to action. Prayer doesn't change God; it changes us. And it's not always blissful. Just the opposite: It jolts us awake to pain and suffering caused by injustice and won't leave us in peace until we do something about it.

I think back on a thirty-day silent retreat I made some years ago at Grand Coteau, Louisiana, where we were supposed to enter prayerfully into all the events in Jesus's life. I did fine with the idea of encountering God in everything around us—and I was having special fun encountering God among the cows in the field, and learning how to ride a bicycle with no hands. But when it came to meditating on Jesus's suffering and death, I felt like a dismal failure. We learned about what St. Ignatius called "the gift of tears," which he obviously had. When he meditated on Jesus's sufferings, he felt them so deeply that he wept. As for me, I knew Jesus died for my sins and the sins of the whole world, and I was truly sorry he suffered—but not enough to cry about it.

The tangible meaning of Christ's suffering was awaiting me down the river. Meditating on Jesus's suffering two thousand years ago wasn't doing it for me. But as I begin to encounter the very real suffering of people I see day in and day out, I find that real tears come naturally.

And I'm learning how liberating it is when I finally rouse myself to act on an issue. The hard part—the paralyzing, confusing part—happens when I'm sorting through all the different, complex options of what I might do—or not do. But when I do act, no matter how small the deed, I can feel the life force coursing through me. And one thing I'm coming to realize is that for me to consistently act for justice is happening only because I am part of a community that lives and breathes and feeds on doing justice. I'm trying to ride the current of grace as it comes. Our founder, Father Jean Pierre Medaille, comes through again with a maxim I sorely need when I'm tempted to rush headlong into action: "Never leap ahead of grace."

THE INTRICACIES OF poverty are exceedingly complex, and it's not that people in St. Thomas bear no responsibility whatsoever for their situation: capable adults lazing about, sipping beer in early afternoon and not looking for a job; fathers walking away after the birth of their children, going to jail for disturbing the peace; young, uneducated single mothers passing up opportunities for self-improvement and raising families on welfare checks—or, maybe worst of all, wallowing in addictions and leaving their children to raise themselves. Figuring out the causes of poverty and possible solutions is way beyond me.

Lory is always talking about the cumulative effect of generation upon generation of poverty being so difficult for an individual to overcome. So many self-defeating habits. So many never-tried new ones. So many instincts of helplessness and defeat. No deeply ingrained work ethic. And not many role models to show the way. Except grandmothers. They're the ones that seem to demonstrate the most enduring sense of responsibility. When I tell Lory about Julius, who showed such promise at the Learning Center, and about my three attempts to set up job interviews for him, all of which resulted in no-shows, she shakes her head: "My rule of thumb is that a comeback from long years of failed attempts is going to take as long as those years or longer." Brand-new terrain for me. It was a lot easier to offer solutions when I didn't have a clue about the gravitational pull of people's daily struggle. Even easier when I could simply pray for them. I never stepped out publicly to stand with people who were victims of injustice. How could I? Until now I've never known real people in struggle.

At Hope House I'm meeting lawyers, civil rights activists, and black educators who are actively engaged in exposing injustice and helping people claim their basic rights. They're teaching us white folks the way racist attitudes insinuate themselves into our institutions, such as our school system (superior Catholic schools for whites who pay tuition; inferior public schools for indigent black people), banks ("redlining" people in poor areas to prevent them from getting loans), housing (gentrification that raises rents sky-high, screening out poor families); and—back then, I was totally blind to this—racially inflected language. The word *white,* like "lily white," always associated with purity, but *black,* like "blacklist" and "blackball," with something sinister or bad.

Barbara Major and Ron Chisom, local African American civil rights leaders who head up a group called the People's Institute for Survival and Beyond, teach a course called "Undoing Racism," in which they (*patiently*) teach us white folk about the ways racism is operative in our society. I hear the term *white privilege* for the first time in my life. I know I'm not a bad person, nor my Mama and Daddy, either, nor many of my white friends and colleagues, including the nuns who taught me. No, not bad people, but also often not awake to the way we are advantaged in this society simply because we show up with "white" (really, we're kind of pink) skin. More important, not brown or black. It's rare that we whites ever have to deal with people who look at us askance or treat us differently simply because of the color of our skin.

In the United States we whites are the *norm setters,* and it's our perceptions and values that get woven into institutional systems, such as the courts, business practices, healthcare, education. To give one example: In the criminal justice system, over 90 percent of judges and prosecutors are white. Dark-skinned people often are the "other," who scare and threaten us. When a person of color excels and rises to the top of the social ladder as a banker or professor or politician, we point to them as beacons of possibility for all black people, when, in fact, they often are rare exceptions. For us whites, when we work hard, we expect to do well, and when we do, we feel like we earned our success. Even in becoming a nun, at least among Catholics, I expected to be exceptional (and holy to boot).

As Barbara Major tells it, "As a woman of color, every time I walk into a room with a lot of white people I have to watch if somebody's going to look at me funny or insult and bait me to get me to react." Barbara takes us through a litany of white privileges we never think twice about:

- When you write a check or use a credit card, ever have somebody question your financial reliability simply because you're white?
- When you hear about national heritage or even "civilization," what color are the people you assume are being talked about as having made it happen?
- When you're facing a challenging situation and you handle it well, ever have anyone tell you that you're a credit to your race?
- When, in a department store, you ask to see the person in charge, what race do you expect them to be?

On and on. I have plenty to write in my journal.

Before Hope House, I had some sense that racial injustice existed but in a general kind of way. I always thought things such as social preference just happened naturally, that it's in our genes to identify with and gravitate toward our "own kind."

Now, I look around in St. Thomas at the ceaseless struggles, especially among the young people, and I have no earthly idea of what to do. I think of the mile-wide Mississippi River that bends its way through New Orleans, on the surface looking smooth and wide, effortlessly flowing toward the sea. And I want to say to every kid in St. Thomas, "*Hey, kid, this is the river of opportunity for everyone, rich and poor alike, including you. This is the Great American Dream, and you can put your little boat in, follow your dream, and glide all the way to the sea. Everybody born in America can do it, kid. Just believe you can and be determined and work hard. Just put your boat in, kid, and start paddling."*

But just below its shining surface, the river swells and lurches, teeming with hidden eddies and whirlpools and sudden hazards like craggy rocks. I look at the kids in St. Thomas. Even if they get a high school diploma, the only careers that await them are minimum-pay, dead-end jobs on the back of a sanitation truck or cleaning motel rooms or unloading and shelving groceries or doing low-end housekeeping in a nursing home. Even a young woman who gets a cashier's job at a department store will be hired only part-time, which means no retirement pension and no health insurance. Upward mobility? Sure. *You just have to paddle your boat a little harder, kid.* Maybe a lot harder, to beat the odds.

I always thought that jobs were the way *out* of poverty. Now I'm learning the meaning of *working poor.* I'm watching how easy it is for a young kid to "run a bag" of white powder down the street for a quick twenty dollars. When you're a kid with nothing but bleak prospects and you look around and the only person you see who's *somebody* is dealing drugs . . . what do you aspire to? Forget the law. Being law abiding has never gotten you anywhere, anyway. Just follow the money.

Hands down, the teachers that impact me most are the residents themselves. I have never in my life heard such stories, nor met people facing such intractable obstacles, such loss, such grief. Like one young mother, who within six months had two sons shot and killed. The police never investigated, nor did she expect them to.

I feel like I'm in another country. And in a way I am, even though I'm a fraction of a mile from the motherhouse in the suburbs. Everything feels different. Without warning, the crack of gunshots erupts from time to time, and once or twice the *rat-a-tat* of an automatic rifle.

The first time I walk through the projects by myself, I'm as nervous as a cat. I'm walking, looking around, super alert, knowing how gunfire can erupt out of nowhere. Then . . . what's this? Is that bacon I smell? "Hey, Sistah, how you doin'?" A lady is cooking breakfast on a grill on the sidewalk outside her apartment. The most delicious whiff and greeting of my life, thanks to Lory's steady presence, which prepared the way for my welcome.

Kenny Singleton, our next-door neighbor, got no such welcome. A couple of weeks after I move in, he gets a bullet to the heart. Sister Therese and I watch in disbelief from our second-story apartment window. One minute, Kenny is arguing with another guy about sunglasses. They are yelling right into each other's faces. It all happens quickly. The other guy runs up the stairs to his apartment and comes back with a gun. *Bang, bang, bang.* Kenny drops to the sidewalk. Kids gather quickly. Shootings like this—blood on the sidewalk—are their big drama of the day. The ambulance comes, the police come. The shooter has fled.

Did that just happen? Lory knows Kenny's family. She'll wait awhile, then visit his mama, ask how we can help. The next day we hear Kenny's family is asking for contributions. Time of wake and funeral will be announced later, so the family has enough time to collect money from neighbors for funeral expenses. A little kid, maybe nine years old, says to a news reporter about the killing: "I'm too young to understand all this." It's the way I feel, too.

.   .   .

MY MOVE TO the projects is a brand-new experience for my family, as well—especially Mama. Our Sisters at Mama's parish, St. Thomas More in Baton Rouge where she attends Mass, say with a chuckle that everybody knows my ministry from my mama's prayers at Mass.

"When you were at Joseph House, your mama prayed for God to send us more nuns. Now you're in St. Thomas and your mama's praying—loudly—'for protection of my daughter in the ghetto!' " It helps that I'm here with my childhood playmate Sister Kathleen Bahlinger. Her mama encourages Mama to venture into the ghetto for a weekend, and now she's talking bravely to Sister Lory, saying that she's not nervous at all, that she sees the good work of Hope House and can feel the people's respect for us nuns.

Meanwhile, her friends, far, far away from the violent, drug-ridden ghetto and very nervous about Mama's descent into the valley of evil, promise to pray "like mad" for her safety, which doesn't exactly bolster her confidence. But visit us she does—joining in the cooking and evening prayers, supervising after-school playtime of the children, sewing on buttons and mending our clothes—and returning home safe and sound. A few months go by and Mama's visiting us again and telling Sister Lory how nervous she had been on her first visit. "But, Mrs. Prejean," Sister Lory says, "you told me you weren't nervous at all," and Mama grins and says, "I was lying through my teeth." Yep, that's Mama.

We nuns take a vow of poverty and talk a lot about "simple living," but it's poor residents in this neighborhood who live the vulnerability of real poverty: eruptions of violence, the raw need for safety unmet, and the ever-present, gnawing worry about unpaid bills, children failing in school, sons in trouble with the police, kids stealing drugs, selling drugs, doing drugs, daughters pregnant at fifteen. Residents talk of having "bad nerves" and taking "nerve pills," and say things like, "That man is gettin' on my last nerve." Not much about goals reached, dreams realized, children to be proud of.

We at Hope House are volunteering to live here, and we're free to leave whenever we choose. Residents in St. Thomas, as well as residents in nine other public-housing projects in this city, don't have that choice. Jaraldine Johnson, a long-time resident and staff member, tells me how she worries about her kids and would love to move but can't begin to afford the rent in another part of the city. "We got no choice. We gotta stay here like we're on a reservation or something."

First lesson: *Poverty reduces choices.* And when experienced by the second, third, or even the tenth generation in a former slave state such as Louisiana, poverty's undertow seems so powerful that it begins to feel permanent, inevitable, a fact of nature. Many young men expect that prison awaits them. Their mamas expect it, too. I used to say things like: Why don't poor people keep their kids in school—don't they realize it's the only way to keep them out of poverty? And Where are the men? Why are the women left alone to raise the family? And Why are they always eating junk food? Why do they always trash things and litter? Why don't *those people . . . ?*

I'm still asking the questions, but now with more urgency and the beginning of understanding, because I know real people in the struggle. Good people who love their children, good people with good hearts and sincere desires. Like my mama.

When Louie was six months old and had contracted double pneumonia and almost died, Mama was like a mother bear, calling, begging, summoning every doctor she knew from her nursing days at Our Lady of the Lake to help her dying son.

They did, and Louie lived. But who does Jaraldine turn to for her sixteen-year-old son when he's grabbed by two policemen as he is jogging to his after-school job, jerked into the back of a police car, and taken under the Mississippi bridge with a gun jammed in his face and told, "We know you robbed a warehouse. Tell us who was with you or we'll throw you into the river and nobody will ever know"? Or Patrick's mama, just finding out her son has serious hypertension—she didn't know he had "high blood," he never felt bad, she and her five kids never got medical checkups—and the unseen, unfelt high blood pressure has taken out both his kidneys and he's going to need dialysis several times a week for the rest of his life. He's twenty-one years old.

At Hope House, I join Kathleen and Sister Lillian Flavin (Irish as they come; just try serving her tea that didn't come to a roaring boil) as teachers at the Adult Learning Center. It's not like a regular classroom in which teachers teach regular classes. We work with each student individually to master the subject areas—reading, math, English, science—that they'll need to get a high-school-equivalency diploma. When students achieve success, it's a big deal, with a full-fledged cap-and-gown commencement ceremony in the neighborhood gym. A big deal, because it's rare. Attrition is sky-high. Residents come through the door with high expectations. They think that because they have made a decision to finish high school it'll be a snap. They have no idea of all they don't know. They also live in the most distracting, conflicted environment imaginable. Few have ever read an entire book, and at home there's constant noise from TV, people talking, arguing, music blaring, in a living space designed for four in which six or even eight people live.

Study habits? Concentration? A quiet place to study?

One day into our Adult Learning Center walks Frank. I

introduce myself to him and explain that I'll be working with him individually on subjects he needs to freshen up on to pass the state high-school-equivalency exam. His head's down, I can't see his eyes, and I have to ask him his name and how far he made it in school several times before I decipher a mumble: "junior." This seems supremely hopeful to me, and I have my pep talk ready saying that with only one year to go before graduation, he'll be done in no time, so what we'll do first is check out his math, English, and reading skills. I flash back to my own junior year at St. Joseph Academy, when I was writing prize-winning essays and beginning to get good at public speaking.

Frank's reading test stuns me. He can barely stumble through a third-grade reader. Here he is, one year from graduation, and he's functionally illiterate? How did this happen?

I know very well the school Frank attended. It's one of the all-black public schools that are always being written about in *The Times-Picayune*: crumbling buildings, paltry teachers' salaries, violence on the school ground, and the highest rate of student dropouts in the nation. I've been vaguely aware of the sad, bad statistics about public education in Louisiana, but until now I've always been part of the tuition-funded Catholic-school system with its highly motivated teachers, the stellar ranking of its students in national merit scholarships, and virtually 100 percent graduation rate. And, it almost goes without saying: mostly all-white student populations.

Now, for the first time, it's dawning on me that I'm not the virtuous, special-to-God person I thought I was. Everything has been handed to me gratis. I didn't have to struggle to have it: my loving family, a good education, and my unfettered freedom to choose a vocation. Take away my cushions and privileges, and who am I? What makes me think I'd be any different from the sixteen-year-old girl who came into the center, cradling her doll-like baby in her arms and saying, "Now I finally have something of my very own"?

Sister Lory told us the first day we arrived that, although we may live among poor people, "we'll never really be poor." Our education will always put us among the privileged. Time to kiss that privileged, special, bride-of-Christ-self goodbye and join the human race. For me, now, being of service isn't virtue—it's flat-out justice. For years and years, black people served me. Now I serve. Long overdue.

EVEN WHEN I'M a hundred years old, I'll still be "too young to understand" the long-standing assault on people of color in my own home state. But learning I am, scribbling furiously in my journal. Mostly I'm sitting at the feet of my new teachers, the residents in St. Thomas. Like Ms. Ruby, seventy-five years old, who has just come to the Adult Learning Center to learn to read the Bible before she dies. As a child she worked in the fields, birthed a bunch of babies, and raised children and grandchildren, with nieces and nephews along the way, never "gettin' round to book learnin'" face-to-face. She always did want to know about Moses, she says, and before she dies, she wants to read God's word with her very own old eyes.

One day, Kathleen and I happen to be on the porch at Hope House and watch a scene unfold between Bobby Leonard and two policemen. Bobby, black and over six feet tall, did time in federal prison for bank robbery but was lucky to land in prison in Atlanta, which collaborated with local colleges to offer degree courses. Unable to read when he was tried and convicted, now with a college degree under his belt, Bobby is fiercely investing his every waking moment to cajole, persuade, or wrangle kids to stay in school. Having just finished talking to our students at the Adult Learning Center, he's nailing a notice on a tree about a meeting for families with loved ones in prison. Suddenly, two policemen drive up and start arguing with him. Kathleen and I watch everything.

First, a loud argument, and then the police handcuff Bobby's hands behind his back and push him against the police car, and he's yelling to us, "Sisters, y'all are my witness, I got no drugs on me, they gonna try to plant 'em in my pocket, *I got no drugs.*" And off they drive with Bobby in the backseat.

Kathleen and I look at each other. I follow her lead. She's already grabbing the car keys. We arrive at Central Lockup and Kathleen asks (demands, really; she's made of strong German stock) to see the officer in charge. Poor Bobby. Here he is, a strong, smart black man having to rely on two white women to intercede for him. He accepts our help and later thanks us. He well knew what would have awaited him at Central Lockup. He'd be searched, the drugs "found" in his pocket, and he'd be charged for possession and maybe intent to distribute. An impossibly high bond would be set, and he'd be thrown in jail to await trial. Which may not have happened for a year or two or even three.

Somewhere along the line, a public defender, shouldering an impossible load of a hundred cases and horribly underpaid, would be assigned to defend him. And it may well be that Bobby would not lay eyes on his defender until the very day of his trial. In all probability there would be no trial at all. In 95 percent of criminal cases, justice is served up bargain-basement style by plea bargains struck between prosecutors and defense lawyers. If your lawyer urges you to take a deal of fifteen to twenty years—saying it's the best the prosecutor is offering—and you say "But I'm innocent," no matter. Here we have the corrupt mess in our justice system in which innocent and guilty alike—overwhelmingly black people and always poor—are thrown into our state prison, Angola, for impossibly long sentences, never to be heard of again. Trouble, trouble, trouble. Poor people have nothing but.

To be sure, policemen on the St. Thomas beat have more than their share of trouble, too. Called to scene after scene of human carnage, including little kids killed in drive-by shootings—like three-year-old Kevin, shot to death while sitting next to his mama on the living room couch—and often in confrontations with fleeing armed suspects, their own lives on the line, how can police possibly not be inured to trauma and its crippling consequences?

I'm taking a fresh look at the American Dream and who gets to live it and who doesn't.

One of the people who is helping me to open my eyes is Bill Quigley, an impassioned civil rights lawyer, who has been meeting with our staff at Hope House to share stories about poor people's struggles for justice—basic justice, such as paved roads, healthcare for kids poisoned by lead-based paint, a long list of unmet maintenance needs in public housing. He and other lawyers become my first teachers of the nuts-and-bolts ways that ordinary people can organize to claim their rights.

Denny LeBoeuf, a lawyer with the ACLU, tells us of a recent lawsuit the civil rights organization filed against the Louisiana Department of Corrections for inhumane conditions in a rural jailhouse, where two young black men died of heat stroke after being locked in cramped steel "hot boxes" for disciplinary infractions. Denny grew up in New York City, and it seems she must have started marching in social justice protests as soon as she learned to walk. I count her as one of the most dedicated, stellar human rights advocates of our day.

Denny and Bill soon become my close friends (they still are), and it is they who introduce me to Amnesty International, the international human rights organization, from whom I first hear the idea of "*inalienable* human rights." *Inalienable* meaning that human beings, simply by being persons, have certain rights that cannot be "alienated," or taken from them, by a government or anyone else. These include the *right to life* and the right to not be subjected to *cruel and degrading punishment or torture*. This foundational moral principle of inalienable rights implants itself in my soul and will become the motivating fire that drives my life's work.

During one of our educational staff meetings, Bill and Ron Chisom tell us about their recent involvement with the struggle of black citizens in rural Ironton, Louisiana, to get running water in their tiny town. Maybe I remember every jot and tittle of the story so vividly because I was so motivated to learn how to translate constitutional ideals into flesh-and-blood action.

Here's what happened: Until the public protest in Ironton, backed by a class-action civil rights lawsuit filed by Bill and other lawyers, every Saturday morning Ironton residents had been forced to wait in long lines for the water truck to come. One by one, the people filled their buckets, pails, and plastic jugs with water. The citizens of Ironton had long been cowed by powerful white folks who basically owned the town and made all the rules. The community organizing effort took a long, fear-filled year. The town had been oppressed so long, and the people were so afraid of losing homes or jobs or being beat up or worse, that it took a whole lot of church prayer meetings and training sessions for people to gain courage and trust in one another to stand together as a united front.

Bill shows us a large black-and-white photograph of the people, eight abreast, holding their signs up high as they marched down the main street of the town: WATER FOR IRON-

TON NOW. Everybody was scared, Bill says, but the community's leaders walked tall as they led the demonstration, and everybody knew what to do if law enforcement moved in to make arrests. The leaders had secured a legal permit to march, and those who marched knew the main rule—to keep moving—so they wouldn't be arrested for blocking traffic. Every marcher had a lawyer's phone number written on his or her arm, and knew their right to make a telephone call if they were handcuffed and taken away. Everyone knew how to curl up and protect their heads if the police moved in with billy clubs.

Bill ends the Ironton story with a quote from Frederick Douglass: "Those who profess to favor freedom and yet depreciate agitation, are men that want crops without plowing up the ground. . . . Power concedes nothing without a demand."

As the months roll by at Hope House, my work with Bill and his wife, Debbie, draws us close, and they invite me to join a small group of friends who meet to pray, reflect on the Gospels, and support one another in efforts for justice. I feel at home. Everyone takes justice seriously. At last I feel that I'm learning to translate Christian ideals into concrete action. I've always known the Christian mandate to love God and my neighbor. But which neighbor? That's the rub. Just the ones like me in my neighborhood? Love them how? Simply by being nice and charitable? I've tried to do that for years. It was never enough.

I'm just beginning to delve into politics, but I do know this: From here on out my perspective will be guided by the effect political policies have on poor and vulnerable people. What's different for me is that now in St. Thomas, in company with neighbors who are suffering the effects of these policies, I can no longer read the misery statistics of my state and nation in a detached way. Doing justice is no longer a superfluous extra in my spiritual life. Taking even small steps, such as going to a community meeting or writing a letter of support for a mother's son in trouble at school, feels integral and right. I'm beginning to actualize my faith, one small act at a time. I'm also learning that getting involved with poor people in the struggle for equality means that controversy starts following you like a hungry dog.

And my nights are different now. Before coming to Hope House, I'd spend most evenings watching TV. Now I spend most evenings going to community meetings or lectures or helping at our Adult Learning Center. Chris and I stay close. She's been right there for me in my move to Hope House, and she visits when she can. I'll always remember her standing up for me at the community meeting when I proposed the fantastical idea of a young people's training center out in the woods. As shy as she is about speaking in large groups, she rose to her feet that day and in her soft voice attempted to explain what she saw as my sincere desire to help young people, despite the impracticalities of my plan.

Chris's speaking up for me at the community assembly was something of a reversal of roles. Usually I've been the one to encourage and support her, as I did by encouraging her to expand her horizons to become a medical doctor. And over seven years' time, with (alleluia—at last!) the blessing of leadership, Chris gets her undergraduate degree from Nicholls State University (she savored the humanities) and, against all odds, gets accepted into Louisiana State University School of Medicine and becomes a family practitioner, the congregation's first physician: Ann Barker, MD. On the day of her graduation from LSU School of Medicine in 1979, we had one big, over-the-top, rollicking celebration—sisters, friends, and our families, including our two mamas. What is it—Doctor Sister or Sister Doctor? Fun, happy talk.

Where would I be without Chris? Now here we are in the 1980s, seasoned friends of twenty years, like a couple of oaks growing side by side.

One day while Chris is in New Orleans for a visit, we attend a lecture at Loyola University by Doug Magee, who tells about his protest in Florida against the 1979 execution of John Spenkelink, the second person executed in the United States after the Supreme Court's reinstatement of the death penalty in 1976. I don't know much at all about the death penalty, and, until now, I haven't given the issue much thought, so I have to say I've supported it, at least by default. The Catholic Church's teaching that the state has the right to execute dangerous criminals to defend society has always sounded morally right to me. I figure that if we allow the state to conduct violent warfare to defend us against foreign enemies, it makes sense to allow government to use violence against dangerous criminals in our own country. In this mindset, Christ's mandate to forgive enemies is solidly put on hold.

Louisiana hasn't executed anyone for the past twenty or so years, even though we have a state statute allowing it. But the mood is rising. I hear it in politicians' and prosecutors' rhetoric—plenty of talk about being "tough on crime," and, with violent crime on the increase, needing the death penalty to "fight fire with fire."

Doug Magee's protest of Spenkelink's execution invites me into a level of engagement I've never thought about before. Here's a young guy whose conscience was so deeply moved by the killing of a convicted criminal that it led him to engage in civil disobedience and get himself arrested. I've read about the priest brothers, Dan and Philip Berrigan, who went to prison for civil disobedience against the Vietnam War, but this is the first time I've actually met someone who knowingly broke the law to protest injustice.

Doug got to know Spenkelink, along with the other Florida death row prisoners, through a photographic assignment for *Life* magazine. It was a simple enough task. Each death row prisoner consenting to be photographed showed up in a small room, exchanged a few words with Magee, who took his picture, and then returned to his cell. What was it in that simple, fleeting exchange that so fired the soul of Doug Magee and led him to chain himself to the front gate of the governor's mansion? All he did was meet the man briefly to take his picture. I leave the meeting wondering about that. I admire Magee for putting himself out there for something he believed in. I don't yet know what that experience feels like, but I want to—I'm longing to catch fire like that.

MEANWHILE, ONE AFTERNOON in the Adult Learning Center, Kathleen and I get some coffee in the kitchen, and Kathleen asks me if I remember that youth program I had proposed to the community.

Augh! Do I remember? About a hundred million times before breakfast. But here's the grace—the sweet, glorious grace. It was the crash of that unreal proposal that has brought me, the latecomer, to be here with the people of St. Thomas.

Kathleen says that maybe we could do a youth program in St. Thomas and invite Catholic suburban kids (white, of course) in the summer months to spend a week or so here with the residents, who will be their teachers. Not us—we'll just be guides, learning along with them. And maybe, just maybe, young people's encounter with real African Americans' struggle will strike a spark of passion in their hearts to join their brothers and sisters in their quest for "equal justice under law." Or at least awaken them to acknowledge the opportunities they've been handed carte blanche (pun intended), which may rouse them to become forces of social transformation.

Kathleen explains that there's already a program that Lory designed called Pathways of Poverty. It takes suburban folks through the criminal justice system, welfare and work, health-care, education in public schools, religious practice (attending Mass at an African American Catholic church), and an after-noon reflection on the U.S. economic system and how poor people of color fare in it. In the final days of the program, participants go into residents' homes as guests to share an eve-ning meal, and on the very last day participants enjoy an after-noon with neighborhood kids at Audubon Park. Each day of the program begins and ends with Gospel reflections and prayer.

We'll call our program BRIDGES. We bang out the pro-gram with incredible ease, thanks to Lory's groundwork, and send invitations across the United States to Catholic high school seniors and college students and wait. In the invita-tional brochure, we stress that participants will not be engaged in projects to "help" poor people but rather, in a humbler vein, are being invited to "sit at the feet of neighborhood residents to learn from them."

The first responses trickle in, but then flow in steadily, and BRIDGES is launched in the summer of 1982. Over the next four summers, five hundred young people travel to New Or-leans to experience a direct personal encounter with African American residents in St. Thomas.

It doesn't take long to understand that it's the personal en-counter with residents that fires hearts. Or not. It's hardly automatic. I withhold judgment. *Just do your part, Helen. Bring them together and leave the results up to God.*

But when I visit white friends in the suburbs, all I meet in their questions about my new neighbors is a barrage of stereotypes: Why don't those people get jobs? Why don't they keep their kids in school? Why do they let their kids get hooked on drugs? Why do they rob and steal and end up in Angola? (I get it. I used to ask the same questions.)

I try to tell them stories of people I've met and what they're up against from every side. I try to take them through the experience of going through a job interview as a person of color in contrast to what they or their sons and daughters might experience. I'm usually not very successful. They have too many preconceived notions—not unlike my own when I lived in the suburbs. Too much translation is needed. What can be done, short of bringing people bodily to Hope House to meet the people directly? What's my personal responsibility to communicate what I'm learning and experiencing?

Statistics about inequality and injustice in the different systems are nonstarters. People don't trust statistics. You give one, they'll counter with another. Sheer, raw data about thwarted lives and untimely deaths seem particularly ineffective at changing hearts and minds. What I'm coming to—what's slowly rising up—is the idea that the way to build bonds of compassion between people of very different backgrounds and experiences is going to be through stories. But how to do that? I know storytelling is an art, not just something you dash off. But I'm seized by the idea. Others write stories. There must be a way to learn to do it—a specific craft that can be passed on from veterans to neophytes.

Enter my life James Hodge, a fellow Catholic and reporter at *The Times-Picayune*. He's over at Hope House one day covering a story and we begin talking about the writing process, and as we talk I wonder out loud about maybe starting a small newspaper that would put faces on the struggling residents of St. Thomas and tell real stories of the people and the systems that enmesh them. What motivates them to keep putting one foot in front of the other?

Two things I like about Jim: He knows how to write good stories, and he believes faith in Jesus is all about getting in there with the "least of these" to strive with them for a digni-fied life. Right up my alley. Without any set plan, Jim and I start meeting at his house, and he becomes my first writing teacher. From him I learn the cardinal rule of good journalistic writing: *Show, don't tell*. And from Hemingway: simple, pared-down sentences, just nouns and verbs, no adjectives or ad-verbs, no descriptive, pumped-up words. Long on scenes, short on personal commentary.

Soon after Jim and I start meeting, we draw in Bill Quigley and Sister Barbara Breaud, O Carm, a Sister of Mount Carmel from the Hope House staff, and launch *Flambeau: A Catholic Voice for Justice*. We choose *Flambeau* for its association with the Mardi Gras night parades, led by African Americans, who hold the burning flambeau (torches) high. We want to com-municate the spirit that working for justice is not a sad, droopy, serious thing—that when you put your hand on your part of the life rope and start pulling, hope and energy flow through you, and you feel *alive*.

THINGS HAPPEN IN life and you don't always see them com-ing. The river that carried me thus far, from Mama and Dad-dy's loving home to the convent in New Orleans, where I studied maxims of perfection, ironed a thousand guimpes, and learned to pray, has led me on a journey I would not have imagined. Along the way, I had to grow up—to find out who I truly was, learn to love, and find deep friendships that nourished my soul and challenged me to grow and push past old boundaries. The river was fed by historical events, by changes in the Church and culture that turned so much of my world upside down. After vowing to be a bride of Christ, I came to know Jesus in a new way, through encounters with poor and struggling people. But some lessons never end.

I'm feeling a fresh sense of purpose and aliveness now, as my life and work continue at St. Thomas. But the river's course is about to take a new turn. I accept an invitation to write a letter to a death row inmate in Louisiana, and a towering new wave rises up in the river. My little boat catches that wave, and I've been riding it ever since.

Here this part of my journey ends, unfurling into the first words on the first page of *Dead Man Walking*:

When Chava Colon from the Prison Coalition asks me one January day in 1982 to become a pen pal to a death row inmate, I say, Sure. The invitation seems to fit with my work in St. Thomas.

Afterword

This book ends where another began. I set out in these pages to tell a story of awakening and discovery, the journey that led to the experiences described in *Dead Man Walking*. That story began in the cradle of my family home when I felt a personal call to follow Jesus. I thought I had answered that call when I entered a religious community, the Sisters of St. Joseph. But that was only the beginning. Once you answer that call, it never ends, and it can take you into places you never dreamed you'd go. The other thing about that call from Jesus—or any deep-souled summons—is that sometimes it takes a form that you don't recognize at first.

When I responded to the invitation to write a letter to Pat Sonnier, a condemned prisoner on death row, I thought I'd only be writing letters. I never dreamed he'd actually be executed, much less that I'd be right there with him. As I accompanied first Pat, and then five other prisoners to their deaths, and came to know their families, as well as some of the families of their victims, I was drawn into the fire that has enkindled my prayers, my energy, and all my efforts over the past thirty-four years. I left Hope House in 1984, six months after Pat Sonnier was executed, to join the national movement to awaken the American people to the moral wrongness and futility of authorizing government officials to set about killing (legally, of course) citizens they consider the "worst of the worst."

As part of that effort, I wrote *Dead Man Walking,* which Random House published in 1993. At the time of publication, U.S. popular support for capital punishment was running at an all-time high and most people didn't give the book the wisp of a chance of having an impact. Yet, against all odds, within a few years of publication, *Dead Man Walking* had become a household word. That was due in no small part to Susan Sarandon, who read my book and persuaded Tim Robbins (it took nine relentless months: "Did you read the nun's book?") to write and direct a soul-searching film of my book. Susan herself played me in the film, and won an Oscar for Best Actress at the 1996 Academy Awards. Over a billion people worldwide watched the awards that night, and the book catapulted to the *New York Times* Best Sellers list for thirty-one weeks.

And that was not the end. In the year 2000, the *Dead Man Walking* opera premiered in San Francisco (Terrence McNally, librettist, and Jake Heggie, composer). Talk about a resurrection narrative! The *Dead Man* walks, then runs, and is running still. As of 2018, there have been sixty international productions of the opera on five continents.

I can't help but think of a line from the Acts of the Apostles: "Awe came upon everyone, and many wonders and signs were done" (Acts 2:43).

But we weren't done. Over two years of correspondence I kept pleading with Tim to write a stage play, saying, "Tim, remember our mantra about the film: The film plows the ground, and the book tills the soil?" I had seen the film's power to draw people to the book, and by then I trusted the book's power to change hearts and minds. From years on the road talking with people in every state of this nation I realized that most folks have never reflected deeply about capital punishment and have almost no information about how the penalty actually works—or doesn't work. In 2004, Tim Robbins wrote a stage play of *Dead Man Walking* for university and high school students, and over the course of five years 250 schools performed the play.

And so it goes, the river flows.

Over the years, as I have accompanied other condemned men to their deaths, I discovered that some of them were actually innocent. That led to my second book, *The Death of Innocents: An Eyewitness Account of Wrongful Executions,* which was published by Random House in 2005. It tells the story of two people: Dobie Gillis Williams in Louisiana and Joseph O'Dell in Virginia. *Death of Innocents* rang one more bell in awakening the American people to the shocking brokenness of our criminal justice system. As of November 2018, 164 wrongly convicted death row inmates have managed to gain their freedom. My relationship with Joseph O'Dell (after his execution O'Dell was buried in Italy; I accompanied his body) brought me into a personal meeting with Pope John Paul II, an encounter that gave me an opening to appeal to the Pope to strengthen the Church's compromised stance on the death penalty: namely, its allowance for state killing in cases of "absolute necessity" and its ready recognition of the dignity of *innocent* life, while remaining silent on the affront to the human dignity of criminals executed after being rendered completely defenseless.

Seeing the plight of murder victims' families, I founded a support group, Survive. True, the group is just one small island of compassion in a sea of sorrow, but the hurting people in this circle are real, and their comfort and support are real.

Publicity from the book, film, opera, and play have made me a public spokesperson on the issue of the death penalty, and I spend many nights and days out on the road talking to U.S. and international audiences and to the media. Southerner that I am, I'm more a storyteller than a lecturer, which for me makes presentations feel natural and creative, and I never have to use notes. I simply ride the wave of the story, which never fails to flow through me whenever I stand before the audience. It's a powerful, spontaneous dynamic, which I've come to trust. I know my job is to be a faithful witness to what I have seen and learned, the inner sanctum of government killing that most people will never ever see close up.

Along the way I have made many new friends: among prisoners and those who advocate for them, among murder victims' families, who let me into their hearts and lives and teach me—*Lord, I'm on my knees, how do they do it?*—their choice of forgiveness rather than "eye-for-an-eye" retribution. I've met Christians who live their faith in the day-in, day-out practice of justice and many courageous folks of other faiths—or no religious faith at all—who struggle passionately to make human rights real in the world. I think gratefully of all who have accompanied me on this journey, and of many—in this story—who have fallen along the way.

I continue to accompany people on death row, currently Richard Glossip in Oklahoma and Manuel Ortiz in my native Louisiana. I firmly believe both these men are innocent of the crimes that sent them to the death house. A way to connect with their lives and their struggle awaits you through my social media contacts at the end of this book.

.   .   .

My friend Chris died of breast cancer on March 22, 1997. We were blessed to have more than thirty years of friendship.

William maintained sobriety until he died peacefully in his sleep on September 6, 2014, in a priests' retirement home. After our big break in the 1970s we were able to resume our friendship, although with "spaces in our togetherness," as the poet Kahlil Gibran put it.

Daddy, a lover of words and books, died in 1974 and never got to see his daughter become a published author. Mama died in June 1993, just as *Dead Man Walking* made its public debut. From her hospital bed she watched me launch the book on the *Today* show in New York City. I interrupted the book tour to return to her side as she died. And in 2016 my beloved sister Mary Ann, ever at my side my whole life long, slipped into eternity.

I remain an active member of my religious community, the Congregation of St. Joseph. When I plunged headlong into death penalty activism, my community plunged in with me. I say with pride that my congregation, along with other Sisters nationwide, are an energizing force of faith-that-does-justice on the issue of the death penalty and many other fronts. I cannot begin to picture where my life would be without the Sisterhood. My Sisters strengthen and inspire me to be generous in service and faithful in prayer, even when God seems to go dark. And now, as we age, they are teaching me how to die. But only when it's time. For now, it's all about riding the life river wherever it leads, full throttle, no-holds-barred. One thing I love about Jesus's spirit is that he was always talking about really living, being truly alive. And as I experience it, that's what the Jesus spirit in us does: quickens us to touch and enliven each other to life.

I rejoice to see a gradual turning of U.S. public opinion

away from the death penalty. When *Dead Man Walking* was published in 1993, 80 percent of the American public supported the death penalty; today that figure hovers closer to 50 percent. In actual practice only a handful of states carry out the vast majority of executions with (no surprise) former slave states leading the way as the chief practitioners of state killing. Not only has the number of executions declined dramatically, but so, too, has the number of death sentences handed out. Even in execution-leading states such as Texas, juries are opting for life over death.

Many factors have moved the public: the voices of the 164 exonerees from death row (the group Witness to Innocence gives exonerees a platform to recount their nightmare stories); corruption scandals plaguing crime labs and overzealous prosecutors; the voices of victims' families who refuse to seek execution of perpetrators ("Don't kill for me"); the glaring racial disparity that prioritizes the death penalty for the murder of white people while devaluing the much more frequent murder of people of color; growing recognition of the enormous cost of pursuing a death sentence, which far outweighs the cost of a life sentence; and the ever-more-evident cruelty of botched executions in our "humane" method of lethal injection. The soul of America is turning from legalized government killings. Bring it on! The day of abolition cannot come soon enough.

On August 2, 2018, Pope Francis gave a seismic boost to worldwide abolition by declaring the death penalty unacceptable in all cases "because it is an attack on the inviolability and dignity of the person" and "contrary to the Gospel of Jesus." I've waited and worked and waited some more to hear these words in my Church. Perhaps my personal dialogue in 1997 with Pope John Paul II about the inviolable dignity of condemned murderers did its small bit to help prepare the way for Pope Francis's principled stance on the inviolable dignity even of murderers.

Central to the dialogue with John Paul II was the question I posed: Is it only the innocent who have dignity? I had noticed—it was blatant—the large number of "pro-life" Catholics who readily condemned abortion, yet supported the death penalty. In my letter I shared with John Paul II how the question of dignity of the condemned first arose in my mind. It happened as I was accompanying Patrick Sonnier to execution in Louisiana's death chamber. With shackled hands and feet and surrounded by guards, Patrick turned to me and whispered: "Please pray God holds up my legs as I walk." He had been rendered completely defenseless. The people of Louisiana would have been safe if he had been sentenced to life behind bars at Angola. It was then I asked: Where's the dignity in this death?

Looking down the road, I hope that the recognition by the Church of the inviolable dignity of every human person, even criminals, will become a guiding moral principle for the Church to rethink its attitudes, teachings, and policies on women and LGBTQ persons. Only when every person's full humanness and gifts are prized and integrated into the life of the church will its wounds be healed and the community made whole. (In the appendix see my appeal to Pope Francis to reform the Church's treatment of its women members.)

Taking the long view, I'm hoping that if it took 1,600 years for the Church to align its teaching on the death penalty with the teachings of Jesus, perhaps this drastically needed transformation in Church teaching might happen in the course of a decade. Or less. Especially given recent growing global awareness of the human rights of women and LGBTQ persons. For this to happen within the Church, a strong, rising chorus of the Catholic faithful will need to cry out for reform—unceasingly—at every level of Church life. That reform can come only through education of laypeople and clergy together, journeying into the challenge of the Gospel to recognize the inherent dignity of all human persons, whatever their gender or sexual orientation.

And so the river rolls . . . and so do we.

As for my faith . . . what has happened to eighteen-year-old me, who joined the convent in search of mystical union with God? The thirst for God is still there, it never goes away; I am haunted by God. No matter how exciting an achievement or sweetly satisfying a personal relationship or dazzling a new insight, there's always this thirst, this aching . . . for what? It drives me to prayer—or to distraction. But often, when prayer does rise, it's the words of St. Augustine that well up: "You have made us for yourself, O God, and our hearts are restless until they rest in you."

As human beings, trying to tackle life's mysteries, we're all struggling in the dark. Rational, logical, philosophical solutions are never going to cut it when it comes to life's Big Mysteries. The Jesus Way I'm learning and will always be learning is to let the big questions lie there—they will always be there—and to reach out and give myself over to loving others as generously as I can. St. John of the Cross gives the coda on this one: "In the evening of life we will be judged by love."

My spiritual practice looks something like this: Every day I set aside time to meditate; guided by the scripture readings of the liturgical year, I attend to happenings in my life and in the world. What's happening on the river? Where is God moving?

Who's suffering? How do I let them into my heart? What am I called to do? I've also learned from women spiritual guides how to attend to my own soul: How am I? Tired? Sad? Anxious? Let me stop and breathe and listen. Time to rest, to simply be and let God, my Creator, gaze upon me. Time to put down the burdens, time to float on the river, time to play, time to dig into a hefty book, time to go to Grand Isle and walk the beach.

From the time of childhood, kneeling next to Mama, I have loved the Mass: the quietness, the solemn reading of scripture, the music that lifts and comforts, and the standing once again before the holy mystery of Christ who calls us to love each other even onto death. I attend Mass at the mostly African American St. Gabriel the Archangel Catholic parish in New Orleans. Just to be in the presence of my struggling black brothers and sisters summons me to live boldly.

I make my yearly retreat with the Trappist monks at the Abbey of Gethsemani in Kentucky, the community where Thomas Merton spent his life. I embrace the days and nights of solitude and rise in (very) early morning to chant sacred verses of scripture with the monks.

I pray with my Sisters, as we gather to read and hear the words of Jesus to discern where we're being called to serve and how we might help one another. And then there is the biggest and scariest of all arenas of my prayer: I'm pleading for the grace to let go of this life I love when the time comes, when my ride on the great river will flow into the vast blue sea.

In April 2018, I turned seventy-nine years old. Mama and Daddy both died at age eighty-one, so I know my death can't be far away. And, from a purely rational point of view, death seems to be such a crapshoot—either it's everything: union in love with all that is, or nothing: disintegration into a puny pile of chemicals. I'm much humbler now about asking others to pray for me, and I find myself praying in earnest for those who are suffering, especially the imprisoned and the victims of their crimes. And those facing death, utterly alone. About my own death I hear Mary Ann, my always-braver-than-me sister: "Buck up, Helen, don't be a sissy, everybody dies; with God's grace I did it, and you will too."

Meanwhile, I keep riding the river and engaging in conversations with people about the death penalty. As of August 14, 2018, 1,490 persons have been executed in the United States and 2,705 persons are in cells awaiting execution, of whom 53 are women. With the recent conservative turn of the U.S. Supreme Court, it looks like we're going to have to do the work of abolition state by state. When a hefty majority of states have abolished the death penalty, the Supreme Court may, perhaps, have satisfactory constitutional grounds for a majority to abolish the penalty by applying the criterion of "evolving standards of decency." But we have a long way to go on that one. Currently only twenty states have abolished government-sanctioned executions, and thirty states still have a statute of approval on their legislative books. So it looks like my work is cut out for me, and I'll need to stay deeply engaged in public discourse and continue traveling to cities to converse with my fellow citizens on this life-and-death issue.

And now, as I travel, I will carry *River of Fire* with me, this one woman's story of awakening to the deepest, most compelling spiritual adventure of my life. I urge you to get in the conversation on human rights and stay in it. It's the only way the arc of the universe ever bends toward justice. And I invite you to join me on the river—in person or online. I look forward to meeting you there.

sisterhelen.org
Facebook.com/sisterhelenprejean
Twitter: @helenprejean
Instagram: @helenprejean

Appendix: A Letter to Pope Francis

An Appeal for the Catholic Church to Fully
Respect the Dignity of Women

Personally delivered to him on January 21, 2016

Dear Pope Francis,

As I pray, I feel the Holy Spirit stirring my heart to use the occasion of meeting you to share a deep concern I have for our Church. An ache and sorrow, actually. I rejoice as I watch your stalwart efforts to renew our Church, especially in the area of collegiality and empowerment of the laity. But over my many years of service within the Church (I'm just two years younger than you), I am saddened to encounter over and over a very deep wound at the heart of the Church, a wound which, I am convinced, infects and weakens every aspect of Church life. That wound, Holy Father, is the way the Church treats women. Except for a few token representatives, women's voices are not directly heard in plenary synods, commissions, and tribunals. This thwarts the dynamic effect we women could have on dialogue and decision-making in the fashioning of church policies and practices.

Women's absence in these arenas is a huge loss, depriving the Church of the practical wisdom women have from faith lived on the ground in daily life and from insights given from our pondering God's word in our hearts. Women's access into Church forums in which we can share these experiences could do much to help our Church become more supple (open to surprises of the Holy Spirit), less cerebral and abstract, less rule-bound and authoritarian. In short, more real. Not to mention less patriarchal and less clerical. How can we have a healthy Church that truly embodies the compassionate mind and heart of Christ if our males are deprived of a steady diet of give-and-take dialogue with women-as-equals (by "equal" I mean fully empowered by the Holy Spirit)? The truth is, Holy Father, in the Church as institution, the baptism of girls and women seems not to be seen as fully empowering us with God's Holy Spirit as is the baptism of boys and men. Thus, in institutional structures of the Church, women's way of "imaging" God is muted. Simply because we are women there are certain opportunities of service from which we are systematically excluded.

If I may use my own life experience as an example: My ministry to awaken citizens on the issue of the death penalty (actually, to evangelize them: Jesus and his teaching are at the heart of every talk I give) has brought me to speak to U.N. commissions, Congress, governors, citizens in civic groups, and religious bodies all over the United States and other countries. In Protestant churches I am allowed to preach, yet, in my own Church I am not permitted to preach a homily. In fact, because I am a woman (a member of the laity, actually), I am not even permitted to proclaim the Gospel at Mass. Present liturgical rules prohibit me or any woman from proclaiming the Gospel. My voice is muted in my own Church, whom I love and have served all of my life. It is a wound, a pain, an ache that never goes away—not only for me, but for all women. No doubt it is one of the reasons why young women as well as older ones distance themselves from the Catholic Church. They know they will never be admitted to full participation.

They feel discounted, disrespected. What a loss of vibrancy to the Body of Christ. This saddens me immensely.

Somehow, over the years, we in the Church have lost the kind of shared ministry Jesus had on the road with his disciples, both women and men, and that Paul shared with women as he established Christian churches far beyond the confines of Palestine. How can we once again recover that vibrancy?

I hope this doesn't weary your spirit. You have already quickened life in our Church in a way I haven't witnessed since Vatican II. I rejoice in your boldness and your joy. I love that you're getting us out of buildings and rigid rule-following and leading us out to the hurting ones on the margins of society and even into the suffering of Mother Earth herself. I thank God for sending you to us, and I pray for you every time I think of you, which is often.

I am in heart and training a religious educator, so I can't help but begin to imagine a three-to-five-year catechetical (educational) pathway whereby the entire Church might be enabled to learn and dialogue and grow together toward a fuller understanding and embodiment of every woman and man as full-fledged, participating members of the Body of Christ. A huge task. But with the fire of the Holy Spirit and with trust in each other, surely . . . surely God will accomplish in us more than we can dream or imagine. One thing I do know, Pope Francis . . . I TRUST YOU.

Love abounding in Christ,
Sister Helen Prejean, CSJ

Acknowledgments

I don't know about other authors, but for me, it has taken a village to write this memoir.

Heartfelt thanks to my Random House editor, Daniel Menaker (who also edited *The Death of Innocents*), for his insights, wit, and superb editing skills in bringing this book to birth; Gina Centrello, president and publisher of Random House, who granted me numerous time extensions over seven years to complete this book (happily, my third for Random House, along with *Dead Man Walking* and *The Death of Innocents*); LuAnn Walther, who, in a year's time is set to publish the Vintage paperback edition of *River of Fire*; Gloria Loomis, my literary agent, who has played such a stellar role in my writing life, and my friend Jason DeParle, and fellow writer Bill McKibben, who led me to her; Robert Ellsberg, editor and publisher of Orbis Books (orbisbooks.com) and dear friend, who for seven years has accompanied me through every page of every draft of this book, pruning away garrulous verbiage, and who as mystic-social-justice-activist has served as my Catholic guide; I count him and his deep-spirited, loving wife, Monica, as precious friends; the African American community in New Orleans, who taught me and continue to teach me about the "other America," in which persons of color must contend with racism in institutional systems all across this nation; Sister Marya Grathwohl, OSF, dearest of friends and fellow writer, who shared her invaluable suggestions and encouragement as I wrote and rewrote this memoir, and who has given me a writing room in her tiny apartment in Billings, Montana, along with a soul-expanding view of Big Sky Country; Sister Margaret Maggio, CSJ (who got a shout-out in the dedication of this book), Elizabeth Ryan, Carolyn Clulee, and Griffin Hardy, friends and working colleagues who have assisted me in ways too numerous to mention; Rose Vines, friend and creative genius of a writer and editor, amazing wizard in all-things-electronic, and my resident guru, who helps me recognize the holy outside the boundaries of mainstream religion; Lillie Eyrich, a brilliant friend and lawyer, who keeps my sense of humor primed through her steady stream of dippy, cornball puns; my friend Manuel Ortiz, an innocent man on Louisiana's death row, who teaches me courage; Susanne Dumbleton, a fellow writer, who read early drafts and offered suggestions; Northern Cheyenne friends, who support me with prayer and ceremonies: Vonda and Francis Limpy, Charlotte and Tom Rock Roads, Marcelline Shoulderblade and Charles Little Old Man; Montana friends: Dorie Green, Pat Feldsein, Sister Cecily Schroepfer, OSF, Chuck and Carol Heath, Sister Kathleen Hanley, CHM, Sister Jeanne Tranell, OP, Mary Fitzpatrick, and Jim and Lin Roscoe, who graciously gave me a writing place in their cabin by the magical Stillwater River; Wyoming friends: Monique Robinson and the Benedictine Sisters of San Benito Monastery; and, finally, my bedrock family: Mama and Daddy, sister Mary Ann and brother Louie, friend-of-my-heart Ann Barker, and Sisters in my beloved Congregation of St. Joseph, with special thanks to Sisters Kathleen Babin, Janet Roesener, Jeannie Masterson, Nancy Conway, Janet Fleischhacker, and Jackie Schmitz.

THE DEATH OF INNOCENTS
An Eyewitness Account of Wrongful Executions

The Death of Innocents tests the moral edge of the debate on capital punishment: What if we're executing innocent men? Two cases in point are Dobie Gillis Williams, an indigent black man with an IQ of 65, and Joseph Roger O'Dell. Both were convicted of murder on flimsy evidence. Both were executed in spite of numerous appeals. As she recounts these men's cases and takes us through their terrible last moments, Sister Helen Prejean brilliantly dismantles the legal and religious arguments that have been used to justify the death penalty. Riveting, moving, and ultimately damning, *The Death of Innocents* is a book we dare not ignore.

Law/Human Rights

DEAD MAN WALKING
The Eyewitness Account of the Death Penalty
That Sparked a National Debate

Sister Helen confronts both the plight of the condemned and the rage of the bereaved, the fears of a society shattered by violence and the Christian imperative of love. On its original publication in 1993, *Dead Man Walking* emerged as an unprecedented look at the human consequences of the death penalty. Now, decades later, this story—which has inspired a film, a stage play, an opera, and a musical album—is more gut-wrenching than ever, stirring deep and life-changing reflection in all who encounter it.

Current Affairs/Law